D0769152

CONTEMPORARY GERMAN PLAYS II

The German Library: Volume 97

Volkmar Sander, General Editor

CONTEMPORARY GERMAN PLAYS II

T. Bernhard, P. Handke, F. X. Kroetz, and B. Strauss

Edited by
Margaret-Herzfeld Sander

CONTINUUM · NEW YORK

2002

The Continuum International Publishing Group Inc
370 Lexington Avenue, New York, NY 10017

The German Library is published in cooperation with
Deutsches Haus, New York University.
This volume has been supported by Inter Nationes,
and by a grant from the funds of
Stifterverband für die Deutsche Wissenschaft.

Printed in the United States of America

Library of Congress Cataloging-in-Publication Data

Contemporary German plays / edited by Margaret Herzfeld-Sander.
v. <1–>; 22 cm. — (The German library ; v. 96–)
Contents: v. 1. The deputy / Rolf Hochhuth. In the matter of J. Robert
Oppenheimer / Heinar Kipphardt. Hamletmachine / Heiner Müller.
ISBN 0-8264-0972-5 (v. 1 : alk. paper).—ISBN 0-8264-0973-3
(pbk. : v. 1 : alk. paper)
1. German drama—20th century—Translations into English.
I. Herzfeld-Sander, Margaret. II. Series.
PT1258.C66   2000
832'.91408—dc21   99-030830

ISBN vol. 97: 0-8264-1313-7 hardcover; 0-8264-1314-5 paperback

Acknowledgments will be found on page 251,
which constitutes an extension of the copyright page.

Contents

Introduction: Margaret Herzfeld-Sander   vii

FRANZ XAVER KROETZ

Farmyard   1
Translated by Michael Roloff and Jack Gelber

PETER HANDKE

Offending the Audience   23
Translated by Michael Roloff

THOMAS BERNHARD

Eve of Retirement   51
Translated by Gitta Honegger

BOTHO STRAUSS

Big and Little   153
Translated by Anne Cattaneo

Introduction

Like most countries, Germany has a long theatrical tradition. The *German Library* in 100 volumes has therefore devoted quite a number of volumes to the subject of drama—this being the last one of more than twenty in the series devoted to the subject.

The line starts with *Theater before 1750* (vol. 8), containing plays by Hrosvitha, H. Sachs, Rebhuhn, Gryphius, Lohenstein, and J. E. Schlegel. Volume 12 is dedicated to Gotthold Ephraim Lessing *(Minna von Barnhelm, Emilia Galotti, The Jews, Nathan the Wise)*, followed by the plays of the *Sturm und Drang* period (vol. 14: plays by Lenz, Wagner, Klinger, Schiller). Four plays by the mature Friedrich Schiller, perhaps Germany's greatest playwright, follow (vol. 15: *Intrigue and Love, Don Carlos;* vol. 16: *Wallenstein, Mary Stuart).*

The 18th century and the era of German classicism end with two volumes of Goethe plays (vol. 18: *Faust;* vol. 20: *Egmont, Iphigenia, Torquato Tasso).*

The 19th century is represented by four important plays by Heinrich von Kleist (vol. 25: *Broken Pitcher, Amphytrion, Penthesilea, Prince Frederick of Homburg),* the complete works of Georg Büchner (vol. 28), and plays by Franz Grillparzer, Friedrich Hebbel and Johann Nepomuk Nestroy (vol. 31).

The plethora of plays during the 20th century is divided into two parts: those of the first half before World War II, and the second half for the period since then. The century begins with Arthur Schnitzler (vol. 55: *Flirtations, La Ronde, Countess Mizzi),* continues with Hauptmann (vol. 57: *Before Daybreak, The Weavers, The Beaver Coat),* plays by Wedekind, Horváth, Fleisser (vol. 58), and a volume on Expressionist short plays during the 1920s (vol. 66: Kokoschka, Stamm, Benn, Sternheim, Hasenclever, Kaiser, Toller). It ends with four of Brecht's major plays (in preparation, vol. 74: *Baal, Threepenny Opera, Mother Courage, Galileo*).

The most recent period from the end of World War II until the present begins with a volume of radio plays, a genre most popular in Germany at that time (vol. 86: Borchert, Eich, Bachmann, Handke, Becker, Lettau). There is a volume on Peter Weiss (vol. 92: *Marat/Sade, The Investigation*), and, of course, a volume each on the two German-Swiss writers Friedrich Dürrenmatt (vol. 89: *Romulus the Great, The Visit*), and Max Frisch (vol. 90: excerpts from six plays) who were widely performed throughout Europe and the United States.

The series is supplemented by a volume on the theory of theater, 34, essays from Lessing to Brecht (vol. 83), and a volume on opera libretti (vol. 52: Mozart's *Figaro*, Beethoven's *Fidelio*, Wagner's *Parsifal*, Strauss's *Rose Cavalier*, Schoenberg's *Moses and Aaron*).

The two volumes in the long line of more than thirty-five plays are the two volumes of *Contemporary German Plays*, the preceding volume 96, and the present one. (A third anthology of contemporary drama is tentatively planned.) Under the subtitle of "Documentary Drama," volume 96 contains Heinar Kipphardt's *In the Matter of J. Robert Oppenheimer*, the play on the trustworthiness and loyalty of the modern physicist and hence the problem of treason in our world, and Rolf Hochhuth's *The Deputy*, the drama of Pope Pius XII and the question of responsibility, both plays written with the help of documentary evidence. The volume is rounded out by Heiner Müller's *Hamletmachine*, a pungent play on responsibility and historical conscience.

The present volume contains plays by Franz Xaver Kroetz, Peter Handke, Thomas Bernhard, and Botho Strauss—all popular during the 1980s and 1990s in German-speaking countries, but very different writers. A common denominator, however, might be helpful to establish some connections as well as a general trend among the plays in the present volume: the retreat from dialectic confrontation, and from public problems and conflicts. The content and structure of these plays return to the private sphere of the dramatic characters. There is also an increasing interest in how human beings construct their social existence and experience—their socialization through language arising out of both local historic environments.

Franz Xaver Kroetz 1946–

Franz Xaver Kroetz was born in Munich, Germany, in 1946. He studied acting in Munich and Vienna and alternately worked as an actor, tourist guide, truck driver, and finally as an independent playwright. Like his contemporaries Rainer Werner Fassbinder and Martin Sperr, he pays particular tribute to two dramatists of the 1920s and 1930s, Ödön von Horváth and Marie Luise Fleisser (see *The German Library*, vol. 58). He recognizes their preoccupation with language and local dialects to characterize the human condition while often restricted by minimal verbal exchanges.

In his early plays *Heimarbeit* (1969), *Stallerhof* (1970; *Farmyard*), *Hartnaeckig* (1970), and *Männersache* (1970), Kroetz presents men and women who are incapable of understanding their own plight or to master their environment and their aggressions. Kroetz wanted to break with the theatrical tradition of an elaborate discourse. The communication of the dispossessed is but a barren speech and an extended silence of those who never had a coherent language. Rural life, social neglect, and sexual male dominance prevent the expansion of human beings, and "that's the way it is, there's nothing one can do." Consciousness of such human conditions lies outside the play with the spectator.

Farmyard represents Kroetz's rage over the narrow and gloomy existence of characters at the fringe of society who are incapable of expressing their feelings and understanding their actions. Beppi— slow, slightly retarded, and short-sighted—daughter of humble farmers in the Bavarian hinterland, is the victim of her dominant parents. Although Sepp, the exploited farmhand, tries to be friendly and caring, he is himself a man of stunted emotions. Beppi, sexually ignorant but pregnant, becomes the shame of the family. She has to submit to parental authority and Sepp has to leave the farm.

Kroetz has mentioned that his early plays are not based on the analysis of social conditions but on his being startled and outraged about the incompleteness of human communication and circumstances.

In the 1970s, Kroetz expressed his misgivings about the limited scope of his characters and his negative position concerning the alienation and humanity of rural life in Bavaria. In a speech at the anniversary of Bertolt Brecht's death in 1975, Kroetz praises Brecht's political insight and his innovative and pluralistic techniques. Although not following Brecht's concepts, he now wanted to create more positive characters who are able to communicate and reveal the social conditions and political contradictions in the lives of ordinary citizens. He maintains that the private and public spheres are closely connected, and that the discourse of his characters must reveal the necessity of change. As a playwright, he aims not to be the slave of dominant dispositions but to become the architect of the future. Neither individual existence nor society are preordained but instead are flexible, and both can be improved. His plays have a certain affinity with the dramas of British playwrights Edward Bond and Nigel Williams.

Franz Xaver Kroetz developed into a very prolific playwright. To date, there are more than thirty theater plays. In addition, he wrote scripts for radio, television, and public addresses. He is the recipient of many literary prizes, and his plays have become standard pieces of the repertory theater in Germany as well as in many theaters abroad.

Peter Handke 1942–

Peter Handke has become a most controversial and celebrated literary figure in modern Europe and also in the United States. He was born in Griffen, Austria, in 1942. He left the secluded valley surrounded by mountains to live with his stepfather's family in the former East Berlin for some time. He later changed his residence frequently, traveled widely, also to the United States (*Short Letter, Long Farewell,* 1972) and to the Far East. At this writing, he lives near Paris, France. Handke studied law but discontinued his academic studies after the publication of his first novel, *The Hornets,* in 1966. He was soon an active writer of plays, novels, essays, poetry, and shorter-prose texts (see The German Library, vol. 86). His dramatic and fictional writings have achieved considerable success in Europe and the United States. His early plays, which he called *Speak-ins,* particularly *Offending the Audience* (1966), *Self-accusation* (1966), *Kaspar* (1967), and *The Ride across Lake Constance* (1970), depart from traditional plays by excluding plot, action, conflicts, representation, characterization, and dramatic discourse. Words are the only means to avoid the illusionary picture of the world, and words alone provide a concept of the world.

Peter Handke's concerns over a new literary form on the stage and his obsession with linguistic experiments stand in the Austrian tradition of the theoretical philosophic investigations of Ludwig Wittgenstein and his treatise on the possibility and limitation of language *(Tractatus logico-philosophicus).* In this, Handke also follows a group of other Austrian playwrights such as Hugo von Hofmannsthal (The German Library, vol. 52), and Karl Kraus and Ödön von Horváth (The German Library, vol. 58), who concentrated their plays on the importance of linguistic subtleties. The socialization of men and women through the process and practice of language in action in these plays often leads to alienation through the manipulative power of words. Peter Handke employs "forms of the expression found in reality" (note on *Offending the Audience*) in order to negate the old and to make the audience aware of a new reality.

Handke also shares Eugène Ionesco's credo that an individual life can be destroyed through the domineering speech of an adversary: in both Ionesco's *The Lesson* and in Handke's *Kaspar,* a person disintegrates under "speech torture." The Speak-Ins, characterized by an uninterrupted flow of words, require both speakers and respondents. Handke admits that Bertolt Brecht helped to educate him, but he rejects Brecht's dialectics on the stage, which reveal the contradictions manifest in a capitalist society, in order to point to the possibility of actively changing circumstances. Handke does not want to revolutionize the audience but to make them conscious of what can be affected through the power of words. The four speakers of *Offending the Audience* treat the audience in the theater as the very subject matter of the play. They have "the standard idea of the world of the theater," which they need to abandon. The people in the audience are being played with in order to recognize their own behavior, actions, reactions, and expectations. The traditional models of what a theater and an audience have to be can only be overcome through offending the audience, and thus provoking them into spontaneous rebuttal. Only when everybody joins the play can the dilemma of the traditional theater, which separates the actor from the passive spectator, be resolved.

Since the 1970s, the mood of Handke's plays and prose fiction have changed from the earlier preoccupation with linguistic concerns. Handke moved to a more detached description of the limitations and futility of language and the soothing effect of nature. He had rediscovered classic and romantic German writers (Goethe, Hölderlin, Stifter, Fontane) and the depiction of landscape as a rejuvenating force. The plays *They are dying out* (1973), and *Über die Dörfer* (1981) are descriptive and reflective evocations of a new human sensibility to overcome false glitter and destructible energy.

In the 1990s, during the breakup of Yugoslavia and the ensuing conflict in the Balkans, Peter Handke traveled through Serbia and published idyllic descriptions of a people and country, neglecting the strife and war crimes reported in European newspapers. Handke's position was hotly discussed and widely rejected by many commentators and intellectuals. His play, *The Journey in the Dugout Canoe; or, the Piece about the Film about the War* (1999), returns to the subject matter of Serbia, now a once war-torn country ten years after the Balkan War. The play turns out to be a fantasy and a mystification of a brutal and bloody nightmare. By contrast, it offers the vision of a beatific landscape, and ends in an apocalyptic message showing an empty stage. Handke has traveled from the world as constituted through language to a very private imagination, evocation, and an ahistorical fantasy.

Peter Handke has received many reputable literary prizes, and his works have been translated into many languages.

Thomas Bernhard 1931–89

Thomas Bernhard was born in Holland in 1931 to Austrian parents. He grew up with his grandparents in Austria and Bavaria. He never knew his father, and his mother died before he reached the age of twenty. Sent to a boarding school in Salzburg, Thomas Bernhard led a lonely, desperate, and suicidal existence. After some temporary jobs and his first attempts at writing, he was forced to spend more than a year as a pulmonic patient in a sanatorium, always on the brink of death. To overcome his boredom there and to combat his hatred of books and his natural aversion to the act of writing, he seriously (and ironically) began to write. After his recovery, he frequently moved from place to place and finally resumed his musical studies in Vienna. Bernhard became a reporter, traveling among other places to Yugoslavia, Sicily, Poland, and Spain. In 1965 he settled in Ohlsdorf, a village in Austria. He continued to write prose, poetry, and numerous controversial but highly successful plays, among others *Ein Fest für Boris* (1970), *Der Ignorant und der Wahnsinnige* (1972), *Die Jagdgesellschaft* (1974), *Der Präsident* (1975), *Die Berühmte* (1976), *Immanuel Kant* (1978), *Der Weltverbesserer* (1980), *Vor dem Ruhestand* (1979, *Eve of Retirement), Der Theatermacher* (1979), and *Heldenplatz* (1988).

Thomas Bernhard soon established himself as an important writer who became well-known beyond his own country. He received important literary prizes, among them the Büchner Prize, Germany's highest literary award. His plays were and are performed regularly. On the occasion of the festivities at the Austrian National Holiday in 1977, he summarized his thoughts on the state of affairs: "Time is always a horrible time and life or existence is always a horrible existence . . . but our contemporary era is for me the most repugnant, wretched time which has ever made its experiment in this world, and to support this contention, Austria is, for me, at every moment the most striking example." Thomas Bernhard was an outsider in his country and his plays were first performed in German theaters. In fact, he forbade performances of his plays in Austria during his lifetime. In his prose writings, both private and public life are overshadowed by sickness, disintegration, closeness to death. A general hopelessness about human nature in general and the political climate in Austria in particular pervade all his work. *Eve of Retirement* and *Heldenplatz* are unmitigated attacks on the survival of the fascist, anti-Semitic, evil mentality of his countrymen.

Eve of Retirement has only three characters, but a constant barrage of words, repetitions, and accusations give impetus to the play. Rudolf Hoeller, former SS-officer, camp commander, spent ten years hidden in a cellar after the war. Now he is chief justice and a respected member of Austrian society. Each year he celebrates the birthday of Reichsführer SS Heinrich Himmler with his two sisters

Vera and Clara. Vera adores her brother and has a secret incestuous relationship with him. Both hate and relentlessly abuse Clara, who is bound to a wheelchair. Clara recognizes her brother's ruthlessness and abhors his and Vera's anti-Semitic outbursts. Rudolf Hoeller rants against an opportunistic, democratic postwar world since "we'd be living in totally different times had we been able to have it our way." At the "eve of retirement," the birthday party ends in horror and brutality. Thomas Bernhard does not spare his audience, and "none of us can escape."

Thomas Bernard died in 1989. His works have been translated into twenty-seven languages and by now he is firmly established in the canon of Austrian literature.

Botho Strauss 1944–

Among contemporary German writers, Botho Strauss is the most conservative author. Born in 1944 in Naumburg-Saale, he became a student of German studies, theater science, and sociology at the Universities of Cologne and Munich. After a professional life as drama critic, Strauss joined the Berliner Schaubühne as dramaturge.

He soon began to publish his plays: *Die Hypochonder* (1971), *Bekannte Gesichter, gemischte Gefühle* (1974), *Trilogie des Wiedersehens* (1976), and—included in this volume—*Gross und Klein* (*Big and Little,* 1978). More plays followed: *Kalldewey Farce* (1982), *Der Park* (1984), *Die Fremdenführerin* (1986), *Die Zeit und das Zimmer* (1989), *Ithaka* (1996), *Schlusschor* (1991), *Der Kuss des Vergessens* (1998), *Lotphantasie* (1999).

Just as controversial as his plays were his novels, essays, and short prose writings. The early comic and satirical elements in his works were later overwhelmed by a reliance on myth and often an elevated, repetitive tone. Botho Strauss emphasizes literary autonomy over the banal but overpowering sociopolitical reality. The apparent alienation of his dramatic and narrative characters from the dominant public sphere and his hermetic aestheticism have led many critics to see him as the veritable protagonist of postmodernism. His negation of present-day culture and the dehumanizing effect of socialization is adamant and absolute. In everyday life, human communications and contemporary forms of information, and entertainment, lack substance. In fact, reason has become instrumentalized and the projects of enlightenment have failed. Therefore it is not surprising that Botho Strauss, on the occasion of receiving the prestigious Büchner Prize in 1989, expressed the superiority of art and the artist as a way to counteract the shallow consumer society. His literary revolt brought him ever closer to embrace traditional and conservative values. Emotion and intuition are the basis of his concept of individual salvation. Instead of references to reality, myth and unspoiled nature are at the core of recent texts.

Botho Strauss abandoned Berlin and its chaotic urban life to live an "authentic" existence in the countryside and to propagate a return to the innocent origin of man.

Big and Little, a play in ten scenes, was first performed in Germany in 1978 and published in America in 1979. It just recently had another revival and again was a huge theatrical success. It still has an uncanny comic touch and offers a persuasive critical view of a cold and meaningless society. At the beginning the protagonist Lotte, a German tourist in Morocco, turns to the audience to ask them, "Can you hear me?," in order to let them participate in the disjointed conversation of two men who are taking a walk on the terrace of her hotel. This dramatic device, which is repeated several times, will be the only genuine contact Lotte can establish with other people. From one scene to the next, she remains the tenacious wanderer through Germany in search of human love—but nothing happens. She fights against the loss of family and friends, and her encroaching loneliness. The saving grace to avoid a depression are her monologues and her attempts to talk to other people. The poverty of modern communication has made room for "confusion, for years of confusion and bad luck, lies and running around." Man, she realizes, has lost the picture of mankind. After each rejection Lotte ponders what to do next, only to conclude that she must stand up and walk to the next encounter. In the final scene she sits in the waiting room of an internist, although physically there is nothing wrong with her—just to be among people, and for the last time she is asked to leave.

M. H.-S

CONTEMPORARY GERMAN PLAYS II

FRANZ XAVER KROETZ

Farmyard

Characters

THE FARMER, his WIFE, BEPPI, SEPP, a DOG (female)

Scenery

Extremely sparse, all of it movable. Simultaneous scenery for each act. Work light. Light changes, blackouts, only at the end of each act.

A note to the director

It is very important for the piece that a dog take part in it. This should be handled in the following manner: In act 1 scene 6, SEPP is alone onstage with the dog; at other moments it is merely desirable to have the dog appear every so often, but it is not absolutely essential. Since the dog's behavior cannot be calculated into the dialogue it is up to the director to improvise as best he can.

Concerning the pauses:
The piece, which is set in a farm environment, becomes clear and comprehensible only if the indicated pauses are strictly adhered to.

— = roughly five seconds

(pause) within the dialogue = caesura of roughly ten seconds

(pause) = silence of at least twenty seconds

(long pause) = silence of at least thirty seconds

Intermission after act 2

Act 1

(Combination living room and kitchen. The WIFE *is cooking.* BEPPI *with a picture postcard. Kitchen utensils.)*

WIFE: From your Godmother. Read it.
BEPPI: Aunt Hilda.
WIFE: She wrote you cause she thinks of you.
BEPPI: Where is she?
WIFE: Don't ask, just read it.
BEPPI: *(reads):* My dear Beppi! *(smiles)* Ssssoon me are going . . .
WIFE: *(gives her a slap):* What is that?
BEPPI: *(reads):* Soon w-we are going to visit you *(smiles)* when me. . . .
WIFE: *(like before)* Again! Open your eyes!!
BEPPI: . . . we. . . . *(hesitates)*
WIFE: What letter is that??? *(writes it large in the air)*
BEPPI: T-t-t-t-t
WIFE: You see!
BEPPI: Me—we has—have time. *(brief pause, then quickly)* Your Godmother, Aunt Hilda.
WIFE: Right. Now you've got it. *(turns back to her work)*
BEPPI: *(looks at the front of the postcard, extended look. Turns the card around and reads it again, faultlessly.):* Dear Beppi! Soon we are going to visit you when we have time. Your Godmother, Aunt Hilda!
WIFE: You're to dry the dishes!!!

*(*BEPPI *and* SEPP *at work in the stable. They are cleaning out dung.* BEPPI *could also be milking.)*

SEPP: And then—they welcomed the captain and said *(pause)* he should pick one out for himself. *(pause)* And then he didn't want to—And then his Indian friend said, the one who understood the language of the Indians, *(pause)* if he don't pick one it's an insult to the chief, and then he went down along into their camp *(pause)* and afterwards—they showed all of them to him. He didn't like any *(pause)* cause they had such funny faces, and afterwards he finally saw one he really liked—But afterwards the Indian chief let him know all right *(pause)* that he's picked the one who's been expelled from the tribe and that no one can touch her cause he gets sick otherwise *(pause)* but then he said: it's her or no one, and simply went up to her and embraced her. *(pause)* Afterwards the Indians all ran apart and said he would die now because he had touched her. *(long pause)* But that was all bullshit, just a superstition, and then of course he didn't die, but married her afterwards *(pause)* and when the wedding night was over and the two of them were still alive the Indians saw that he was right. *(pause)* I mean they felt that he—the "white man"—had supernatural powers and that he destroyed the bad magic. *(pause)* Afterwards all of them came and wanted him to become their medicine man. But because he was really a doctor he became the first white man the Indians trusted and let themselves be cured by. And then the woman he married said to him *(pause)* that the tribe had made a plan as revenge for the attack by the whites *(pause)* and afterwards he talked with them, and then they made him their deputy, and afterwards he worked out a ceasefire. And that's the way it was.
(pause)
BEPPI: And then!!?

SCENE 3

(SEPP is sitting on the toilet, taking a shit and masturbating.)

SCENE 4

(In the room. Evening. SEPP and THE FARMER at the table. THE WIFE is cooking. BEPPI is playing with pieces of firewood.)

SEPP: I just ain't got no luck in life, that's it. If someone got no luck there's nothing can be done.

(pause)

FARMER: Everyone makes his own luck, they say.

SEPP: Not everyone.

FARMER: Excuses.

WIFE: That's the way it is if he says so.

SEPP: Right. That's something I'd know about—In six years I'm gonna retire, then my worries is over. That'd be a whole lot better then. If I'm lucky I'm gonna do it earlier.

FARMER: If I was you I'd go out and get myself a steady job.

WIFE: But he says it ain't easy!

(pause)

FARMER: We're having an economic boom!

WIFE: Still.

FARMER: Anyone who wants to work can work. When the harvest is in, you can go down to that unemployment place till they got something for you. That's it.

SEPP: To find something steady ain't easy for me, the man at the unemployment office said, cause I ain't young no more. And that's it.

FARMER: Just like a gypsy.

SEPP: I used to have a steady job in the old days.

(pause)

Or if I was in the city, that'd be a whole lot better. But I ain't in the city.

FARMER: You bet.

SEPP: One time I was on a farm ten times the size of yours. A real farm, that was a REAL farm.

FARMER: Musta been a real spread.

SEPP: Right.

(pause)

FARMER: And why'd you leave it?

SEPP: Cause I wanted to go to the city.

FARMER: The city.

SEPP: That's right.

FARMER: Then what the hell are ya doing here?

SEPP: My, now that's hard to say.

WIFE: *(to* BEPPI*)* Don't pull the wood apart; it's for stoking the fire.
(*pause*)

FARMER: She's outgrown her dolls.

WIFE: It's a shame.

SEPP: She just wants to play.

WIFE: Shouldn't play no more, should do something real.

FARMER: Retarded she is.

WIFE: Retarded you are, you hear what your pa is saying? Ain't
makin' us happy.

FARMER: Others your age already go to high school.

WIFE: When I was your age I was up in the mountain pastures.

SEPP: That was in the old days, wasn't it?

WIFE: Alone up in the mountains. I had to work hard all day; at
night I was afraid. Once I almost came down, but then I didn't
dare after all.

FARMER: There, you hear it?

WIFE: Give me the wood, have to stoke up. *(takes the pieces from*
BEPPI, *puts them in the stove)*

BEPPI: Don't burn Dollie.

WIFE: Set the table, we gonna eat now.
(*pause*)

SEPP: It's bad if someone can't see proper.

WIFE: Can see all right cause she got glasses.

FARMER: The fourth pair . . . cause they're free.

WIFE: Would have everything if she wasn't retarded.

SEPP: I can still see with no glasses. And read the papers.

FARMER: Ain't none of us ever got bad eyes, only her.
(they start to eat)

BEPPI: It's county fair time now.

WIFE: Eat and shut up.

SCENE 5

(The stable in the evening. SEPP *and* BEPPI *watch cats at play.
They're working.)*

SEPP: All cats look the same at night.
(long pause)

SEPP: You see them, the two?

BEPPI: *(nods)*
SEPP: Which is the one and which is the other?
BEPPI: *(looks)*
SEPP: *(smiles)*
        (pause)
SEPP: The left one is the one who's red and the right one's the other.
BEPPI: *(nods)*
SEPP: So you can see!
        (pause)
SEPP: Everyone sees what the Lord gives him to see.
        (pause)
SEPP: Now they're fighting, you see?
BEPPI: *(nods)*
SEPP: You can see everything?
        (pause)
BEPPI: No more now.
SEPP: Well, it's over now. Now they're starting. Now he's jumping
        her, you see?
        (pause)
SEPP: Look. . . . It's her own fault she lets him, the tomcat's only a
        year old, right?
BEPPI: *(nods)*
        (pause)
SEPP: What's young is desirable. I don't like them, the young ones.
        (he laughs)
        (pause)

SCENE 6

(Evening. SEPP *in his room with his dog, which is eating. Watching the dog.)*

SEPP: Come on, eat. *(pause)* Don't you like it? *(pause)* I got nothing
        else. *(pause)* And if I did you wouldn't get it. Cause you can't
        pick and choose.
        (pause)
        If you don't eat it, I'll give it to the cat. Then you can see
        where you go if you get hungry. A good dog eats what's put
        in front of him, don't you know that?

(pause)
He's picky, that's what.

Act 2

SCENE 1

(A small county fair, early afternoon, a dead time. BEPPI and SEPP. BEPPI completely fascinated. SEPP slightly drunk.)

SEPP: You gotta wish?
BEPPI: *(doesn't react)*
SEPP: Want to ride the merry-go-round? *(It's a ghost train)* You afraid? Look at those big dolls.
BEPPI: *(afraid, fascinated)*
SEPP: Come, let's take a ride.
　　(takes her by the hand to the box office)
SEPP: One adult and one child.
　　(they take the ghost train)
　　(return)
BEPPI: *(disturbed)*
SEPP: It was nice wasn't it?
BEPPI: *(uncertain)*
SEPP: What's the matter?
BEPPI: *(walks stiffly)*
SEPP: Something hurting you?
BEPPI: *(denies it)*
SEPP: You dirtied your pants. You did. Come on now. Were you scared?
BEPPI: *(completely confused)*
SEPP: Or was it the soda pop? Come on we'll clean you up. *(They go behind a tent or away from the crowd.)* Here, wipe yourself with these leaves.
　　(She cleans herself; diarrhea runs down her legs.)
SEPP: You shit in your pants. Here let me. *(He cleans her up.)* Take off your pants, you can't run around like that. (BEPPI *cleans herself with his help.)* Wipe yourself with this. Here let me. *(He takes his handkerchief and wipes her with it.)*

It's all right again. *(pause)* Come here.
(He takes her and deflowers her.)

SCENE 2

(In SEPP'S *room.* SEPP *and* BEPPI.)

SEPP *(gives* BEPPI *a purse):* This is for you. From the city.
BEPPI: *(looks)*
SEPP: Say if you don't like it and I'll take it back.
BEPPI: No.
SEPP: Well, doesn't a person say "thank you" or not?
BEPPI: Thank you.
SEPP: So that you see that there is someone who thinks of you.
   (looks at the purse himself) That wasn't cheap, you can say
   that again. Genuine leather. *(puts a dollar inside)* There, so
   you have a start.
BEPPI: *(takes the purse)*
SEPP: When the time comes when you have money—so you don't
   lose it.
BEPPI: *(smiles)*

SCENE 3

(A restaurant that extends into a garden outdoors. SEPP *and* BEPPI
arrive on a motorscooter. BEPPI *on the back seat. They get off and
go into the garden, etc.)*

SEPP: *(while dismounting):* Did I go too fast?
BEPPI: *(denies that he did)*
SEPP: Want me to go slower on the way home?
BEPPI: No.
   (pause)
BEPPI: I like to drive with you.
   (They go into the garden.)
   (sit down at a table)
SEPP: We won't eat nothing, costs too much.
BEPPI: *(nods in agreement)*
SEPP: Or do you want a hot dog?

BEPPI: *(denies that she does)*
(pause)
SEPP: It's nice here, isn't it?
BEPPI: *(nods)*
SEPP: You like it?
BEPPI: Yes.
(pause)
SEPP: You can have a hot dog if you want.
BEPPI: A soda.
SEPP: Ain't you hungry?
SEPP: No . . . soda.
(SEPP looks around; no one's coming.)
SEPP: I'm gonna have a beer. I'm gonna go inside cause no one's serving out here.
Coming?
BEPPI: *(nods)*
SEPP: *(goes inside the restaurant)*
BEPPI: *(uncertain, looks around. Then straightens her dress, neckerchief, pulls up her knee socks, etc. Then folds her hands on the table.)*
SEPP: *(comes back)* It's coming right away. *(He sits back down.)* *(long pause)* In five years if I'm lucky—I'm gonna retire *(pause)* then I'm a free man. No one's gonna tell me what to do, no way, nothing, no way.
(long pause)
Then I'm going to the city and get an apartment. Afterward you can come if you like.
(pause)
To the apartment, in the city.
BEPPI: The city.
SEPP: Right, the city. At the outskirts cause it's cheaper there. You got the most luck and opportunities in the city. They want people there. Everywhere. They don't even check who it is; they're happy with anyone they got.
(pause)
SEPP: One day you'll understand what I'm telling you. Time passes faster than you think. You just turn around and a year is over.
BEPPI: *(turns and looks around)*

(In a shed. SEPP *and* BEPPI *together after sexual intercourse.)*

SEPP: I didn't mean to hurt you. Couldn't be helped.
BEPPI: *(denies it)*
SEPP: Of course not.
BEPPI: Why?
SEPP: Cause that's the way it is; you don't understand that. *(pause)*
BEPPI: Do unto others as you want them to do unto you.
SEPP: *(remains silent)*
      (pause)
SEPP: That's different.
      (pause)
SEPP: What're you looking for?
BEPPI: Glasses.
SEPP: Won't find 'em no more.
BEPPI *(nods):* They're where you put them.
BEPPI: Where?
SEPP: I see them.
BEPPI: *(looks)*
SEPP: Close.
BEPPI: Where?
SEPP: Gotta say "please."
BEPPI: Please.
SEPP: You're cold . . . cold . . . warm . . . warmer. . . .
BEPPI *(smiles):* Play?
SEPP: Cold.—Cold.—Warmer.—Cold.—Warmer.—Warm.—Very
    warm. So hot you're gonna burn yourself.
BEPPI: Where?
SEPP: Real hot. You don't look nice with glasses.
BEPPI: Want to see?
SEPP: No need to look now.
BEPPI: . . . red.
SEPP: That's normal. Doesn't matter. It'll stop again. You'll see. It's
    like I said.
BEPPI: When?
SEPP: When it's over. *(pause)* Tomorrow.
BEPPI: *(nods)*

SEPP: *(uncertain)*
    (pause)
SEPP: Now I'm gonna go out, so no one notices that I'm gone.
BEPPI: Stay.
SEPP: You can stay a little if you want, I'll keep a lookout. Then
    you can come out too.
    (gets up and goes out)
BEPPI: Glasses. *(looks for them)*

SCENE 5

(In the room. WIFE and BEPPI. BEPPI nicely dressed.)

WIFE: Let me look at you.
BEPPI: *(lets her)*
WIFE: Yes. You're pretty. All you need now is a ribbon, then you
    can march off.
BEPPI: *(nods)*
WIFE: *(ties a ribbon around her braids)*
WIFE: Now go on, and after confession come straight home. To
    help me make jam.
BEPPI: Yes.
WIFE: Now get going.
BEPPI: Good-bye.
WIFE: Don't be gone forever.
    (BEPPI goes off.)
    (WIFE gets ready to make jam.)

SCENE 6

(In the field, lying down. BEPPI and SEPP.)

BEPPI: Had to confess.
SEPP: Of course, but ya didn't say with who.
BEPPI: "I was unchaste."
SEPP: Right. That's enough—Is no one's business, just ours. And
    we ain't gonna let ourselves be asked questions of by nobody.
    (pause)
SEPP: Now we do it.

BEPPI: Later.

SEPP: Don't want to? Make an effort. All you need is a little good will.

BEPPI: Tell something.

SEPP: Afterwards I'll tell you a story, if you're a good girl to me.

(BEPPI *undresses herself.*)

It's over in a jiffy now. It's over before you even notice.

(pause)

BEPPI: Was confessed already.

(pause)

SEPP: And what'd the priest say?

BEPPI: Six Our Fathers and two Aves.

SEPP: Confessed everything?

BEPPI: *(nods)* Otherwise a mortal sin.

SEPP: Right. How'd you say it?

BEPPI: First Commandment: Thou shalt love and honor the Lord thy Father. Second Commandment: Thou shalt love and honor father and mother. I made trouble for father and mother. Third Commandment: Sundays and holidays. Fourth Commandment: I've never cursed, never. Fifth Commandment: . . . Sixth Commandment: I was unchaste.

SEPP: How'd you say it?

BEPPI: Sixth Commandment: I was unchaste.

SEPP: Nothing else?

BEPPI: That I lied.

SEPP: The priest ask something?

BEPPI: Nothing.

SEPP: Penance?

BEPPI: Six Our Fathers and two Aves.

SEPP: Did you do it?

BEPPI: Ten Our Fathers and three Aves.

SEPP: You're real eager!

BEPPI: *(smiles)*

SEPP: You did real well. *(He pats her.)*

BEPPI: *(smiles)*

SEPP: Now everything's forgiven and forgotten. You'll see.

BEPPI: *(nods)*

(starts coitus)

SEPP: You're a real good girl. (BEPPI *emits a few sounds; she has an orgasm.*)

SEPP: Be quiet so that no one hears nothing—Don't you hear me?

BEPPI: *(doesn't hear)*

SEPP: *(uncertain, stops)* Did I hurt you? Didn't want to—be quiet, afterwards I'll tell you a story. *(pause)*

BEPPI: A real nice one!

SCENE 7

(FARMER and SEPP in SEPP'S room.)

FARMER: That's gonna cost you ten years and me my honor.

SEPP: But not cause it was on purpose.

FARMER: That's a big help. *(long pause)*

FARMER: It leaves you speechless. *(pause)*

FARMER: And we put our trust in him.

SEPP: That's the way it goes.

FARMER: Three months.

SEPP: No one counted the days. *(pause)*

FARMER: Want to know a secret? She's pregnant.

SEPP: Why?

FARMER: She just is.

SEPP: That ain't true, that's a lie.

FARMER: We have proof.

SEPP: Not possible.

FARMER: You bet.

SEPP: Nothing is.

FARMER: We had to make a test. Cost ten dollars.

SEPP: Why?

FARMER: It's made with piss.

SEPP: Whose?

FARMER: Hers.

SEPP: At the doctor's?

FARMER: At the doctor's; what do you know. At the drugstore. They do it with a frog. They shoot piss into the frog and then he changes color. That's it.

SEPP: I didn't know that.

FARMER: Now you do. If she's pregnant it changes color.

SEPP: Did it change color?
FARMER: Right. That's proof of pregnancy. *(pause)*
SEPP: But it wasn't on purpose.
FARMER: Cause you're a pig, no two ways about that.
SEPP: Yeah, right.
FARMER: We'll also tell the priest. We'll tell everyone.
SEPP: I'm leaving.
FARMER: Where you going?
SEPP: To the city. *(pause)*
FARMER: We'd never have hired you if we'd known.
SEPP: Leaving anyhow.
FARMER: You'll stay a while yet. There's got to be a punishment. You'll see.
SEPP: What?
FARMER: Just you wait and see. *(pause)*
FARMER: An underage child and retarded. It leaves you speechless.
SEPP: Didn't want to, I swear.
FARMER: Couldn't find nobody else? You don't shit where you eat, and a child besides. . . .
SEPP: Didn't dare never nowhere.
FARMER: Why?
SEPP: Won't say.

SCENE 8

(In the stable. Young cats in the corner. SEPP and BEPPI.)

SEPP: That's a nice litter. But only one can stay.
BEPPI: *(looks at the animals)*
SEPP: Just the way small cats are. Pick one out.—Since you gave me away, you'll see what that gets you.
BEPPI: *(looks)*
SEPP: Which one you want?
BEPPI: Nothing.
SEPP: They're all the same. But one of them gets caught.
BEPPI: EENIE, MEENIE, MINEE, MOE,
     Catch a tiger by the toe
     If he hollers, make him pay
     fifty dollars every day. This one!

SEPP: Yours it is. Pa and Ma know everything now.
BEPPI: *(looks)*
SEPP: You gave me away.
BEPPI: Nothing. Mama knew.
SEPP: You tell her?
BEPPI: *(denies it)*
SEPP: Believe you, sure.

SCENE 9

(In the yard. SEPP and FARMER.)

FARMER: What are you looking at? No work to do?
SEPP: The dog.
FARMER: Your dog ain't on my yard.
SEPP: Where else she gonna be?
FARMER: It'll be somewhere all right.
SEPP: Can't a person look?
FARMER: You got nothing left to look at in my yard.
SEPP: Right.
FARMER: There, you knew it.
     (pause)
SEPP: I'm just looking for my dog.
FARMER: Then look for her. "Seek and ye shall find."
SEPP: Right.
FARMER: Was here.
SEPP: Where?
FARMER: By the barn.
SEPP: Why?
FARMER: Ask her yourself. No concern a dog that don't belong
     to me.
SEPP: She's a roamer, that's it.
FARMER: You'll find her all right. *(pause)*
FARMER: And if I catch you on my farm once more I'll blow your
     head off; now you knows it.
SEPP: You don't have no gun.
FARMER: You'd be the one to know. *(pause)*
SEPP: I'm just looking for my dog.
FARMER: Yeah.

SEPP: *(by the barn)* There she is. Nell! Nell! Come here. *(whistles)*
Heel! Don't you hear me? You want a kick???? *(The dog
is dead.)*
FARMER: Found her?
SEPP: Yeah, that's her. . . .
FARMER: Then make sure you get going, the two of you.
SEPP: . . . Murderer.
FARMER: Probably ate some rat poison; there was some laid out in
the barn.
SEPP: *(picks up the dead dog)*
Let's go home. *(goes away with the dog)*
FARMER: That does it.

SCENE 10

(In SEPP'S *room.* SEPP *is packing his stuff into a small bag.* BEPPI.*)*

SEPP: No need to look inside, it's nothing for you.
BEPPI: Want to.
SEPP: She's in there.
BEPPI: I know. *(looks inside the bag)*
SEPP: *(stops the pacing)* You see her?
BEPPI: *(nods)*
SEPP: She's dead?
BEPPI: *(nods)*
SEPP: Nothing can be done anymore, eh?
BEPPI: *(agrees)* Nothing no more.
SEPP: *(cries)* Just go, don't need you no more.
BEPPI: *(smiles)* Pretty dog. *(affirms it)*
SEPP: Everything's done. Go on now.
BEPPI: *(shakes her head, yes and no, stands up, walks around the
table, looks uncertain; then she takes the things and helps
pack)*
SEPP: What ya doing?
BEPPI: nothing *(stops again)*
(pause)
SEPP: Everything's over but the shouting.
BEPPI: Why?
SEPP: It's over.

BEPPI: I'm with you.
SEPP: A lot of good that does me.
BEPPI: *(nods)*
SEPP: You got no right; you're nothing; that's it.
BEPPI: *(nods)*
SEPP: Now I'm going to the city to report what happened.
BEPPI: Stay.
SEPP: You don't need me; you'll be all right by yourself.
BEPPI: Please.
SEPP: Nothing keeps me here now the dog is dead.
BEPPI: I'm askin' real nice.
SEPP: No way.
    (pause)
SEPP: *(starts to pack again)*
BEPPI: Comin' back?
SEPP: When you get the child I'll come look if it's turned out good.
BEPPI: Don't go, stay.
SEPP: It's over between us.
BEPPI: Why?
    (pause)
SEPP: Bought a chocolate for you.
BEPPI: *(takes it, cries)*
SEPP: No need to cry.
BEPPI: No need.

Act 3

SCENE 1

(On the way to church in bad weather. FARMER and WIFE. BEPPI slightly in front.)

FARMER: Can people see something already?
    (pause)
WIFE: Can't see nothin' yet.
    (long pause)
FARMER: I see something.
WIFE: That's your imagination. There's nothing to see.

FARMER: No one should ever see nothing.

WIFE: Don't worry.

(long pause)

WIFE: They say someone who's slightly off doesn't feel death the way we do.

FARMER: Of course a fly don't feel nothing either.

(pause)

WIFE: Fifth Commandment: thou shalt not kill.

FARMER: Sixth: thou shan't be unchaste.

(pause)

That's something between me and the Lord.

(pause)

WIFE: They say the child goes on living in the mother's belly for hours after.

FARMER: Not this one.

(long pause)

WIFE: I wouldn't forget that my whole life. I know that.

FARMER: God helps those who help themselves.

WIFE: Yes.

(pause)

WIFE: Blessed are the meek, for theirs is the kingdom of heaven.

FARMER: I don't believe that.

WIFE: The ideas people get. It's unheard of.

FARMER: Just talking.

WIFE: But to go into your ruin with your eyes wide open, that's not right either.

FARMER: No.

WIFE: When one thinks about it.

FARMER: I know that my daughter who's still a child that's retarded shouldn't be pregnant by an old bum. What would people say? No!

WIFE: Why a bum?

FARMER: That's what you say.

SCENE 2

(Daytime, in the kitchen. The centrifuge is attached to the bench. BEPPI is churning. The WIFE is wet-mopping the floor.)

WIFE: That's no way to make butter, just mush.
BEPPI: *(churns)*
    (long pause)
WIFE: Pick it up.
BEPPI: It's heavy.
WIFE: Didn't used to be heavy for you.—You'll have to lick up
    what you spill.

SCENE 3

(Evening in the room. FARMER *at the table with his paper.* WIFE.
BEPPI *writes in a notebook.)*

FARMER: Whatcha doing? *(to* WIFE*)*
    (pause)
    (to BEPPI*)* What's the matter? *(to* WIFE*)* She belongs in bed.
WIFE: Leave her be, she's doing her homework.
FARMER: At night!
BEPPI: Handwriting.
WIFE: She's been good.
    (pause)
FARMER: *(to* WIFE*)* Whatcha doing?
WIFE: I'm makin' a solution.
FARMER: What for?
    (pause)
WIFE: You'll see.
    (pause)
FARMER: Wanna do it?
WIFE: Talk he can, that's all.
    (pause)
FARMER: And if she doesn't do it?
WIFE: She's gotta obey.
FARMER: That doesn't help any.
WIFE: Know something better?
BEPPI: *(listens)*
WIFE: Do your homework and don't bother about what don't con-
    cern you.
    (pause)
FARMER: Everybody would do it if they knew it would work.

WIFE: Cause it ain't usual, most folks don't know about it.
   (pause)
   *(*FARMER *goes on reading the paper.)*
WIFE: Well *(to the* FARMER*)* go outside now; we do that amongst
   ourselves. We don't need no Peeping Toms.
FARMER: *(gets up)* Going anyhow since that's your business.
   (goes offstage)
WIFE: Well, we'll get it over with in no time at all.
BEPPI: *(looks)*
WIFE: Come here now. Take down your pants, lie down there.
BEPPI: Noo.
WIFE: We gotta wash so the dirt goes off; take down your pants.
BEPPI: *(does it)*
WIFE: Cause you have made such a mess that the dirt has to go out
   where it came in. That pinches a little but that don't matter,
   that's the soap that cleans everything. Pull up your skirt and
   spread your legs.
BEPPI: *(has undressed completely, stands there)*
WIFE: You're freezing, you dumbhead.
   (pause)
WIFE: *(takes the rag from the stove, the scrub brush, wets it in the
   soap solution and proceeds to scrub the floorboards)*
   (pause)
WIFE: Well, can't you hear what I said? You're supposed to go wash
   yourself outside in the tub, and then straight to bed, you gotta
   be up again by tomorrow. I got my work to do.

SCENE 4

(Night. WIFE *and* FARMER *in their double bed.)*

WIFE: I tried my best, that's for sure. I can't blame myself anymore,
   that's for sure.
FARMER: Did I say something?
   (long pause)
WIFE: That's the way it is; there's nothing one can do.
FARMER: No we can't. Other people can; others know how to help
   themselves.
WIFE: If it's no use, then it's no use.

FARMER: That's what I thought right away, that it makes no sense.
WIFE: Right.
> *(pause)*
FARMER: If we had another child, a boy, at least that would be a real comfort.
WIFE: Why?
FARMER: It's obvious, ain't it?
WIFE: When I couldn't get a second child when I was young I'm sure not gonna get one now; everybody knows that.
> *(pause)*
FARMER: I can think out loud if I want to, can't I?
WIFE: Yup.

SCENE 5

(Hillside with cranberry bushes. WIFE and BEPPI are picking berries. BEPPI very pregnant.)
> *(long pause)*
BEPPI *(has found a very productive spot):* So many!
WIFE *(smiles, softly):* Then pick 'em, and don't talk.
> *(pause)*

SCENE 6

(Evening in the room. WIFE and FARMER and BEPPI having supper.)
> *(long pause)*
BEPPI: *(stops eating, looks at FARMER and WIFE. Her labor pains begin.)*
> *(pause)*
BEPPI: Daddymommy.

CURTAIN

Translated by Michael Roloff
and Jack Gelber

PETER HANDKE

Offending the Audience

for Karlheinz Braun, Claus Peymann,
Basch Peymann, Wolfgang Wiens, Peter Steinbach,
Michael Gruner, Ulrich Hass, Claus Dieter Reents,
Rüdiger Vogler, John Lennon

Note on *Offending the Audience* and *Self-accusation*

The speak-ins *(Sprechstücke)* are spectacles without pictures, inasmuch as they give no picture of the world. They point to the world not by way of pictures but by way of words; the words of the speak-ins don't point at the world as something lying outside the words but to the world in the words themselves. The words that make up the speak-ins give no picture of the world but a concept of it. The speak-ins are theatrical inasmuch as they employ natural forms of expression found in reality. They employ only such expressions as are natural in real speech; that is, they employ the speech forms that are uttered *orally* in real life. The speak-ins employ natural examples of swearing, of self-indictment, of confession, of testimony, of interrogation, of justification, of evasion, of prophecy, of calls for help. Therefore they need a vis-à-vis, at least *one* person who listens; otherwise, they would not be natural but extorted by the author. It is to that extent that my speak-ins are pieces for the theater. Ironically, they imitate the gestures of all the given devices natural to the theater.

The speak-ins have no action, since every action on stage would only be the picture of another action. The speak-ins confine themselves, by obeying their natural form, to words. They give no pictures, not even pictures in word form, which would only be pictures the author extorted to represent an internal, unexpressed, wordless circumstance and not a *natural* expression.

Speak-ins are autonomous prologues to the old plays. They do not want to revolutionize, but to make aware.

PETER HANDKE

Cast: Four Speakers

Rules for the actors:

Listen to the litanies in the Catholic churches.
Listen to football teams being cheered on and booed.
Listen to the rhythmic chanting at demonstrations.
Listen to the wheels of a bicycle upturned on its seat spinning until the spokes have come to rest and watch the spokes until they have reached their resting point.
Listen to the gradually increasing noise a concrete mixer makes after the motor has been started.
Listen to debaters cutting each other off.
Listen to "Tell Me" by the Rolling Stones.
Listen to the simultaneous arrival and departure of trains.
Listen to the hit parade on Radio Luxembourg.
Listen in on the simultaneous interpreters at the United Nations.
Listen to the dialogue between the gangster (Lee J. Cobb) and the pretty girl in *The Trap*, when the girl asks the gangster how many more people he intends to kill; whereupon the gangster asks, as he leans back, How many are left? And watch the gangster as he says it.
See the Beatles's movies.
In *A Hard Day's Night*, watch Ringo's smile at the moment when, after having been teased by the others, he sits down at his drums and begins to play.
Watch Gary Cooper's face in *The Man from the West*. In the same movie watch the death of the mute as he runs down the deserted street of the lifeless town with a bullet in him, hopping and jumping and emitting those shrill screams.
Watch monkeys aping people and llamas spitting in the zoo.
Watch the behavior of bums and idlers as they amble on the street and play the machines in the penny arcades.

When the theatergoers enter the room into which they are meant to go, they are greeted by the usual pre-performance atmosphere. One might let them hear noises from behind the curtain, noises that make believe that scenery is being shifted about. For example, a table is dragged across the stage, or several chairs are noisily set up and then removed. One might let the spectators in the first few rows hear directions whispered by make-believe stage managers and the whispered interchanges between make-believe stagehands behind the curtain. Or, even better, use tape recordings of other performances in which, before the curtain rises, objects are really shifted about. These noises should be amplified to make them more audible, and perhaps should be stylized and arranged so as to produce their own order and uniformity.

The usual theater atmosphere should prevail. The ushers should be more assiduous than usual, even more formal and ceremonious, should subdue their usual whispering with even more style, so that their behavior becomes infectious. The programs should be elegant. The buzzer signals should not be forgotten; the signals are repeated at successively briefer intervals. The gradual dimming of the lights should be even more gradual if possible; perhaps the lights can be dimmed in successive stages. As the ushers proceed to close the doors, their gestures should become particularly solemn and noticeable. Yet, they are only ushers. Their actions should not appear symbolic. Late-comers should not be admitted. Inappropriately dressed ticket holders should not be admitted. The concept of what is sartorially inappropriate should be strictly applied. None of the spectators should call attention to himself or offend the eye by his attire. The men should be dressed in dark jackets, with white shirts and inconspicuous ties. The women should shun bright colors.

There is no standing-room. Once the doors are closed and the lights dim, it gradually becomes quiet behind the curtain too. The silence behind the curtain and the silence in the auditorium are alike. The spectators stare a while longer at the almost imperceptibly fluttering curtain, which may perhaps billow once or twice as though someone had hurriedly crossed the stage. Then the curtain grows still. There is a short pause. The curtain slowly parts, allowing an unobstructed view. Once the stage is completely open to view, the four speakers step forward from upstage. Nothing impedes their progress. The stage is empty. As they walk forward noncommittally, dressed casually, it becomes light on stage as well as in the audience. The light on stage and in the auditorium is of the same intensity as at the end of a performance and there is no glare to hurt the eyes. The stage and the auditorium remain lighted throughout the performance. Even as they approach, the speakers don't look at the audience. They don't direct the words they are speaking at the audience. Under no circumstance should the audience get the impression that the words are directed at them. As far as the speakers are concerned, the audience does not yet exist. As they approach, they move their lips. Gradually their words become intelligible and finally they become loud. The invectives they deliver overlap one another. The speakers speak pell-mell. They pick up each other's words. They take words out of each other's mouths. They speak in unison, each uttering different words. They repeat. They grow louder. They scream. They pass rehearsed words from mouth to mouth. Finally, they rehearse one word in unison. The words they use in this prologue are the following (their order is immaterial): *You chuckleheads, you small-timers, you nervous nellies, you fuddy-duddies, you windbags, you sitting ducks, you milquetoasts.* The speakers should strive for a certain acoustic uniformity. However, except for the acoustic pattern, no other picture should be produced. The invectives are not directed at anyone in particular. The manner of their delivery should not induce a meaning. The speakers reach the front of the stage before they finish rehearsing their invectives. They stand at ease but form a sort of pattern. They are not completely fixed in their positions but move according to the movement which the words they speak lend them. They now look at the public, but at no one person in particular. They are silent for a while. They collect themselves. Then they begin to speak. The order in which they speak is immaterial. The speakers have roughly the same amount of work to do.

You are welcome.

This piece is a prologue.

You will hear nothing you have not heard here before.
You will see nothing you have not seen here before.

You will see nothing of what you have always seen here.
You will hear nothing of what you have always heard here.

You will hear what you usually see.
You will hear what you usually don't see.
You will see no spectacle.
Your curiosity will not be satisfied.
You will see no play.
There will be no playing here tonight.
You will see a spectacle without pictures.

You expected something.
You expected something else perhaps.
You expected objects.
You expected no objects.
You expected an atmosphere.
You expected a different world.
You expected no different world.
In any case, you expected something.
It may be the case that you expected what you are hearing now.
Bu even in that case you expected something different.

You are sitting in rows. You form a pattern. You are sitting in a certain order. You are facing in a certain direction. You are sitting equidistant from one another. You are an audience. You form a unit. You are auditors and spectators in an auditorium. Your thoughts are free. You can still make up your own mind. You see us speaking and you hear us speaking. You are beginning to breathe in one and the same rhythm. You are beginning to breathe in one and the same rhythm. You are beginning to breathe in one and the same rhythm in which we are speaking. You are breathing the way we are speaking. We and you gradually form a unit.

You are not thinking. You don't think of anything. You are thinking along. You are not thinking along. You feel uninhibited. Your thoughts are free. Even as we say that, we insinuate ourselves into your thoughts. You have thoughts in the back of your mind. Even as we say that, we insinuate ourselves into the thoughts in back of your mind. You are thinking along. You are hearing. Your thoughts

are following in the track of our thoughts. Your thoughts are not
following in the track of our thoughts. You are not thinking. Your
thoughts are not free. You feel inhibited.

You are looking at us when we speak to you. You are not watching
us. You are looking at us. You are being looked at. You are unpro-
tected. You no longer have the advantage of looking from the shelter of darkness into the light. We no longer have the disadvantage
of looking through the blinding light into the dark. You are not
watching. You are looking at and you are being looked at. In this
way, we and you gradually form a unit. Under certain conditions,
therefore, we, instead of saying *you,* could say *we.* We are under
one and the same roof. We are a closed society.

You are not listening to us. You heed us. You are no longer eavesdropping from behind a wall. We are speaking directly to you. Our
dialogue no longer moves at a right angle to your glance. Your
glance no longer pierces our dialogue. Our words and your glances
no longer form an angle. You are not disregarded. You are not
treated as mere hecklers. You need not form an opinion from a
bird's or a frog's perspective of anything that happens here. You
need not play referee. You are no longer treated as spectators to
whom we can speak in asides. This is no play. There are no asides
here. Nothing that takes place here is intended as an appeal to you.
This is no play. We don't step out of the play to address you. We
have no need of illusions to disillusion you. We show you nothing.
We are playing no destinies. We are playing no dreams. This is not
a factual report. This is no documentary play. This is no slice of
life. We don't tell you a story. We don't perform any actions. We
don't simulate any actions. We don't represent anything. We don't
put anything on for you. We only speak. We play by addressing
you. When we say we, we may also mean you. We are not acting
out your situation. You cannot recognize yourselves in us. We are
playing no situation. You need not feel that we mean you. You
cannot feel that we mean you. No mirror is being held up to you.
We don't mean you. We are addressing you. You are being addressed. You will be addressed. You will be bored if you don't want
to be addressed.

You are sharing no experience. You are not sharing. You are not following suit. You are experiencing no intrigues here. You are experiencing nothing. You are not imagining anything. You don't have to imagine anything. You need no prerequisites. You don't need to know that this is a stage. You need no expectations. You need not lean back expectantly. You don't need to know that this is only playing. We make up no stories. You are not following an event. You are not playing along. You are being played with here. That is a wordplay.

What is the theater's is not rendered unto the theater here. Here you don't receive your due. Your curiosity is not satisfied. No spark will leap across from us to you. You will not be electrified. These boards don't signify a world. They are part of the world. These boards exist for us to stand on. This world is no different from yours. You are no longer kibitzers. You are the subject matter. The focus is on you. You are in the crossfire of our words.

This is no mirage. You don't see walls that tremble. You don't hear the spurious sounds of doors snapping shut. You hear no sofas squeaking. You see no apparitions. You have no visions. You see no picture of something. Nor do you see the suggestion of a picture. You see no picture puzzle. Nor do you see an empty picture. The emptiness of this stage is no picture of another emptiness. The emptiness of this stage signifies nothing. This stage is empty because objects would be in our way. It is empty because we don't need objects. This stage represents nothing. It represents no other emptiness. This stage *is* empty. You don't see any objects that pretend to be other objects. You don't see a darkness that pretends to be another darkness. You don't see a brightness that pretends to be another brightness. You don't see any light that pretends to be another light. You don't hear any noise that pretends to be another noise. You don't see a room that pretends to be another room. Here you are not experiencing a time that pretends to be another time. The time on stage is no different from the time off stage. We have the same local time here. We are in the same location. We are breathing the same air. The stage apron is not a line of demarcation. It is not only sometimes no demarcation line. It is no demarcation line as long as we are speaking to you. There is no invisible circle here.

There is no magic circle. There is no room for play here. We are not playing. We are all in the same room. The demarcation line has not been penetrated, it is not pervious, it doesn't even exist. There is no radiation belt between you and us. We are not self-propelled props. We are no pictures of something. We are no representatives. We represent nothing. We demonstrate nothing. We have no pseudonyms. Our heartbeat does not pretend to be another's heartbeat. Our bloodcurdling screams don't pretend to be another's bloodcurdling screams. We don't step out of our roles. We have no roles. We are ourselves. We are the mouthpiece of the author. You cannot make yourself a picture of us. You don't need to make yourself a picture of us. We are ourselves. Our opinion and the author's opinion are not necessarily the same.

The light that illuminates us signifies nothing. Neither do the clothes we wear signify anything. They indicate nothing, they are not unusual in any way, they signify nothing. They signify no other time to you, no other climate, no other season, no other degree of latitude, no other reason to wear them. They have no function. Nor do our gestures have a function, that is, to signify something to you. This is not the world as a stage.

We are no slapstick artists. There are no objects here that we might trip over. Insidious objects are not on the program. Insidious objects are not spoil-sports because we are not sporting with them. The objects are not intended as insidious sport; they are insidious. If we happen to trip, we trip unwittingly. Unwitting as well are mistakes in dress; unwitting, too, are our perhaps foolish faces. Slips of the tongue, which amuse you, are not intended. If we stutter, we stutter without meaning to. We cannot make dropping a handkerchief part of the play. We are not playing. We cannot make the insidiousness of objects part of the play. We cannot camouflage the insidiousness of objects. We cannot be of two minds. We cannot be of many minds. We are no clowns. We are not in an arena. You don't have the pleasure of encircling us. You are not enjoying the comedy of having a rear view of us. You are not enjoying the comedy of insidious objects. You are enjoying the comedy of words.

The possibilities of the theater are not exploited here. The realm of possibilities is not exhausted. The theater is not unbounded. The theater is bound. Fate is meant ironically here. We are not theatrical. Our comedy is not overwhelming. Your laughter cannot be liberating. We are not playful. We are not playing a world for you. This is not half of one world. We and you do not constitute two halves.

You are the subject matter. You are the center of interest. No actions are performed here, you are being acted upon. That is no wordplay. You are not treated as individuals here. You don't become individuals here. You have no individual traits. You have no distinctive physiognomies. You are not individuals here. You have no characteristics. You have no destiny. You have no history. You have no past. You are on no wanted list. You have no experience of life. You have the experience of the theater here. You have that certain something. You are playgoers. You are of no interest because of your capacities. You are of interest solely in your capacity as playgoers. As playgoers you form a pattern here. You are no personalities. You are not singular. You are a plurality of persons. Your faces point in one direction. You are an event. You are *the* event.

You are under review by us. But you form no picture. You are not symbolic. You are an ornament. You are a pattern. You have features that everyone here has. You have general features. You are a species. You form a pattern. You are doing and you are not doing the same thing: you are looking in one direction. You don't stand up and look in different directions. You are a standard pattern and you have a pattern as a standard. You have a standard with which you came to the theater. You have the standard idea that where we are is up and where you are is down. You have the standard idea of two worlds. You have the standard idea of the world of the theater.

You don't need this standard now. You are not attending a piece for the theater. You are not attending. You are the focal point. You are in the crossfire. You are being inflamed. You can catch fire. You don't need a standard. You are the standard. You have been discovered. You are the discovery of the evening. You inflame us. Our words catch fire on you. From you a spark leaps across to us.

This room does not make believe it is a room. The side that is open to you is not the fourth wall of a house. The world does not have to be cut open here. You don't see any doors here. You don't see the two doors of the old dramas. You don't see the back door through which he who shouldn't be seen can slip out. You don't see the front door through which he who wants to see him who shouldn't be seen enters. There is no back door. Neither is there a nonexistent door as in modern drama. The nonexistent door does not represent a nonexistent door. This is not another world. We are not pretending that you don't exist. You are not thin air for us. You are of crucial importance to us because you exist. We are speaking to you because you exist. If you did not exist, we would be speaking to thin air. Your existence is not simply taken for granted. You don't watch us through a keyhole. We don't pretend that we are alone in the world. We don't explain ourselves to ourselves only in order to put you in the know. We are not conducting an exhibition purely for the benefit of your enlightenment. We need no artifice to enlighten you. We need no tricks. We don't have to be theatrically effective. We have no entrances, we have no exits, we don't talk to you in asides. We are putting nothing over on you. We are not about to enter into a dialogue. We are not in a dialogue. Nor are we in a dialogue with you. We have no wish to enter into a dialogue with you. You are not in collusion with us. You are not eyewitnesses to an event. We are not taunting you. You don't have to be apathetic any more. You don't have to watch inactively any more. No actions take place here. You feel the discomfort of being watched and addressed, since you came prepared to watch and make yourselves comfortable in the shelter of the dark. Your presence is every moment explicitly acknowledged with every one of our words. Your presence is the topic we deal with from one breath to the next, from one moment to the next, from one word to the next. Your standard idea of the theater is no longer presupposed as the basis of our actions. You are neither condemned to watch nor free to watch. You are the subject. You are the playmakers. You are the counterplotters. You are being aimed at. You are the target of our words. You serve as targets. That is a metaphor. You serve as the target of our metaphors. You serve as metaphors.

Of the two poles here, you are the pole at rest. You are in an arrested state. You find yourself in a state of expectation. You are no subjects. You are objects here. You are the objects of our words. Still, you are subjects too.

There are no intervals here. The intervals between words lack significance. Here the unspoken word lacks significance. There are no unspoken words here. Our silences say nothing. There is no deafening silence. There is no silent silence. There is no deathly quiet. Speech is not used to create silence here. This play includes no direction telling us to be silent. We make no artificial pauses. Our pauses are natural pauses. Our pauses are not eloquent like speech. We say nothing with our silence. No abyss opens up between words. You cannot read anything between our lines. You cannot read anything in our faces. Our gestures express nothing of consequence to anything. What is inexpressible is not said through silences here. Glances and gestures are not eloquent here. Becoming silent and being silent is no artifice here. There are no silent letters here. There's only the mute *h*. That is a pun.

You have made up your mind now. You recognized that we negate something. You recognized that we repeat ourselves. You recognized that we contradict ourselves. You recognized that this piece is conducting an argument with the theater. You recognized the dialectical structure of the piece. You recognized a certain spirit of contrariness. The intention of the piece became clear to you. You recognized that we primarily negate. You recognized that we repeat ourselves. You recognize. You see through. You have not made up your mind. You have not seen through the dialectical structure of the piece. Now you are seeing through. Your thoughts were one thought too slow. Now you have thoughts in the back of your mind.

You look charming. You look enchanting. You look dazzling. You look breathtaking. You look unique.

But you don't make an evening. You're not a brilliant idea. You are tiresome. You are not a thankful subject. You are a theatrical blunder. You are not true to life. You are not theatrically effective. You don't send us. You don't enchant us. You don't dazzle us. You don't entertain us fabulously. You are not playful. You are not sprightly. You have no tricks up your sleeve. You have no nose for the theater.

You have nothing to say. Your debut is unconvincing. You are not with it. You don't help us pass the time. You are not addressing the human quality in us. You leave us cold.

This is no drama. No action that has occurred elsewhere is reen-acted here. Only a now and a now and a now exist here. This is no make-believe which re-enacts an action that really happened once upon a time. Time plays no role here. We are not acting out a plot. Therefore we are not playing time. Time is for real here, it expires from one word to the next. Time flies in the words here. It is not alleged that time can be repeated here. No play can be repeated here and play at the same time it did once upon a time. The time here is *your* time. Space time here is your space time. Here you can compare your time with our time. Time is no noose. That is no make-believe. It is not alleged here that time can be repeated. The umbilical cord connecting you to your time is not severed here. Time is not at play here. We mean business with time here. It is admitted here that time expires from one word to the next. It is admitted that this is your time here. You can check the time here on your watches. No other time governs here. The time that gov-erns here is measured against your breath. Time conforms to your wishes here. We measure time by your breath, by the batting of your eyelashes, by your pulsebeats, by the growth of your cells. Time expires here from moment to moment. Time is measured in moments. Time is measured in your moments. Time goes through your stomach. Time here is not repeatable as in the make-believe of a theater performance. This is no performance: you have not to imagine anything. Time is no noose here. Time is not cut off from the outside world here. There are no two levels of time here. There are no two worlds here. While we are here, the earth continues to turn. Our time up here is your time down there. It expires from one word to the next. It expires while we, we and you, are breathing, while our hair is growing, while we are sweating, while we are smelling, while we are hearing. Time is not repeatable even if we repeat our words, even if we mention again that our time is your time, that it expires from one word to the next, while we, we and you, are breathing, while our hair is growing, while we sweat, while we hear. We cannot repeat anything, time is expiring. It is unrepeat-able. Each moment is historical. Each of your moments is a historical moment. We cannot say our words twice. This is no make-believe. We cannot do the same thing once again. We cannot repeat the same gestures. We cannot speak the same way. Time expires on our lips. Time is unrepeatable. Time is no noose. That is no make-believe. The past is not made contemporaneous. The past is dead and buried. We need no puppet to embody a dead time. This is no puppet show. This is no nonsense. This is no play. This is no sense. You recognize the contradiction. Time here serves the wordplay.

This is no maneuver. This is no exercise for the emergency. No one has to play dead here. No one has to pretend he is alive. Nothing is posited here. The number of wounded is not prescribed. The result is not predetermined on paper. There is no result here. No one has to present himself here. We don't represent except what we are. We don't represent ourselves in a state other than the one we are in now and here. This is no maneuver. We are not playing ourselves in different situations. We are not thinking of the emergency. We don't have to represent our death. We don't have to represent our life. We don't play ahead of time what and how we will be. We make no future contemporaneous in our play. We don't represent another time. We don't represent the emergency. We are speaking while time expires. We speak of the expiration of time. We are not doing as if. We are not doing as if we could repeat time or as if we could anticipate time. This is neither make-believe nor a maneuver. On the one hand we do as if. We do as if we could repeat words. We appear to repeat ourselves. Here is the world of appearances. Here appearance is appearance. Appearance is here appearance.

You represent something. You are someone. You are something. You are not someone here but something. You are a society that represents an order. You are a theater society of sorts. You are an order because of your kind of dress, the position of your bodies, the direction of your glances. The color of your clothes clashes with the color of your seating arrangement. You also form an order with the seating arrangement. You are dressed up. With your dress you observe an order. You dress up. By dressing up, you demonstrate that you are doing something that you don't do every day. You are putting on a masquerade so as to partake of a masquerade. You partake. You watch. You stare. By watching, you become rigid. The seating arrangement favors this development. You are something that watches. You need room for your eyes. If the curtain comes together, you gradually become claustrophobic. You have no vantage point. You feel encircled. You feel inhibited. The parting of the curtain merely relieves your claustrophobia. Thus it relieves you. You can watch. Your view is unobstructed. You become uninhibited. You can partake. You are not in dead center as when the curtain is closed. You are no longer someone. You become something. You are no longer alone with yourselves. You are no longer left to your own devices. Now you are with it. You are an audience. That is a relief. You can partake.

Up here there is no order now. There are no objects that demonstrate an order to you. The world here is neither sound nor unsound. This is no world. Stage props are out of place here. Their places are not chalked out on the stage. Since they are not chalked out, there is no order here. There are no chalk marks for the standpoint of things. There are no memory props for the standpoint of persons. In contrast to you and your seating arrangement, nothing is in its place here. Things here have no fixed places like the places of your seating arrangements down there. This stage is no world, just as the world is no stage.

Nor does each thing have its own time here. No thing has its own time here. No thing has its fixed time here when it serves as a prop or when it becomes an obstacle. We don't do as if things were really used. Here things *are* useful.

You are not standing. You are using the seating arrangements. You are sitting. Since your seating arrangements form a pattern, you form a pattern as well. There is no standing room. People enjoy art more effectively when they sit than if they stand. That is why you are sitting. You are friendlier when you sit. You are more receptive. You are more open-minded. You are more long-suffering. Sitting, you are more relaxed. You are more democratic. You are less bored. Time seems less long and boring to you. You allow more to happen with yourself. You are more clairvoyant. You are less distracted. It is easier for you to forget your surroundings. The world around you disappears more easily. You begin to resemble one another

more. You begin to lose your personal qualities. You begin to lose
the characteristics that distinguish you from each other. You become a unit. You become a pattern. You become one. You lose your
self-consciousness. You become spectators. You become auditors.
You become apathetic. You become all eyes and ears. You forget to
look at your watch. You forget yourself.

Standing, you would be more effective hecklers. In view of the anat-
omy of the human body, your heckling would be louder if you
stood. You would be better able to clench your fists. You could
show your opposition better. You would have greater mobility. You
would not need to be as well-behaved. You could shift your weight
from one foot to the other. You could more easily become conscious
of your body. Your enjoyment of art would be diminished. You
would no longer form a pattern. You would no longer be rigid. You
would lose your geometry. You would be better able to smell the
sweat of the bodies near you. You would be better able to express
agreement by nudging each other. If you stood, the sluggishness of
your bodies would not keep you from walking. Standing, you
would be more individual. You would oppose the theater more resolutely. You would give in to fewer illusions. You would suffer more
from absentmindedness. You would stand more on the outside. You
would be better able to leave yourself to your own devices. You
would be less able to imagine represented events as real. The events
here would seem less true to life to you. Standing, for example, you
would be less able to imagine a death represented on this stage as
real. You would be less rigid. You wouldn't let yourself be put under
as much of a spell. You wouldn't let as much be put over on you.
You wouldn't be satisfied to be mere spectators. It would be easier
for you to be of two minds. You could be at two places at once with
your thoughts. You could live in two space-time continuums.

We don't want to infect you. We don't want to goad you into a
show of feelings. We don't play feelings. We don't embody feelings.
We neither laugh nor weep. We don't want to infect you with
laughter by laughing or with weeping by laughing or with laughter
by weeping or with weeping by weeping. Although laughter is more
infectious than weeping, we don't infect you with laughter by
laughing. And so forth. We are not playing. We play nothing. We

don't modulate. We don't gesticulate. We express ourselves by no means but words. We only speak. We express. We don't express ourselves but the opinion of the author. We express ourselves by speaking. Our speaking is our acting. By speaking, we become theatrical. We are theatrical because we are speaking in a theater. By always speaking directly to you and by speaking to you of time, of now and of now and of now, we observe the unity of time, place, and action. But we observe this unity not only here on stage. Since the stage is no world unto itself, we also observe the unity down where you are. We and you form a unity because we speak directly to you without interruption. Therefore, under certain conditions, we, instead of saying you, could say we. That signifies the unity of action. The stage up here and the auditorium constitute a unity in that they no longer constitute two levels. There is no radiation belt between us. There are no two places here. Here is only one place. That signifies the unity of place. Your time, the time of the spectators and auditors, and our time, the time of the speakers, form a unity in that no other time passes here than your time. Time is not bisected here into played time and playtime. Time is not played here. Only real time exists here. Only the time that we, we and you, experience ourselves in our own bodies exists here. Only one time exists here. That signifies the unity of time. All three cited circumstances, taken together, signify the unity of time, place, and action. Therefore this piece is classical.

Because we speak to you, you can become conscious of yourself. Because we speak to you, your self-awareness increases. You become aware that you are sitting. You become aware that you are sitting in a theater. You become aware of the size of your limbs. You become aware of how your limbs are situated. You become aware of your fingers. You become aware of your tongue. You become aware of your throat. You become aware how heavy your head is. You become aware of your sex organs. You become aware of batting your eyelids. You become aware of the muscles with which you swallow. You become aware of the flow of your saliva. You become aware of the beating of your heart. You become aware of raising your eyebrows. You become aware of a prickling sensation on your scalp. You become aware of the impulse to scratch yourself. You become aware of sweating under your armpits. You become aware of your sweaty hands. You become aware of your parched hands. You become aware of the air you are inhaling and exhaling through your mouth and nose. You become aware of our words entering your ears. You acquire presence of mind.

Try not to blink your eyelids. Try not to swallow any more. Try not to move your tongue. Try not to hear anything. Try not to smell anything. Try not to salivate. Try not to sweat. Try not to shift in your seat. Try not to breathe.

Why, you are breathing. Why, you are salivating. Why, you are listening. Why, you are smelling. Why, you are swallowing. Why, you are blinking your eyelids. Why, you are belching. Why, you are sweating. Why, how terribly self-conscious you are.

Don't blink. Don't salivate. Don't bat your eyelashes. Don't inhale. Don't exhale. Don't shift in your seat. Don't listen to us. Don't smell. Don't swallow. Hold your breath.

Swallow. Salivate. Blink. Listen. Breathe.

You are now aware of your presence. You know that it is *your* time that you are spending here. You are the topic. You tie the knot. You untie the knot. You are the center. You are the occasion. You are the reasons why. You provide the initial impulse. You provide us with words here. You are the playmakers and the counterplotters. You are the youthful comedians. You are the youthful lovers, you are the ingénues, you are the sentimentalists. You are the stars, you are the character actors, you are the bon vivants and the heroes. You are the heroes and the villains of this piece.

Before you came here, you made certain preparations. You came here with certain preconceptions. You went to the theater. You prepared yourself to go to the theater. You had certain expectations. Your thoughts were one step ahead of time. You imagined something. You prepared yourself for something. You prepared yourself to partake in something. You prepared yourself to be seated, to sit on the rented seat and to attend something. Perhaps you had heard of this piece. So you made preparations, you prepared yourself for something. You let events come toward you. You were prepared to sit and have something shown to you.

The rhythm you breathed in was different from ours. You went about dressing yourself in a different manner. You got started in a different way. You approached this location from different directions. You used the public transportation system. You came on foot. You came by cab. You used your own means of transportation. Before you got underway, you looked at your watch. You expected a telephone call, you picked up the receiver, you turned on the lights, you turned out the lights, you closed doors, you turned keys, you stepped out into the open. You propelled your legs. You let your arms swing up and down as you walked. You walked. You walked from different directions all in the same direction. You found your way here with the help of your sense of direction.

Because of your plan you distinguished yourselves from others who were on their way to other locations. Simply because of your plan, you instantly formed a unit with the others who were on their way to this location. You had the same objective. You planned to spend a part of your future together with others at a definite time.

You crossed traffic lanes. You looked left and right. You observed traffic signals. You nodded to others. You stopped. You informed others of your destination. You told of your expectations. You communicated your speculations about this piece. You expressed your opinion of this piece. You shook hands. You had others wish you a pleasant evening. You took off your shoes. You held doors open. You had doors held open for you. You met other theatergoers. You felt like conspirators. You observed the rules of good behavior. You helped out of coats. You let yourselves be helped out of coats. You stood around. You walked around. You heard the buzzers. You grew restless. You looked in the mirror. You checked your makeup. You threw sidelong glances. You noticed sidelong glances. You walked. You paced. Your movements became more formal. You heard the buzzer. You looked at your watch. You became conspirators. You took your seat. You took a look around. You made yourself comfortable. You heard the buzzer. You stopped chatting. You aligned your glances. You raised your heads. You took a deep breath. You saw the lights dim. You became silent. You heard the doors closing. You stared at the curtain. You waited. You became rigid. You did not move any more. Instead, the curtain moved. You heard the curtain rustling. You were offered an unobstructed view of the stage. Everything was as it always is. Your expectations were not disappointed. You were ready. You leaned back in your seat. The play could begin.

At other times you were also ready. You were on to the game that was being played. You leaned back in your seats. You perceived. You followed. You pursued. You let happen. You let something happen up here that had happened long ago. You watched the past which by means of dialogue and monologue made believe it was contemporaneous. You let yourselves be captivated. You let yourselves become spellbound. You forgot where you were. You forgot the time. You became rigid and remained rigid. You did not move. You did not act. You did not even come up front to see better. You followed no natural impulses. You watched as you watch a beam of light that was produced long before you began to watch. You looked into dead space. You looked at dead points. You experienced a dead time. You heard a dead language. You yourselves were in a dead room in a dead time. It was dead calm. No breath of air moved. You did not move. You stared. The distance between you and us was infinite. We were infinitely far away from you. We moved at an infinite distance from you. We had lived infinitely long before you. We lived up here on the stage before the beginning of time. Your glances and our glances met in infinity. An infinite space was between us. We played. But we did not play with you. You were always posterity here.

Plays were played here. Sense was played here. Nonsense with meaning was played here. The plays here had a background and an underground. They had a false bottom. They were not what they were. They were not what they seemed. There was something in back of them. The things and the plot seemed to be, but they were not. They seemed to be as they seemed, but they were different. They did not seem to seem as in a pure play, they seemed to be. They seemed to be reality. The plays here did not pass the time, or they did not only pass the time. They had meaning. They were not timeless like the pure plays, an unreal time passed in them. The conspicuous meaninglessness of some plays was precisely what represented their hidden meaning. Even the pranks of pranksters acquired meaning on these boards. Always something lay in wait. Always something lay in ambush between the words, gestures, props and sought to mean something to you. Always something had two or more meanings. Something was always happening. Something happened in the play that you were supposed to think was real. Stories always happened. A played and unreal time happened. What you saw and heard was supposed to be not only what you saw and heard. It was supposed to be what you did not see and did not hear. Everything was meant. Everything expressed. Even what pretended to express nothing expressed something because something that happens in the theater expresses something. Everything that was played expressed something real. The play was not played for the play's sake but for the sake of reality. You were to discover a played reality behind the play. You were supposed to fathom the play. Not a play, reality was played. Time was played. Since time was played, reality was played. The theater played tribunal. The theater played arena. The theater played moral institution. The theater played dreams. The theater played tribal rites. The theater played mirrors for you. The play exceeded the play. It hinted at reality. It became impure. It meant. Instead of time staying out of play, an unreal and uneffective time transpired. With the unreal time an unreal reality was played. It was not there, it was only signified to you, it was performed. Neither reality nor play transpired here. If a clean play had been played here, time could have been left out of play. A clean play has no time. But since a reality was played, the corresponding time was also played. If a clean play had been played here, there would have been only the time of the spectators here. But since reality was part of the play here, there were always two times: your time, the time of the spectators, and the played time, which seemed to be the real time. But time cannot be played. It cannot be repeated in any play. Time is irretrievable. Time is irresistible. Time is unplayable. Time is real. It cannot be played as real. Since time cannot be played, reality cannot be played either. Only a play where time is left out of play is a play. A play in which time plays a role is no play. Only a timeless play is without meaning. Only a timeless play is self-sufficient. Only a timeless play does not need to *play* time. Only for a timeless play is time without meaning. All other plays are impure plays. There are only plays without time, or plays in which time is real time, like the sixty minutes of a football game, which has only one time because the time of the players is the same time as that of the spectators. All other plays are sham plays. All other plays mirror meretricious facts for you. A timeless play mirrors no facts.

We could do a play within a play for you. We could act out happenings for you that are taking place outside this room during these moments while you are swallowing, while you are batting your eyelashes. We could illustrate the statistics. We could represent what is statistically taking place at other places while you are at this place. By representing what is happening, we could make you imagine these happenings. We could bring them closer to you. We would not need to represent anything that is past. We could play a clean game. For example, we could act out the very process of dying that is statistically happening somewhere at this moment. We could become full of pathos. We could declare that death is the pathos of time, of which we speak all the time. Death could be the pathos of this real time which you are wasting here. At the very least, this play within a play would help bring this piece to a dramatic climax.

But we are not putting anything over on you. We don't imitate. We don't represent any other persons and any other events, even if they statistically exist. We can do without a play of features and a play of gestures. There are no persons who are part of the plot and therefore no impersonators. The plot is not freely invented, for there is no plot. Since there is no plot, accidents are impossible. Similarity with still living or scarcely dead or long-dead persons is not accidental but impossible. For we don't represent anything and are no others than we are. We don't even play ourselves. We are speaking. Nothing is invented here. Nothing is imitated. Nothing is fact. Nothing is left to your imagination.

Due to the fact that we are not playing and not acting playfully, this piece is half as funny and half as tragic. Due to the fact that we only speak and don't fall outside time, we cannot depict anything for you and demonstrate nothing for you. We illustrate nothing.

We conjure up nothing out of the past. We are not in conflict with the past. We are not in conflict with the present. We don't anticipate the future. In the present, the past, and the future, we speak of time.

That is why, for example, we cannot represent the now and now of dying that is statistically happening now. We cannot represent the gasping for breath that is happening now and now, or the tumbling and falling now, or the death throes, or the grinding of teeth now, or the last words, or the last sigh now, that is statistically happening now this very second, or the last exhalation, or the last ejaculation that is happening now, or the breathlessness that is statistically commencing now, and now, and now, and now, and so on, or the motionlessness now, or the statistically ascertainable rigor mortis, or the lying absolutely quiet now. We cannot represent it. We only speak of it. We are speaking of it *now*.

Due to the fact that we only speak and due to the fact that we don't speak of anything invented, we cannot be equivocal or ambiguous. Due to the fact that we play nothing, there cannot exist two or more levels here or a play within a play. Due to the fact that we don't gesticulate and don't tell you any stories and don't represent anything, we cannot be poetical. Due to the fact that we only speak to you, we lose the poetry of ambiguity. For example, we cannot use the gestures and expressions of dying that we mentioned to represent the gestures and expressions of a simultaneously transpiring instance of sexual intercourse that is statistically transpiring now. We can't be equivocal. We cannot play on a false bottom. We cannot remove ourselves from the world. We don't need to be poetic. We don't need to hypnotize you. We don't need to hoodwink you. We don't need to cast an evil eye on you. We don't need a second nature. This is no hypnosis. You don't have to imagine anything. You don't have to dream with open eyes. With the illogic of your dreams you are not dependent on the logic of the stage. The impossibilities of your dreams do not have to confine themselves to the possibilities of the stage. The absurdity of your dreams does not have to obey the authentic laws of the theater. Therefore we represent neither dreams nor reality. We make claims neither for life nor for dying, neither for society nor for the individual, neither for what is natural nor for what is supernatural, neither for lust nor for grief, neither for reality nor for the play. Time elicits no elegies from us.

This piece is a prologue. It is not the prologue to another piece but the prologue to what you did, what you are doing, and what you will do. You are the topic. This piece is the prologue to the topic. It is the prologue to your practices and customs. It is the prologue to your actions. It is the prologue to your inactivity. It is the prologue to your lying down, to your sitting, to your standing, to your walking. It is the prologue to the plays and to the seriousness of your life. It is also the prologue to your future visits to the theater. It is also the prologue to all other prologues. This piece is world theater.

Soon you will move. You will make preparations. You will prepare yourself to applaud. You will prepare yourself not to applaud. When you prepare to do the former, you will clap one hand against the other, that is to say, you will clap one palm to the other palm and repeat these claps in rapid succession. Meanwhile, you will be able to watch your hands clapping or not clapping. You will hear the sound of yourself clapping and the sound of clapping next to you and you will see next to you and in front of you the clapping hands bobbing back and forth or you will not hear the expected clapping and not see the hands bobbing back and forth. Instead, you will perhaps hear other sounds and will yourself produce other sounds. You will prepare to get up. You will hear the seats folding up behind you. You will see us taking our bows. You will see the curtain come together. You will be able to designate the noises the curtain makes during this process. You will pocket your programs. You will exchange glances. You will exchange words. You will get moving. You will make comments and hear comments. You will suppress comments. You will smile meaningfully. You will smile meaninglessly. You will push in an orderly fashion into the foyer. You will show your hatchecks to redeem your hats and coats. You will stand around. You will see yourselves in mirrors. You will help each other into coats. You will hold doors open for each other. You will say your goodbyes. You will accompany. You will be accompanied. You will step into the open. You will return into the everyday. You will go in different directions. If you remain together, you will be a theater party. You will go to a restaurant. You will think of tomorrow. You will gradually find your way back into reality. You will be able to call reality harsh again. You will be sobered up. You will lead your own lives again. You will no longer be a unit. You will go from one place to different places.

But before you leave you will be offended.

We will offend you because offending you is also one way of speaking to you. By offending you, we can be straight with you. We can switch you on. We can eliminate the free play. We can tear down a wall. We can observe you.

While we are offending you, you won't just hear us, you will listen to us. The distance between us will no longer be infinite. Due to the fact that we're offending you, your motionlessness and your rigidity will finally become overt. But we won't offend *you*, we will merely use offensive words which you yourselves use. We will contradict ourselves with our offenses. We will mean no one in particular. We will only create an acoustic pattern. You won't have to feel offended. You were warned in advance, so you can feel quite unoffended while we're offending you. Since you are probably thoroughly offended already, we will waste no more time before thoroughly offending you, you chuckleheads.

You let the impossible become possible. You were the heroes of this piece. You were sparing with your gestures. Your parts were well rounded. Your scenes were unforgettable. You did not play, you *were* the part. You were a happening. You were the find of the evening. You lived your roles. You had a lion's share of the success. You saved the piece. You were a sight. You were a sight to have seen, you ass-kissers.

You were always with it. Your honest toiling didn't help the piece a bit. You contributed only the cues. The best you created was the little you left out. Your silences said everything, you small-timers.

You were thoroughbred actors. You began promisingly. You were true to life. You were realistic. You put everything under your spell.

You played us off the stage. You reached Shakespearean heights, you jerks, you hoodlums, you scum of the melting pot.

Not one wrong note crossed your lips. You had control of every scene. Your playing was of exquisite nobility. Your countenances were of rare exquisiteness. You were a smashing cast. You were a dream cast. You were inimitable, your faces unforgettable. Your sense of humor left us gasping. Your tragedy was of antique grandeur. You gave your best, you party-poopers, you freeloaders, you fuddy-duddies, you bubbleheads, you powder puffs, you sitting ducks.

You were one of a kind. You had one of your better days tonight. You played ensemble. You were imitations of life, you drips, you diddlers, you atheists, you double-dealers, you switch-hitters, you dirty Jews.

You showed us brand-new vistas. You were well advised to do this piece. You outdid yourselves. You played yourselves loose. You turned yourselves inside out, you lonely crowd, you culture vultures, you nervous nellies, you bronco busters, you moneybags, you potheads, you washouts, you wet smacks, you fire eaters, you generation of freaks, you hopped-up sons and daughters of the revolution, you napalm specialists.

You were priceless. You were a hurricane. You drove shudders up our spines. You swept everything before you, you Vietnam bandits, you savages, you rednecks, you hatchet men, you subhumans, you fiends, you beasts in human shape, you killer pigs.

You were the right ones. You were breathtaking. You did not disappoint our wildest hopes. You were born actors. Play-acting was in your blood, you butchers, you buggers, you bullshitters, you bullies, you rabbits, you fuck-offs, you farts.

You had perfect breath control, you windbags, you waspish wasps, you wags, you gargoyles, you tackheads, you milquetoasts, you mickey-mice, you chicken-shits, you cheap skates, you wrong numbers, you zeros, you back numbers, you one-shots, you centipedes, you supernumeraries, you superfluous lives, you crumbs, you cardboard figures, you *pain* in the mouth.

You are accomplished actors, you hucksters, you traitors to your country, you grafters, you would-be revolutionaries, you reactionaries, you draft-card burners, you ivory-tower artists, you defeatists, you massive retaliators, you white-rabbit pacifists, you nihilists, you individualists, you Communists, you vigilantes, you socialists, you minute men, you whizz-kids, you turtledoves, you crazy hawks, you stool pigeons, you worms, you antediluvian monstrosities, you claquers, you clique of babbits, you rabble, you blubber, you quivering reeds, you wretches, you ofays, you oafs, you spooks, you blackbaiters, you cooky pushers, you abortions, you bitches and bastards, you nothings, you thingamajigs.

O you cancer victims, O you hemorrhoid sufferers, O you multiple sclerotics, O you syphilitics, O you cardiac conditions, O you paraplegics, O you catatonics, O you schizoids, O you paranoids, O you hypochondriacs, O you carriers of causes of death, O you suicide candidates, O you potential peacetime casualties, O you potential war dead, O you potential accident victims, O you potential increase in mortality rate, O you potential dead.

You wax figures. You impersonators. You bad-hats. You troupers. You tear-jerkers. You potboilers. You foul mouths. You sell-outs.

You deadbeats. You phonies. You milestones in the history of the theater. You historic moments. You immortal souls. You positive heroes. You abortionists. You anti-heroes. You everyday heroes. You luminaries of science. You beacons in the dark. You educated gasbags. You cultivated classes. You befuddled aristocrats. You rotten middle class. You lowbrows. You people of our time. You children of the world. You sad sacks. You church and lay dignitaries. You wretches. You congressmen. You commissioners. You scoundrels. You generals. You lobbyists. You Chiefs of Staff. You chairmen of this and that. You tax evaders. You presidential advisers. You U-2 pilots. You agents. You corporate-military establishment. You entrepreneurs. You Eminencies. You Excellencies. You Holiness. Mr. President. You crowned heads. You pushers. You architects of the future. You builders of a better world. You mafiosos. You wiseacres. You smarty-pants. You who embrace life. You who detest life. You who have no feeling about life. You ladies and gents you, you celebrities of public and cultural life you, you who are present you, you brothers and sisters you, you comrades you, you worthy listeners you, you fellow humans you.

You were welcome here. We thank you. Good night.

[*The curtain comes together at once. However, it does not remain closed but parts again immediately regardless of the behavior of the public. The speakers stand and look at the public without looking at anyone in particular. Roaring applause and wild whistling is piped in through the loudspeakers; to this, one might add taped audience reactions to pop-music concerts. The deafening howling and yelling lasts until the public begins to leave. Only then does the curtain come together once and for all.*]

Translated by Michael Roloff

THOMAS BERNHARD

Eve of Retirement

Characters

RUDOLPH HOELLER, Chief Justice and former SS Officer
CLARA, his sister
VERA, his sister

Place

The house of Chief Justice Hoeller

Act 1

What is character but the determination of incident.
                                                    —Henry James

Large room on the first floor. Two high windows in the back, a door on either side. Various chairs, easy chairs, a dresser, an ironing board at the window, a piano. Late afternoon on October 7, Himmler's birthday.

VERA *(Closing the door on the left):* She's gone
CLARA *(In a wheelchair, mending her brother's socks.):*
      Are you sure
VERA: She's going to her grandmother
      and will stay until tomorrow
      Poor child
      with her coughing fits
      But if we put her in an institution
      she'll waste away
      this place is good for her
      this place is like home to her
      (Moves her right index finger across one of the window sills.)
      dust everywhere
      dirt
      (Looks at the barometer.)
      It's way down
      it's falling
      She could use a little sun
      but since she's going to her grandmother
      it doesn't make any difference anyway
      It's not easy for me either
      with an illiterate
      It's really an art

dealing with a deaf mute
at her age they are so stubborn on top of it
especially when they come from the country
and don't know anything
(Pulls at the curtain.)
here she's certainly treated
with kid gloves
(Looks through the window.)
It's always gloomy on this day
But that adds a certain solemnity
I've already chilled three bottles of champagne
Fuerst Von Metternich the brand Rudolph likes so much
(Starts to iron RUDOLPH's *judge's robe, which has been hanging on the wall.)*
He has reached the highest position
a judge can reach
he is afraid of retirement
Our Olga is a blessing
for him too
he enjoys her
she's nice to look at
after all
If you only knew
where I dredged her up
that such poor squalid conditions
still exist even today
But these people have only themselves to blame
for their misery
Poverty is no longer necessary
Poverty is caused
by the poor themselves
Don't ever help the poor
father used to say
you pull them out of their filth
but it won't do any good
I had two pretty dresses made for her
she wanted one in baby blue
but that was out of the question
one black and one dark brown

very pretty very pretty
I tied her braids exactly the way
I used to wear them
remember
how mother tied our braids
very slowly
and always with a bit of advice
Sometimes I think of myself
when I look at that child
when she's by herself and thinks no one is watching
she sits on the floor and plays with her hands
either with her hands or with her braids in turns

CLARA: We are only exploiting her
It's disastrous for her
to be here
We only ruin this child
She'll collapse one day
You knew what you were doing
when you chose a deaf mute
for a maid

VERA: You always think the worst of me
That's your habit
That's your weapon against me
(Looks out the window.)
Of course someone who can hear and talk
would certainly be better in a way
On the other hand it's lucky
that she can't hear that she can't talk
everything hinges on just that
that she cannot hear or talk
imagine if she could talk
if she could hear

CLARA: Out of pity
you keep saying
but that too is a perversion

VERA: Maybe
maybe you're right
Soon it will be my last time
to iron his robe

Then we'll take a trip
to the sea
The three of us
CLARA: You exploited every one of your maids
until they collapsed
then you discarded them
Deaf and mute
the ideal tool
for your mental and emotional paralysis
VERA: When I look at you
What gives you the right
to talk to me like that
for years I've put up with everything
you said
CLARA: She's here primarily for you
you take up all her time
she knows full well
that if she suddenly
could hear and speak
you would kill her instantly
VERA: Sometimes I feel
like wheeling you up a cliff
up there where it's the steepest
and pushing you off
into the water
with all your misery
CLARA: That's all you can think of
But you keep controlling yourself
Control means everything to you
just like father
your life depends on it
in fact you don't really live at all
you just drag yourself from lie to lie
VERA: When she's with her grandmother
she is in good care
I don't have to worry about her
I know everything is fine
when she's with her grandmother

CLARA: Wouldn't you love to run after her
    and check
    if she really went
    to her grandmother
VERA: Where else could she go
    poor thing
CLARA: What if some day
    she won't be going to her grandmother
    what if she suddenly were able to talk
VERA: You and your vicious imagination
CLARA: You always had luck
    with your maids
    they all came from the country
    poverty cases as they say
VERA: Where would you be without her
    as long as I want her here
    and as long as she can manage
    she'll be at our disposal
    at your disposal
    to be more exact
    Her illness isn't all that bad
    an occasional fit
    She has become much calmer
    As long as we keep her busy
    People who work don't get sick
    She just has to have something to do
    all the time
    keep her busy
    and she'll get better
    not worse
CLARA: She is terrified
VERA *(Laughs.)*
    Terrified
    is that so
    she was less than human
    when she first got here
    she was nothing nothing
    a zero
    Your pity for her is also

a weapon against me
Father saw right through
that so-called solidarity with servants
and called it by its proper name
vulgarity
I only want what's best for you
as long as she is here
this household functions
otherwise everything would fall apart
and you would be institutionalized at once
that you are here at all is only possible
because of her
don't you forget it
She's literally blossomed
since she's come here
She wouldn't be alive any more
without my kindness
I am her teacher
and I even pay her very well
I pay her more than she deserves
but that's not the point
Here she has everything she needs
At home she has nothing
All that socialist talk everywhere
yet nothing has changed
basically
A primitive vulgar mother
running around in rags
An alcoholic father
eight brothers and sisters choking on their own dirt
because they're too lazy to wash themselves
So much bodily filth
is bound to suffocate the soul
as father used to say
I pulled that child out of the muck
and she has changed to her advantage
Born into that proletarian filth
she would have choked on it
very soon very soon

   believe me
   if I hadn't come along
   The parents were happy
   that I took her on
   When I left
   her mother kissed me on the cheek
   it was repulsive
   The child was happy
   as soon as she set foot
   in this house
CLARA: Into this horrible house
VERA: She doesn't see it as horrible
   she is grateful
   what she came from
   wasn't fit for humans
   You must put yourself in the place of such simple people
   This is paradise for that kind of person
CLARA: This ghastly atmosphere
VERA: Your knowledge of human nature
   is not the best
   It comes straight out of books
   and newspapers
   You really have no personal experience
   This child is well off with us
   and it's just as well
   that she is deaf and dumb and can't be cured
   it saves her
   and of course us
   a lot of trouble
   She has learned a lot around here
CLARA: You mean she saw a lot around here
VERA: You certainly are out of touch with reality
   destructive
   ungrateful
   that's what you are
   Deaf and dumb
   what a blessing
   I don't care
   what she sees

as long as she doesn't talk about it
and that she can't do
Two dresses for her
and of very expensive material
while I haven't bought myself a new dress
in eight years
The sister of Chief Justice Hoeller
has been wearing the same dress for years
I know what people are saying
it's obvious that they envy me
they envy Rudolf for everything
and they wish you the worst
those hypocrites talk about you
as if you were a saint
it's disgusting
By the way I gave her
the dressing gown with the red trim
for her grandmother

CLARA: Generous
    Philanthropic

VERA: Say what you like
    It's all right
    I love you and protect you
    but it's hard with a person
    who despises me unnecessarily
    who thinks she knows better
    Our lot has not been the worst
    What if Rudolf hadn't returned from the war
    What if they had brought him to trial
    Isn't it nice that everything turned out all right
    We are respected people aren't we
    and we are well off
    Whatever we want
    we can have
    With so much misery in the world
    we can't complain
    we have it good
    we don't have to be afraid
    only you are never content

always plagued by your obsessions
I couldn't take care of you myself
dressing and undressing you three times a day
it's out of the question
Rudolf often wonders
if you wouldn't be better off
in a sanitarium
Don't worry
we wouldn't dare
The three of us are a conspiracy
aren't we
You have the best life here
you don't lack anything
you have everything you need
nice surroundings
helpful people
who love you
you always get
your wishes
this we owe one another
to always grant each other every wish
all in all it's an ideal mechanism
you and I and Rudolf
Things could be much worse
(Picks up the robe and holds it against the light.)
We are full of affection for one another
(Looks out.)
It will all stay the same
once he retires
Once we start traveling
Rudolf wants to go to Egypt
We will even find a way
for you to come along
all four of us will go
Olga will be all yours
Who has it easy nowadays
(Directly to Clara.)
No no that child is in good hands here
but you mustn't confuse her

you terrify her
leave her alone
be happy she's here
she does her work
that's all
You're always racking your brains
over trifles
You haven't changed
We don't need a witness on October seventh
(Takes the robe, hangs it on the wall, looks it over.)
Days before the seventh
Rudolf starts to change
everything in him is geared toward the seventh
*(Takes the robe off the wall, puts it back on the ironing board
and continues ironing.)*
He talked to Himmler only once
a man who wasn't to be contradicted
and Rudolf swore that as long as he lives
he would celebrate Himmler's birthday
That he never married
has something to do with this
None of us can get away
(Suddenly directly to Clara.)
And just before October seventh
you keep having those strange dreams
(Questioning her.)
You always wake up
just before he crushes you to death
CLARA: At first I thought
it was an animal
but then it was a man after all
VERA: Well just consider your condition my dear
CLARA: A huge animal you know
a wild animal
completely covered with hair
and it gets bigger and bigger
and I can't get away
I am afraid he will crush me to death

But the moment he crushes me
I wake up
VERA: You always dream of a man
crushing you to death
that's your condition my dear
it's at its worst on October seventh
it's quite obvious that you are afraid
the man will crush you to death
CLARA: I faint and then I wake up
VERA: You still haven't asked him
for his name
it's of utmost importance
that you ask him for his name
CLARA: No
VERA: You must ask him
you must ask him immediately
CLARA: Yes
VERA: You must ask him
you must confront him
your monster
before it crushes you to death
before it turns into a man
CLARA: Yes
VERA: That's the problem
you never ask him for his name
You have to know his name
We simply fell into this that's all
You have to play your part
in your wheelchair you understand
It's always worst before October seventh
but it's also quite wonderful
don't you think so
(*Laughs.*)
You can't fool nature
We keep making the same crucial mistakes
we set up a system for ourselves
and we keep making the same mistakes
(*Suddenly.*)
Shall I wheel you outside

before Rudolf gets home
Afterwards it will be too late you know
For him October seventh
is the most important day of the year
(Looks out.)
It's foggy
you can't see a thing
I can't even see the tree
As long as we keep warm inside
and we have enough food
and we have our Olga
we should be content
Another year gone by already
eight years without a new dress
at least on October seventh
to make Rudolf happy
but I don't have the energy
(Looks out.)
A dangerous afternoon
Always be on your guard
father used to say
He was right
He would be proud of Rudolf
(Hangs the finished robe on the wall, examines it, then:)
And now I'll make us some coffee
You'll have a cup with me won't you
CLARA: Yes of course
VERA: *(As she exits.)* Our father taught us mistrust
    how fortunate
    that we listened to him
CLARA: *(To herself.)* Never suppress mistrust
    always obey mistrust
    always approach people with mistrust
    always listen to nature
VERA: *(Offstage.)* How right he was
    we should have listened to him more
    maybe then he'd still be alive
    how old would father be today

CLARA: *(Calling out.)* He wouldn't have liked
    what happened afterward
VERA: *(Calling back.)* What do you mean
CLARA: You and Rudolf
VERA: You don't understand
    It just happened
    It simplifies so much
    You have no right
    to pass judgment
    it's all to your advantage
    if things were different
    if Rudolf were married
    this way he is with us
    everything is kept between us
CLARA: He always praised you
    he hated me
    He loved you
    he hated me
VERA: How fortunate that you can't walk
    you'd be in jail by now
    with your crazy ideas
    you'd be sitting in some prison
    That wheelchair saves you
    from imprisonment
    Father always knew
    how dangerous you were
    Family killer that's what he called you
    There's some truth to it
    Our little socialist can consider herself lucky
    that she can't move
    they would have caught you long ago
    locked you up and sentenced you
    you would have disappeared
CLARA: It's in my nature
    to be bad
    father used to say
    He always loved you
VERA: You'd be dangerous out there
    I know you

You'd be throwing bombs
and killing people
everyone you hate
you hate them all
Because you're insane
a fanatic
(Enters with a tray of coffee and sits down next to CLARA.)
Your tragedy saved you my dear
you owe everything to that air raid and to the bombing
Rudolf says so too
you'd be a terrorist by now
CLARA: What do you know about that
VERA: From the same parents
yet such completely different children
Be happy you are here
in protective custody so to speak
you are very fortunate
even though everything in you keeps rebelling
that's only natural
this way you are limited
to an occasional nasty letter to the editor
Out there the world is quite different my dear
(Pours herself and CLARA *some coffee.)*
Father liked it
when we went to the park
all dressed in white
he'd let us play
and watch us
sometimes he'd call us My Beauties
Mother always wanted to see Paris
it was her obsession
he hated this idea
he always promised
that he'd take her to Paris
but he had no intention of going
Do you think he loved her
Your father does nothing but abuse me she used to say
He is inhuman
I am ashamed for him she used to say

(Looks at the left door.)
How dirty these doors are
First thing tomorrow
when Olga comes back
the doors must be cleaned
and the windows
there's so much dust on the window sills
You don't see any of this
but its drives me crazy
You should see the kitchen
and today of all days
Actually everything here disgusts me too
but the mere thought
that something might be changed
In fact this place should be repainted
(Looks around.)
See the cracks in the ceiling
they're getting worse
it's an old house
the curtains are gray
everything grimy and gray
We haven't had a visitor in years
because that's how Rudolf wants it
It wouldn't do any harm
to have an occasional visitor
Then again
who would be suitable
Rudolf's cut himself off completely
because of his position
and because in truth he's always been a lonely man
he's always hated company
even though he can be so charming at parties
people are quite surprised
when they see him completely open and relaxed
entertaining a large crowd
who'd be dying of boredom otherwise
he got that from father
who at home was withdrawn
and an absolute tyrant

but a real charmer at parties
it was a big problem for mother
Well from time to time we do get to see the acting Prime
Minister
and Professor Wackernagel
I don't care for that boring man
who only talks about his research
which no one understands and which is worthless I'm sure
there's nothing more boring than that kind of scientist
And he started an argument with Doctor Fromm
which is a pity
the doctor always lightened the mood
As soon as the doctor arrived
everyone's spirits began to brighten up
But it's been two years
since the doctor was last here
He's bought himself a beautiful home
Doctors are rolling in money
They are the only ones who can afford to live in luxury today
The true saints as father used to call them
Maybe I should talk to Rudolf
about making up with the doctor again
don't you think it's a shame
that the doctor has stopped coming
Rudolf was jealous that's true
but now he has no more reason
and you
you liked him too
CLARA: Maybe
VERA: Such people can make a house a home
    they even make the world more livable
CLARA: But even people like him finally conform
    They stagnate they grow stale
VERA: You should have seen the doctor the other day
    I ran into him downtown
    as he was coming out of the jewelry shop
    he looked more elegant than ever
CLARA: I know what you like
VERA: You drag everything through the mud

CLARA: Through the mud where it belongs
VERA: You and your sick views
  You should be pitied my dear
  If you could just once see things from a normal perspective
  Your revolutionary ruined you
  Sometimes I think what a blessing
  that he disappeared from your life
  It's always so crucial whom one meets
  You took up with the devil
  Sometimes I think it's just as well
  he's dead
  He destroyed you that's a fact
  He infected your mind
  fed you disgusting literature
  and completely destroyed you for good
  He took the easy way out
  a bullet through his head
  and not a second thought for you
  But just think if you were
CLARA: Not paralyzed you're about to say
VERA: Of course
  how awful it would be with you
  Yet this is the way things are
  In the meantime you too got old
  it's far better you let me wheel you to his grave
  than being dead yourself
  The bad ones drag the others down
  father used to say
  It's a good thing that I have everything
  already prepared
  Justice Roesch
  won't be coming this year
  he has a cold
  And it's better for Rudolf to be alone
  I don't like that man
  Colleagues are always dangerous
  Perhaps it's just an excuse
  A year ago on his way here
  he was stopped

harassed
by some young hoodlums who recognized him from court
and nearly dragged him into a bar with them
luckily he was able to get away
Imagine they had torn off his coat
and he just stood there in his SS uniform
Maybe he feels it's too dangerous this year
he called and said he had a cold
he felt miserable and couldn't come
he would celebrate Himmler's birthday at home by himself
A despicable man really isn't he
But a loyal friend to Rudolf
His lips are sealed you understand
I know you hate me
when I talk like this
But I get so excited
when October seventh comes around
It's Rudolf's obsession
to celebrate this day
After all it was the high point of his life
The time will come Rudolf says
when he'll no longer be forced
to celebrate Himmler's birthday
hiding away in our house
but out in the open my dear
openly quite openly
in front of everyone
Of course it's madness
the way he clings to it
but why should I spoil his fun
We have to support him
Who knows what's ahead of us
We are a conspiracy
It means so much to him
I'm forever grateful to you
that you leave us in peace
I know what this means to you
Then again what else could you do
And in return first thing tomorrow morning

I'll put all your leftist books back on the table again
and buy you all the newspapers you want
CLARA: You make me sick
 but I listen to you
 I promised
 and you are right
 what else can I do
 I am at your mercy
 It's no secret
 that on Himmler's birthday
 you two also go to bed together
 after the second bottle of champagne
 I'm not even embarrassed anymore
 My poor sister what else can she do
 but submit to her brother's madness
 You are still worse off than I
 and only because you are such a liar
 can you bear to stand it at all
 more perverted than your brother
 more abominable
 much more vicious
 (VERA gets up and exits with the coffee tray.)
 Everything you do is admirable
 I admire you
 I always admire you
 (Calls after her.)
 my big sister
 whom I always admired
 (To herself.)
 We are condemned to viciousness
 (Picks up the pair of socks again, starts mending, calls out.)
 None of us deserves any better
 But your perversity beats Rudolf's
 by far
 (VERA enters and opens the dresser.)
 I admire you
 I really admire you
 but I also despise you

VERA: It's to be expected
    You haven't changed
    (Takes a framed picture of Himmler out of the dresser, walks
    to the window with it and polishes it.)
CLARA: You're not to blame
    Nobody's to blame
VERA: What are you talking about
    just stop it will you
    I know what you really think
    (Breathes on the picture.)
    People are the way they are
    and they have to get along with each other
    You've learned that too
    (Looks out.)
    Everything grimy and gray
    that's the way it was
    even when we were children
    nothing's changed
    Father wouldn't tolerate the slightest change
    We are a true lawyer's family
    with everything that goes with it you understand
    that's not easy
    The lawyer's children people used to say
    when we walked through town by ourselves
    (Breathes on the picture.)
    This picture was taken
    when Himmler visited the camp
    Rudolf had lunch with him alone
    the day after his thirty-ninth birthday
    There was nothing more difficult
    than being camp commander
    A commander that was the worst
    Rudolf was quite impressed
    with what Himmler had to say
    (Puts the picture on the window sill, looks at it.)
    And it was Himmler after all
    who gave him the forged passport
    with which Rudolf disappeared
    Rudolf owes it to him

that he is still here
and we owe it to Rudolf
that we are still here
If they had caught him
they would have killed him on the spot
this way he got off
And then ten years later
no one asked any more questions
That's the way it is
(Takes the picture, exits, and enters again without the picture,
walks to the judge's robe, looks it over.)
Rudolf is a decent man
you know that
If he weren't
we wouldn't live the way we do
People applaud him every time
he talks about love of country
as he did the other day at the Legal Society
Every time he says love and country
he gets applause
They didn't want to see him go
but his retirement can't be put off
(Looks around.)
Father wouldn't tolerate the slightest change
and mother acquiesced
women always acquiesce
that won't change
they won't admit it
but they acquiesce
and they don't mind
at first mother resisted that's true
then she gave up
all of a sudden
from one moment to the next
she gave up quickly don't you think
how old and gray she was already at thirty
and ugly quite frankly
then everything happened very quickly
Paris she said again and again

until she stopped saying it
First father ignored her
then she stopped saying it
(Pulls on the curtain.)
when she was dead he said
I should have taken her to Paris
How would that have changed anything
I think Paris is dreadful
Everyone wants to see Paris
I always found Paris the ugliest city
a desolate wasteland
they all talk of a Paris
that doesn't exist
better dead than living in Paris
Close to home that's where it's nicest
But they all talk of Paris
because it's been the fashion for two hundred years
CLARA: She wasn't ugly
VERA: Mother
CLARA: Yes
VERA: She certainly was
On her thirtieth birthday
a horrible sight my dear
You are lucky
because you don't remember
ugly and bitter that's what she was
old and alone
although she lived in our midst
and father was mean and brutal to her
I'm embarrassed to speak of him like that
but it's the truth
(Holds up the robe.)
Another six months
and he won't be putting on his robe anymore
His Honor the Chief Justice
it will be hard for him
the older they get our dear men
the vainer they get
of course he says he can't wait for the last time

he'll be putting on his robe
but it will be hard on him
His Honor the Chief Justice
a long hard climb
that Paragon of Justice
as they say
(Exits with the robe.)
CLARA: I cleared my own path to the top
father used to say
and I didn't soil my hands in the process
unlike the others
When we went out
we had to walk in front of him
which always frightened us
(Calls out.)
It's a good thing that mother
didn't put up with it any longer
Rudolf was ashamed of her suicide
What sort of lawyer's family is this
where the mother kills herself
Will you bring me the papers
(To herself.)
We inherit the insecurity
that drags out our lives
Hated by father
because unwanted
as well as by mother
*(VERA comes back with a SS officer's uniform and with news-
papers, which she gives to her sister.)*
VERA: Every day you bury your head
in this printed filth
*(Takes the uniform to the ironing board, puts the trousers on
the ironing board, hangs the jacket on the window and starts
ironing.)*
All of us killed mother
she had no resilience
as father used to say
she was made of the fragile matter
which isn't meant for this brutal world

it didn't take much
to break her
(Directly to CLARA.*)*
He didn't want you
and he didn't love you
he was a lawyer through and through
and he would be proud to see Rudolf now
If he knew
that his children ended up alone
he enjoyed
ceremony
he liked being a soldier an officer
Mother foresaw everything
that's why she broke
And under what circumstances did we end up alone
getting there old and alone
the three of us
that's no coincidence
no doubt about that
*(*CLARA *reads the newspapers.)*
You can't wait
for these obscenities
You devour this printed garbage
and you rejuvenate
It's your only passion
you don't have any others
You live on newspapers
nothing else
you think through newspapers
all your values come straight out of newspapers
Nothing is more abominable
than the newspaper business Rudolf says
selling the crap that goes on nowadays
to people who grab it eagerly
The filthiest papers are published
by the Jews
I know you don't like hearing this
but it's a fact
Your father was a Jew hater

like ninety-eight percent of the population
only very few admit
that they are anti-Semitic
but the Germans hate the Jews
even as they claim just the opposite
that's the German nature
you can't get around it
because you can't get around nature
in a thousand years the Jews will still be hated in Germany
in a million years
if there'll be any Germans or Jews left at all
that's what Rudolf says
(After a pause.)
At first it's always an animal
then a large violent man
who crushes you to death
your dreams are a precise reflection
of your condition
you couldn't have any other dreams
My condition isn't much better
(Looks out.)
The days are already getting so short
(Turning toward CLARA *again.)*
Or do you think that my condition is better
that I'm the lucky winner
you know very well this isn't true
and my going to bed with Rudolf
is the most logical solution
I find it perfectly natural
We are a conspiracy
We close the curtains when it's time
Nobody knows what we're doing
We don't keep any secrets from each other do we
(Suddenly resolutely.)
I'll wheel you outside if you want me to
(Looks out.)
But that would be silly
it's cold and almost dark
We've been acting our parts for so many years

we can't get out anymore
if they were alive
we might kill them who knows
I've killed mother many times in my dreams
knifing strangling bludgeoning her
You hide your head behind those papers
but I know what you look like
I know your face
you keep on living in your paper world
you won't be bothered
not by the worst monstrosity
not even if I tell you
that I'd kill my mother
if she were still around
This is how you punish me
this is how we punish each other
How I always hated those papers
all those special magazines I got for you
because I can see
how they gradually ruin you
you're disintegrating from all this reading
It clearly shows what this filth does to you
But the point is
that we keep acting our parts
to perfection
sometimes we don't understand it ourselves
then we get scared
but we know full well what we have to do
You and your wheelchair
that's at least as cruel
as I and Rudolf
We can't help ourselves
we keep lying to ourselves
but how nice it is in the end
doing what we do
by acting it
and acting what we act
by doing it
It is no longer possible

to go against our own rules
(Leaves the ironing board, goes toward CLARA *and strikes the newspaper away from her face.)*
Your face is already ruined
from your papers
You are even uglier
than our mother
It has all been decided my dear
*(*CLARA *tries to smooth out the paper and read it again.)*
The real art lies in keeping
the ones we hate alive
but just enough to torment them
again and again
without really killing them
(Irons the trousers.)
I don't even know
what made me
do it
he didn't resist
your brother
it is quite natural my dear
*(*CLARA *hides her face behind her papers again.)*
You swore
you would never again mention
the names Rosa Luxemburg and Clara Zetkin
you kept your promise
You are one of us all right
and how
We have rehearsed our play
the parts were cast thirty years ago
each of us got his role
a despicable and dangerous one
each got his costume
and woe to the one who slips into the other's costume
The point at which the curtain will come down
must be a joint decision made by the three of us
No one has the right to lower the curtain at will
that's against the law
Sometimes I actually see myself

on a stage
and I am not ashamed in front of the audience
unlike you who is always ashamed
who nearly goes crazy with shame
We only go on
living
because we keep giving each other the cues
you and I and Rudolf
as long as it suits us
we shall see
It's so artificial so cold sometimes
for days
then it eases up again
(Listens.)
For a minute I thought I heard Rudolf
He will sit here and suddenly not say a word
and that means
he wants me
to bring him the photo album
I have to turn the pages
and I have to look at it with him
picture after picture
the same every year
he arranged them in perfect order
that orderly man
for every picture he has a story
a horror story
as if his memory
consisted of nothing but piled-up corpses
This album frightens me more
than anything else
Last year he made me
shave your head
and dress you up
as an inmate of a concentration camp
We must do what he wants
He is a sick man of course
or don't you think so
You bury your head in your papers

because you can't run away
(Looks at the watch.)
Would you like something to eat
I think we should wait
otherwise we'll spoil our appetite for the birthday dinner
I never knew
that Himmler only lived to be forty
a young idol don't you think
I would have liked to have seen Hamlet
I can't see how you can live without Shakespeare
Hamlet
Our brother the Chief Justice
treats us to the center box
and you say no
a new Hamlet
a famous actor
the one who played the Prince of Homburg
I would have enjoyed it
What would people say
if I were to sit alone in the box
without you
Where did you leave your poor sister
that's what they'd say
I've been through it before
that poor child
who was struck by a ceiling beam
by an American bomb
paraplegic how awful
They are always saying the same thing
I know what everyone's saying
If I go by myself everybody keeps asking for you
Your poor sister where is she
helpless
hopeless
pitiful thing
Everything really depends on you
if you won't see Hamlet
I can't see it either
if you won't go to the concert

I can't go either
if you don't care for art
I won't have it either
and you know how much I need cultural stimulation
At least once a month
if not weekly
a cultural stimulant
My love for the theater comes from father
my love for music from mother
you deprive me of plays as well as concerts
We used to go to every chamber recital
that was when we still played the cello of course
CLARA: *(Laughs.)* The cello
When we still played the cello
how out of key we used to play
what ghastly amateurs we were
VERA: You think so
I don't
(Holds the trousers up against the light.)
It was so nice
when we made music
(Looks at the piano.)
It must be years
since I last touched the piano
Making music
in this horrible house
saturating these cold walls with music
bringing them to life with music
CLARA *(Cynically.)*: Saturating with music
you can't be serous
to think you managed
to bring life to this ghastly house
this morgue
VERA: I thought I did
Even when we were children
and mother used to play
on those wonderful long winter evenings
What a shame that Rudolf
gave up the violin

I miss it a lot
he had such a soft touch
The war spoiled it for him
It was so different here
when we made music together
(Goes to the piano, opens it, wants to play something.)
No no
there is no more time to make music
(Turns toward CLARA.*)*
The arts are a means
of saving oneself
but you reject everything beautiful of course
(Closes the piano, gets up and goes back to the ironing board.)
You reject all means of salvation
anything that might bring pleasure
You're shrouded in gloom

CLARA: What a liar you are
how can you be such a liar
you're full of lies and deceit
It was always awful
when our parents were alive
and it was unbearable
when we made music
and nothing has changed
since their deaths
except that the two of you grew more vicious and brutal
you don't even know
what music or art is all about
in your hands music always became
something atrocious
And there was nothing more atrocious
than father reading poetry
how many times did you butcher music
fiction poetry
you always violated art
You always say
when our parents were alive
but nothing has changed

the way you lie
the way you always lied
you always lied to yourself
and to Rudolf and everyone else
The cello how dare you
In your hands it became an abomination
and Rudolf with his violin
I can't think of a greater perversion
It was nothing but a mad idea of our father
and a mad idea of our unfortunate mother
they wanted us to make music
because children from good families always made music
and read fiction and poetry
Deep down father hated music
and he had no idea of Literature
he abhorred poetry
One day he even proved himself stupid enough
to buy a Bösendorfer
he would have done better buying me a pistol instead
to shoot him
to shoot all of you

VERA: You're insane
just like your father
you're getting more like him every day
I get chills
when I hear you
talk like him
now I know exactly why he hated you
and vice versa

CLARA: Music in this cold house
in this abominable pit

VERA: When he read to us
we weren't allowed to move
he always read to us from books
we didn't understand
he tortured us with Schopenhauer

CLARA: And Nietzsche

VERA *(Holds up the trousers against the light and continues ironing.)* When they are doing Strindberg
will you go

CLARA: No
VERA: For months no theater
　　no concert
　　I feel like I'm in prison
　　(Suddenly inquisitive.)
　　What are you punishing me for
　　What did I do
　　If only we could go to court again
　　to amuse ourselves
　　Not if it's Rudolf case of course
　　how about a jury trial
　　one of Roesch's
　　I don't think Rudolf would mind
　　if I tell him
　　we need to get out
　　you're so pale my dear you look sick
　　We're always only dealing with each other
　　I with you
　　you with me
　　and with Rudolf
　　You shouldn't hate me dear
　　I don't deserve it
　　The most interesting trials are coming up now
　　In the old days you were always ready to go
　　No murder trial without you
　　you couldn't wait to go
　　Let's go
　　we never do anything else
　　it's free
　　and it's the most exciting entertainment
　　they made ramps for the handicapped
　　now I can wheel you right into the courtroom
　　Let's go there let's
　　What's the theater
　　compared to a trial
　　(Goes over to the desk and looks at the calendar.)
　　The thirteenth
　　against Amon
　　the twenty-second against Harreiter

Amon's the one who killed the industrialist's widow
remember
CLARA: Of course I remember
VERA: Harreiter is also Roesch's case
not Rudolf's
we'll go yes we'll go there
we'll have lunch with Rudolf in the court house cafeteria
if he's around
(Puts the calendar away, goes back to the ironing board to continue with her ironing, looks out the window.)
The park twice a week
isn't enough
Every day the doctor says
You have to want it my dear
you have to force yourself
it's not enough if I wheel you
in front of the open window
and you breathe in the fresh air
that's not enough
you need a change of scenery
Believe me dear
I want what's best for you
(The telephone rings off-stage.
VERA *exits.*
CLARA *looks after her.)*
VERA *(Speaks off-stage, but she can't be understood. She returns with a striped inmate's jacket.)* Rudolf
if everything is ready
he's on his way
(Referring to the inmate's jacket.)
Maybe he wants you
to put it on
it's possible
(Hangs the SS trousers on the wall and irons the inmate's jacket.)
Suddenly it may occur to him
that you should put it on
and he'll want me to shave your head
You'll ruin your eyes my dear

(Walks over to CLARA *and turns a light on for her.)*
Come on give me the papers
Rudolf will be here any moment
He doesn't like you
reading those papers
(Takes the stack of papers and exits.)
Tomorrow morning you can read again
*(*CLARA *examines the pair of socks which she mended.)*
VERA *(Enters.)* Once he's no longer at court
he'll be home all day
he isn't much of a walker as you know
he'll just sit around all day
and wait
*(Walks to the ironing board and holds the inmate's jacket up
against the light.)*
Sometimes I think
he's much too good natured
Some of his sentences are much too lenient
he didn't make the best of our penal code
even though he had the opportunity
then again he can be so tough it's hard to understand
(Exits with the inmate's jacket.)
CLARA: *(Calling after her.)* I won't put it on
even if he wants me to
not today
VERA: *(Enters with* RUDOLF's *boots, sits down and polishes them.)*
Wait and see
how everything goes
we mustn't irritate him
you have to control yourself
If he wants you to
just put on the jacket
you've got to you know that
(Gets up, takes the SS uniform from the wall and takes it out.)
CLARA: Not today
I can't
I won't
VERA: *(Comes back and continues to polish the boots.)* It's just for
tonight

let him have his fun
we all have our follies
But he is serious about it
deadly serious
(Gets up, sits down in front of the mirror and combs her hair.)
At first I thought
it's just a quirk
but then I realized that he is serious
about this birthday
I never resisted him
And what else could you do
but go along with it
after thirty years
it's too late to change anything
You know how Rudolf is
I am glad
that Justice Roesch won't be coming today
that we can be by ourselves
(Turns toward CLARA.*)*
But for you the company of Justice Roesch
would mean a welcome distraction
(Starts to braid one braid.)
I can easily go back in time
(Lifts up her head and looks in the mirror.)
Of course I'm no longer the young maiden in braids
but he wants it this way
Why shouldn't I do what he wants
I must admit I think it's very nice of you
to go along
even though you hate it
I admire you
CLARA: Now you look as you did forty years ago
but even forty years ago
I couldn't stand you
You always tortured me
you never missed an opportunity to torture me
as if all you ever did was devise
new ways to torture me
always new humiliations

like my father
wasn't really my father
you told me that one often
you lied to me
you humiliated me
whenever you could
At night when I slept and you didn't
you pulled me by my braids out of bed
You locked me in the cellar
you secretly tore up my clothes
(Starts combing herself.)
You started it with Rudolf didn't you
you took advantage of the situation
it's disgusting

VERA: You simply don't know
what's going on inside a person
you don't even know what's going on inside yourself
you just keep nagging
and drag everything through the mud
What's between Rudolf and me
is completely clean it is pure
you should be hit every time you open your mouth
but you're my sister
it's not my fault that I can walk and you can't
I'm punished in other ways
(Sticks out her tongue in front of the mirror.)
It just happened this way
all you ever see is some plot against you
it's not immoral my dear
Good God the way you carry on
instead of being glad
you're not in pain
What if you were in pain all the time
There you sit and you're all right
you have every wish taken care of
but that you can't walk and run off
is something you can't blame on anyone
You see us as the guilty parties
Rudolf and myself that is

I can't drive this madness out of your head
What a good life you could have
if you could simply be content
Rudolf and I we suffer more from you than you suffer yourself
that's the truth
he is such a kindhearted man
who gives his all
and I too am I not at your disposal day and night
but you don't see that
you don't want to see that
although you know it very well
We hate those who help us
(Works on her second braid.)
The truth is that we sacrificed ourselves for you
We could have left
we didn't leave
so that you wouldn't be left alone
we could have sold this house
we didn't
for your sake
We could put you into an institution
then we would be by ourselves
how nice it would be sometimes
and how often do I wish
you were in an institution
and would leave me alone and in peace
Do you really believe Rudolf is happy
this is no constellation
to give happiness
to a man his age and in his position
Rudolf's life deserved quite another final chapter
we sacrificed it for you
(Sticks out her tongue.)
and all we get is your relentless hate
for myself and Rudolf
You are our enemy
not like someone of our own flesh and blood
Every cripple torments his nurse

father used to say
until they drop dead
In fact you are the strongest of us all
You will outlive us all
I am sure
you will outlive us all
How much longer can Rudolf go on
with his bad heart
You are the healthiest
that makes it even more grotesque
You control us
not the other way around
we are the ones who need help
not you
you determine what happens
whether I get to the theater or not
You sit in your wheelchair as if it were a throne
and you give the orders
A bomb put you in first position
your immobility has paralyzed us
Rudolf and myself
I dread the day
he takes off his robe
never to put it on again
It is his retirement
I fear
then all three of us will be sitting here
in this room
just waiting to die
But who knows how long it will take
a process of gradual mortification
Then you will sit in judgment of us
that's what I'm afraid of
Rudolf of course suspects what lies ahead of him
but he doesn't have the strength to say it
(Looks around.)
How I hate all this furniture
I am never alone
I am under your constant surveillance

If I do go out it means rushing back home
to my poor sister
People will never know what it means
to be watched that closely
by someone like you
and to be judged
You deny me a heart
yet yours is cold as ice
(Gets up, walks over to CLARA *and combs her hair.)*
How contradictory each of us is
how vicious we can be
combing your hair relaxes me
(Gives the comb to CLARA *and walks back to the dresser, sits
down in front of the mirror.)*
Your misery isn't just yours alone
it's our misery too
above all our misery
Once Rudolf is retired
things will change perhaps
We will travel
You'll see Rudolf will take you out
every day off to the park
into the city with Rudolf
Then he'll have the time to sit with you in the park
(Pins her braids to her head.)
He is a kind man
Everyone says so
Everyone who knows him knows how kind he is
All these insidious rumors
(Exclaims.)
And even what they say is true
it happened so long ago
I don't think Rudolf is guilty
of a crime
not he
(Turns toward CLARA *and shows her her braids pinned to her
head.)*
That's how he likes me
just like that

Do you remember
us running around this way as little girls
during the war
during the Nazis
(Turns toward the mirror, looks into it and undoes her hairdo,
untying her braids.)
First Rudolf takes a bath
What if
Rudolf hadn't come back
if he had gone on under his own name
Ten years in the military underground
After that no one asked any more questions
Now they start dredging up the past again
hunting down every decent law-abiding citizen
(Turns toward CLARA.*)*
Rudolf is a good good man
You are proof of it
What's past doesn't matter
And who's to know how it really was
Now they are digging up the dirt again
You should have seen
how the children loved him
they all love him
Kindness creates enemies
father used to say
During war there are no laws
father used to say
(Listens.)
Do you hear something
I thought it was Rudolf
If only he can make the transition
if only he doesn't fall apart
The Government automatically exiles
its most accomplished people into retirement
the best ones far too soon
But the Government can afford it right
Rudolf would love to stay in office
but no the authorities stick to the date of birth
and send him home

They never had a better judge
If only all judges were like him
How quickly time passes
it seems only yesterday
that Rudolf became Chief Justice
It's the most difficult
public office Rudolf says
the most responsible one
Being a judge means setting the perfect example
He always was the sickliest among us
do you remember
a cold every moment
and if he'd jumped out of a window just for the fun of it
you could be sure he'd land on a rusty tin
every other moment he'd be walking with a limp
or have to stay in bed
mother loved him
he was her favorite
she always took his side
(Gets up and walks to the window. Takes the uniform from its hanger.)
He is the only one
She's paid attention to
without Rudolf we wouldn't be here anymore
(Takes the clothes brush and brushes the uniform.)
Rudolf has proven
who he really is
We know
and love our brother
He still is the child
he once was
(Looks through the window.)
the timid shy child
We must stick by him you understand
very very closely
(Brushes the uniform.)
he needs us
(Looks through the pockets for something and finally pulls out the Iron Cross of the First Order.)

Our hero
(Pins the Iron Cross on the uniform jacket.)
I beg you
don't cause any trouble
you've got to control yourself
for my sake
for our sake
promise me
maybe it is the last time
I always dread this day
He must celebrate this day
his own way you understand
you've got to control yourself
(Looks through the window, suddenly:)
Rudolf is here
How lucky everything is ready
I even got the azaleas
Rudolf's favorite flowers
(Exits with the uniform.)

CURTAIN

Act 2

Ten minutes later. RUDOLF *in his chair, exhausted.* CLARA *mending* RUDOLF's *socks.* VERA *enters with* RUDOLF's *winter coat.*

RUDOLF: Here's the button here
(Searches his jacket for his button and finally finds it.)
There
They tried to stop me again
near the school
as I was passing by with Roesch
VERA: Those Jew boys
RUDOLF: I'll have a talk with their father some time
I'm sure Mr. Schwartz is behind all this
always the same place
(To CLARA.*)*

Now the Jew boys are hanging out
where your tragedy occurred
If you hadn't been in school that day
everything would have been different
Right on target smack into the school
And only two days before the end

VERA: Schwartz of all people
who do they think they are
that they can carry on like that
(RUDOLF gives VERA the button to his coat and VERA fixes the button.)
I'll be glad when you are retired Rudolf
Then all these troubles will be over
But maybe those kids were just playing

RUDOLF: Today of all days
There is a connection
between today's date
and the way those youngsters came at me

VERA: Maybe it's just your imagination
Mr. Schwartz always treats me very kindly
I always get the best service in his shop

RUDOLF: Maybe you're right
maybe it is just my imagination
I am a little exhausted that's true
But why me of all people
They didn't go after Roesch
A year ago they stopped me
at the very same place

VERA: They're just children Rudolf
they don't know what they're doing
Unruly undisciplined like everyone else
nowadays
Everything's changed
children nowadays can do as they please
Besides at our age we just can't take children anymore
You would have never put up with children
What a thought you and children
(Has fixed the button and bites off the thread.)
We were still brought up well

Today's children grow up like savages
This descent into barbarity comes from America
Savage children are ruling the world today
There's nothing but chaos all around
(RUDOLF *gets up, gets into his coat.* VERA *is helping him.*)
VERA: Where will it all end
    with everyone heading toward chaos
RUDOLF: *(Buttoning his coat.)* I've been wearing this coat for ten
    years
    I should have a new one made
    But not before I retire
    Ten years in the same coat
    You won't find that among my colleagues
    (Goes to the window, looks out.)
    There they're suddenly pushing me around
    pulling on me and the button is off
    (Takes off the coat again.)
    There is a connection between all this
VERA: You are overworked Rudolf that's all
    you overdid it lately
    All this devotion to duty
    and who thanks you for it
    I'll be glad when everything is over
    As Chief Justice you get a handsome pension
    then we won't have to give a damn
    then all we care about is ourselves
RUDOLF: *(Gives the coat back to* VERA *and sits down.)* We have no
    reason to complain of course
    Things could have been quite different
    Everyone has his own cross to bear
    (To CLARA.*)*
    Our victim how is she today
    are you in pain
    All day I'm haunted by the thought of you
    sitting at home in pain
    Just think though
    soon we'll be going to Egypt
    all three of us
    (To VERA.*)*

We'll pack up and go
to Genoa and from there by boat
to Alexandria
I've been dreaming about this for decades
I can hardly wait
(Gets up and goes toward CLARA.*)*
You shall always have a good life my dear
We can consider ourselves lucky
Others have turned to dust years ago
(Walks to the window and looks out.)
The factory was voted down
I got it through
It certainly would be unbearable
to have a factory wall in front of our window

VERA: Now see how influential you are
You only have to want something
and you get it

RUDOLF: Now they'll build it on the other side of town
it won't bother us there
What a depressing view it would be
Instead of trees
we would see a wall
behind which they manufacture poison
(To CLARA.*)*
For your sake I put up a fight
against the construction of that plant
The decision came this morning at eleven

VERA: Oh Rudolf we have to celebrate this too

RUDOLF: Of course I made a lot of enemies

VERA: They can't harm you anymore
You've achieved everything you ever wanted

RUDOLF: Destroying nature
cutting down trees
cutting down those beautiful old trees
for the sake of a chemical plant
which produces nothing but poison
The profit mongers get their hands on everything
The world has never been so brutal
profit guides and governs everything

Wherever some land has still been preserved
you can be sure that industry moves in
But not here I told them
not here
not in front of my window
where nature is still untouched
I love our view
CLARA: But you can't see a thing
RUDOLF: Not now
but that doesn't alter the fact that this view
is my favorite view
When the fog is gone
even in winter when the branches are all ice
and all is white like made of glass
(Turns around and goes toward CLARA.*)*
Roesch asked me
why we didn't put you in an institution
But I told him
the thought never entered our minds
having you institutionalized
We and that means Vera and I and you
we shall stay together
no matter how long
I swore to it
We must endure one another my child
It will all be better once I'm at home
then I can take on some of Vera's work
we can go to the park every day
and into town twice a week maybe
Your brother likes to see you happy
Once I'm no longer in office
I'll be free
and that means all three of us will be free
(Goes to VERA.*)*
Now I often think
it is time to quit
it really is too much for me
then again when I look at Roesch
married

(Sits down.)
two children
what you might call a family
he's not as fit as I
yet he's much younger
Family life burns you out very quickly
we've managed fairly well
we can't complain
Luckily the house is paid off
now we have our peace
Marriage is something horrible
people run into it blindly
craving this marital bliss
they can hardly wait for it
at seventeen or eighteen that soon
they make their child
and get married
We've had it better the three of us
A higher level of consciousness
(VERA sits down.)
A higher degree of difficulty
not without its troubles of course
not without despair as father used to say
Things were just the way they were that's all
*(To CLARA who had put away the socks and is reading a book
now.)*
If you hadn't been wrecked
and you'll forgive me such harsh words
you would have married
you would be gone
to who knows where
in any case you would have married
living your own life
but most likely you wouldn't even be alive
you would have destroyed yourself
your tragedy saved you from destruction
the bomb that hit the school
only as a cripple
did you have a chance to survive

(Facing VERA.*)*
am I not right
this is how we became what we are
a conspiracy against the stupidity of life
(Looks at CLARA.*)*
She pretends to read
one of her books of lies
and she despises us
(To VERA.*)*
We all deserve what we are
(Looks at the watch.)
Six o'clock
(VERA *gets up and goes to the piano.)*
RUDOLF: *(To* CLARA.*)* That's a good idea
play something
I haven't heard you play in a long time
maybe you can't anymore
it's been so long
In the old days music used to count so much
(VERA *starts to play. She improvises on "A Little Night Music" by Mozart.)*
RUDOLF: *(To* CLARA.*)* I used to love it
when she sat down and played
at twilight
like old times
When I lived in hiding
behind closed curtains
during my cellar days
I'd venture upstairs around nine at night
and listen to her
that's when she'd play for me
And you'd sit exactly where you're sitting now
and watch me
You hated me then as you hate me now
I got used to it
I got tough just like you
we all got tough
For ten years I had to hide
then it was time

to see the daylight again
Who would have thought
that I would end my career as Chief Justice
and retire with an enormous pension
(Looks at VERA.*)*
Who would have thought so Vera
That's how times change
At first ten years hidden in a cellar
hidden by you and Clara
And then suddenly this rise
I have no bad conscience
Now and then things get a bit sticky for me
that's true even today
but I don't have a bad conscience
if that were the case all the others
would have to feel much worse than I
I only did my duty
and I paid my dues
I did my work and I accomplished more
than could be expected of me
I paid my dues
I owe no apologies
(Turns around.)
On this day the seventh of October a day of reckoning
I swore
to go through with it my way
(To CLARA.*)*
You always find it quite repulsive
but to me it's a necessity
to Vera too it's a necessity
and we do celebrate this birthday
in all due modesty
just the three of us in the quiet of our home
If it weren't for Himmler
this house wouldn't be here
you know what would be here instead
a poison plant
isn't it strange Vera that today
I too could prevent

the construction of a toxic gas plant
right in front of our windows
Forty years ago Himmler prevented it
today I prevented it
There's no such thing as coincidence
If I could have said in front of the city council
what was really on my mind
when the city council rejected the project
Of course I had to hold my tongue
I exercised my power
I really did
categorically
and maybe for the last time
His Honor the Chief Justice showed his muscle
his word counts
they all listened to me
they all accepted my arguments
now of course I have the other part of town
against me
Once they start construction work there
But in our part of town which is prettier more valuable
they'll thank me forever
In a hundred years hence
when we won't even be alive anymore
They will still talk about this council meeting
the one in which Chief Justice Hoeller
was able to have the final word
saving this district from the worst possible fate
VERA: You are really enjoying this
You really are in your element
and today of all days
RUDOLF: What a coincidence
which it isn't
that today of all days was the day of the meeting
and that a decision was reached
People don't even realize
how much they owe me
For generations to come
I saved nature in this district

VERA: Oh Rudolf one day they'll build you
    a monument a real statue
RUDOLF: I couldn't have done any more
    (Looks toward CLARA.*)*
    Yet I kept only thinking of us
    how we must not let them destroy
    the view from our window
    this barbarous industrial society
    that already destroyed ninety percent of our globe
    The war bred its own kind of profiteers
    but peace time wheeler-dealers are much worse
    The Jews destroy annihilate the surface of the earth
    and some day they will have achieved
    its final destruction
    The Jews sell out nature
    Democracy is a fraud
    But woe to the man who raises his voice these days
    to give away such truths
    they cut his throat no less
    (Looks at CLARA.*)*
    But it's obvious of course
    that the exceptions prove the rule
    and I myself met hundreds and thousands
    of decent Jews
    I'm not talking about those
    I'm talking about the criminal ones
    it's the ruthless Jew I'm talking about
    who under the guise of democracy
    exploits nature and wrecks the earth
    unscrupulously
    *(*VERA *closes the piano.)*
    We are living in terrible times
    we Europeans did everything wrong
    once this is understood it will be too late
    Americanism has poisoned us
    Those who glorify democracy
    are in fact its murderers
    But we live in a thoroughly opportunistic world
    which only knows the language of hypocrisy

not one truthful word is spoken by anyone
thus we are heading toward a dreadful situation
(Gets up, goes to the window and looks out.)
The worst degeneration has affected
all walks of life
Sometimes I wish I were no longer alive
when it's this gray and cold outside
and there is no one I can openly talk to
always functioning with a paralyzed tongue
filled with lies and shameless through and through
We'd be living in totally different times
had we been able to have it our way
Things will be different again mark my words
but we won't live to see it
the young will wake up
and not stand for what's happening now

VERA: *(Goes to* RUDOLF.*)* Why rack your brains
it won't do any good
but of course this day
makes you think this way
We are doing all right
no one is bothering us really
(Kisses his forehead.)
Just think what you are
and who you are
None of this filth can harm you

RUDOLF: One day the Germans will realize
what the Americans did to them

VERA: We will have a nice party
and no one can stop us
no one
(Turns toward CLARA.*)*

RUDOLF: *(Also facing* CLARA.*)* We shall win
the enemy will destroy itself

VERA: *(Takes both of* RUDOLF's *hands and leads him back to the
chair at the window. They both sit down.)* I'm proud of you
of what you accomplished today
Chief Justice Hoeller
kept the toxic gas plant away from our window

RUDOLF: I knew of course
    that the crucial meeting was to be on October seventh
    I staked all my bets on one deal
    I was a one man conspiracy against all
    for the prevention of this plant
    first most of the votes were against me
    but then I felt
    the force of my arguments coming through
    and soon the majority of the votes were on my side
    even Roesch initially against me
    finally voted down the construction of the plant
    in this spot
    with the meeting still in session I crossed the room
    and thanked him
    I even convinced the Socialists
VERA: Now you are the old Rudolf again
    whom I always admired
    whom I love
    (To CLARA *while she is holding* RUDOLF's *wrist.)*
    Isn't it true
    Rudolf is his old self again
    strong willed unbending tough
    The road we walked on
    was strewn with many stones
    but now it is clear
    Every man's goodness
    will assert itself one day
    and you are a good man Rudolf
    (With a glance at CLARA.*)*
    we know it
    Often it was tough going
    You took completely after father
    if he could see
    what you've achieved
    He had to die so soon
    before he could have the slightest idea
    of what would become of you
RUDOLF: I owe you two so much

VERA: It's your own energy Rudolf
Because you never gave in
and because you paid no attention
to other people's opinions
God forbid you had listened to them
you would have perished
they would have trampled you to death
(RUDOLF stretches out his legs and VERA takes off his shoes.)
VERA: It's just awful to think
that they might have had it their way
had they discovered your hiding place
For almost ten years you didn't venture
into the streets
It's a disgrace for our country
(Looks at his feet.)
Your feet are swollen Rudolf
Soon all this standing in the cold courtroom will be over
Everything there is inhuman
What was going on today
RUDOLF: The Meissner murder case
A cold blooded individual
Everything was clear from the beginning
but the Law demands
that we deal with such animals
for over half a year
What's the use of a lifetime sentence
if after fifteen years these people
are on the loose again
VERA: One really lives in constant fear
(With a glance at CLARA.)
Clara mended your socks
Five pairs today
she works hard
I use these woollen socks to trick her
into forgetting about her reading
Every day a dozen papers
plus the books
The money it costs
But that's not even the point

> She already has
> a thoroughly twisted mind
> What it took me today of all days
> to keep her
> away from her papers
> I simply snatched them away from her
> As soon as she is done with her mending
> her head's back in the books again

RUDOLF: And to what papers did you write today
> Your letters to the editor always
> exaggerate
> because you write so many
> nobody takes you seriously any more
> She got herself hopelessly stuck
> in this political fanaticism
> we must consider our sister a lost case
> Just imagine us without our enemy
> *(Takes off* RUDOLF's *socks.)*
> It will be good
> when you're no longer in office
> My dear Chief Justice

RUDOLF: *(Takes off his jacket.* VERA *helps him.)* It's much too hot
> in here

VERA: *(Who has helped him into a pair of slippers.)* I keep it that
> way for Clara
> all she does is sit in her wheelchair
> and read all day

RUDOLF: But it's not healthy
> in such overheated rooms
> *(*VERA *gets up and opens the window.)*
> I shall spend much time out in nature
> and I will pursue my music again
> You can get my violin ready
> get the dust off
> Do you think I still can play it

VERA: It's something you don't forget Rudolf
> not a master like you

RUDOLF: It won't click anymore

VERA: Nobody ever played the violin as well as you
> a born virtuoso that's what you are

RUDOLF: I can't even read music anymore
    She got herself hopelessly stuck
    in this political fanaticism
    we must consider our sister a lost case
    Just imagine us without our enemy
VERA: *(Takes off* RUDOLPH's *socks.)*
    It will be good
    when you're no longer in office
    My dear Chief Justice
RUDOLF: *(Takes off his jacket.* VERA *helps him.)* It's much too hot
    in here
VERA: *(Who has helped him into a pair of slippers.)* I keep it
    that way for Clara
    all she does is sit in her wheelchair
    and read all day
RUDOLF: But it's not healthy
    in such overheated rooms
    *(*VERA *gets up and opens the window.)*
    I shall spend much time out in nature
    and I will pursue my music again
    You can get my violin ready
    get the dust off
    Do you think I still can play it
VERA: It's something you don't forget Rudolf
    not a master like you
RUDOLF: It won't click anymore
VERA: Nobody ever played the violin as well as you
    a born virtuoso that's what you are
RUDOLF: I can't even read music anymore
VERA: In your sleep you can
RUDOLF: In my sleep
    the things we can do in our sleep
    We can hardly believe
    all the things we can do in our sleep
    Without the music it's so empty here
    don't you agree
    (Takes off his vest, slips down his suspenders with a glance at
    CLARA.)*
    I'm not appreciated

sitting around like this I know
but I can't stand it any other way
where else but at home
can I let myself go
VERA: All day long the severest discipline
RUDOLF: Mask of dignity over my face
his Honor the Chief Justice
You have no idea
how impertinent people are nowadays
how shrewd
(Takes a deep breath.)
No we must hold together
it won't be easy
(Looks at the ceiling.)
Then we'll have the place painted
and perhaps the furniture rearranged
maybe the dresser here
and the two chairs over there
The piano should be more in the light
And different curtains
these were already our grandparents'
VERA: Yes how well they used to make things
they last and last
The things they're making now
are worthless
by the time one gets used to them
they're already falling apart
RUDOLF: Let them build their plant in this district
I said
I said it very loudly very clearly
but then you'll have destroyed
the face of this town our home town
utterly
forever
just for a momentary profit's sake
Then there was a pause
Then I spoke about
what this district means to our town
what it's always meant to me

one must get personal if one wants to convince
I described a few childhood impressions
this and that from our childhood
how we used to play in the park with our parents
such happy parents such happy children
I said
You are destroying all that
if you vote for the plant
the whole town will be wrecked
Think it over think what you're doing
Then they voted against the plant

VERA: Oh Rudolf isn't it nice
such agreement
such solidarity
(Gets up and kisses his forehead.)
They know what they have in you
(Leaves with the shoes.)

RUDOLF: *(To* CLARA.) Every now and then
the thinking man has the obligation
to intervene in world affairs
and even if it is only
to prevent a gas plant in a place
where it doesn't belong

VERA: *(Enters with Himmler's photograph.)* You see I got a new
frame for the Reichsführer SS
that's my gift for this day
for Himmler's birthday
solid silver
come on take it
*(*RUDOLF *takes the photograph.)*
If the jeweler had only known
what picture was going in that frame
Do you like it

RUDOLF: Very precious very precious

VERA: I had to look for a long time
to find just the frame
(Takes the picture and leaves again.)

RUDOLF: *(To* CLARA.) You are so considerate
As one grows older and older

one gets more considerate
(VERA enters and sits down.)
Incidentally I met Doctor Fromm
(To CLARA.)
he asked about you
I told him you were fine
no complications whatsoever
he still thinks
you should be institutionalized
However I assured him
that we are determined
to never have you institutionalized
even though all things considered
that's what I said
it might be better for your health
there's nothing we can do for you in medical terms
I said that yes
since this is October seventh after all
I didn't mention that
but I thought so to myself
if the Americans hadn't attacked the school
Two days before the war was over
innocent people
this poor helpless child I said
I called it a terror attack
but he didn't react to that
Ninety-two dead children I said and he
What ninety-two
I completely forgot
Yes said I
one easily forgets these horrible figures
If my sister Clara
the most intelligent of us I said to him
had not been struck by that falling beam
Oh yes of course said Doctor Fromm that beam
A terror attack just two days before the end I said
Wouldn't he like to visit us
not for medical purposes I said
medically speaking he has no business in our house

for a chat I said
my two sisters Vera and Clara would certainly be pleased
a man with such extraordinary abilities
such knowledge
with so profound an education
and so charming I said
he took his leave
he was clearly upset because
I spoke of a terror attack
that shows right away he's a Jew
Medical people are a strange breed
I never got along with them
You ask them something
they talk around the answer
they can't look you in the face
Doctors have had a bad conscience
for centuries father said
he was right
If you believe a doctor you are lost
father used to say
getting involved with a doctor
means getting involved with death no less
If we put ourselves in the hands of doctors
we are doomed to death
If we happen to run into a doctor
it's best to turn the other way
and we will save ourselves from horrendous lifelong ailments
and in most cases we'll even escape death itself
Doctors are death's delivery boys father said
Of course if we only use them for our own purposes
to have them at our command as it were
to cut out an appendix or cut off a leg
since otherwise we would kick off anyway
but otherwise
the company of doctors is the most dangerous
you do better as our father said
inviting the first violinist of the Philharmonic Orchestra
that can't do any harm
if we only do it once or twice a year

And you know what he said
our Doctor Fromm
before he took off
and after I conversed with him
in the most civilized manner
Weren't you substitute camp commander
he put special emphasis on substitute
before I realized what he meant
he was off and away
People have started
to dig up the past again
something's been set in motion
it's not hard to guess by whom
it's a good thing we cut off all social contacts
we don't need anybody

VERA: Oh Rudolf nothing can happen to you
ten years in a cellar that's something
way down there with the rats

RUDOLF: *(With a glance at* CLARA.*)* I can imagine what's going on
inside your sister Clara
but let's leave it at that
The fact is that we did everything humanly possible
for our country
that we spent our lives breaking our backs
for its people
corrosion and destruction are the result
but it will change
Something is brewing
in our favor
people can't fool me
most of them are good Germans
who want no part
in what is going on today
The good German detests what's going on in this country
Depravity hypocrisy general stupefaction
The Jewish element has taken root everywhere
again you can see it everywhere in every nook and cranny

VERA: Oh Rudolf
You must take it easy
you must take care of yourself

RUDOLF: There is a criminal in each of us
　　he just has to be called upon
　　that's how it has always been
　　that's how it will always be
　　(Takes a handkerchief from his trousers, wipes his forehead,
　　and points outside with his handkerchief.)
　　There right there
　　an enormous wall
　　behind which poison is produced
　　poison to exterminate insects
　　gas
VERA: Today's a big day for you
　　the day you prevented an enormous disaster
RUDOLF: It is inconceivable
　　right on this beautiful piece of land
　　Industry has the main say
　　industry not democracy
　　Democracy is the biggest nonsense
　　that ever existed
　　Democracy is the biggest business for those
　　in charge of democracy
　　(To CLARA.*)*
　　Speechless as always
VERA: *(Sits down.)* And merciless
　　From her vantage point she watches us and waits
　　until the day she'll strike out
RUDOLF: *(Jumping up, angrily.)* Where do you get all your hate you
　　and your kind
　　who gives you the right
VERA: *(Calming him down.)* Sit down Rudolf sit down
　　*(*RUDOLF *sits down.)*
VERA: It's just a game
　　it's nothing serious
　　it can't be serious
　　It's a real comedy
　　sometimes we forget that
　　Why shouldn't we play this comedy
　　especially today
　　I admire you Clara

she plays the hardest part
We only give her the cues
With her speechlessness
she keeps the comedy in motion

RUDOLF: Now the office is beginning
to get to me
We used to say we're getting old
and now we already are
(VERA *starts to massage his neck first and then his whole back.*)
One thing is sure
there's no one you can trust
they're all spies
Follow your distrust
father said
All life long alone
everyone by himself
And all for what
Sometimes I think it were better
to have died in Siberia
like our nephew
instead of having gone through all this
how strenuous it is
how it's dragging on
we have to live and don't even want to
for the few hours we can count on one hand
Where did we get all that energy
If I had taken up music
or mathematics
But that's not for a lawyer's son
(*Recoils from pain.*)

VERA: Here it is

RUDOLF: Yes right in that spot
After three o'clock my whole body aches
but this feels good
(VERA *opens his shirt and massages him lower down.*)
If you had married taken a husband
most likely a lawyer whom else
with a fortune

from a wealthy family
had you moved into a modern house
had children
you'd still be alone now
old age leaves everyone alone
first they have children so that they won't be alone
and then they are completely alone
I can see them all around me
growing old and lonely
what's left to a man is him alone
and old

VERA: Whom could I have married
I can't think of one man
You maybe

RUDOLF: If I hadn't been around
if circumstances hadn't been what they were
Didn't you have to come down to the cellar
and take care of me
And of Clara
You are a brave girl Vera
how different from your mother
you made it through everything
she quit
a tiny breeze and she was gone
(VERA wants to take off his shirt, but in order to do so, he has
to unbutton his pants.)
You are the bravest of us all
the most dependable one
First they couldn't find me
because you were hiding me
then the dust could settle
for ten years
and then it all happened very quickly
(Now VERA takes off his shirt completely and puts it on his
shoulders.)
I grew into my office as they say
a man takes on the features of his office
he merges with his office
I had no other choice

whatever I did I was forced to do
and I did nothing
I couldn't justify
on the contrary

VERA: You are racking your brains
for no reason at all
All those people digging up the past
totally incompetent
He who acts in good faith and conscience
shall prevail in the end father said

RUDOLF: I have no bad conscience

VERA: Of course not
One day you will be able to speak openly
about everything you have to keep silent about now
The time will come sooner than you think

RUDOLF: If it can be arranged
we will go to sea
to Egypt of course
that's what I've always missed
a cultural excursion
back to antiquity
the pyramids
Persepolis
we are all victims of the war
A life dear Vera
utterly devoted to the penal code
You should have seen that bastard
at the scene of the crime
cold to the bone
cynical
complete indifference toward his victim
killing a man for four thousand
but they are all alike
that didn't exist in our days
such elements simply didn't exist
they never surfaced to begin with
each trial opens your eyes
to a human cesspool
now I'm just about sick of it

VERA: Only a few more months
    and it will all be over
RUDOLF: Actually I'm glad
    When I think that
    fifteen years after I retire
    people will still be sitting out their sentences
    the ones I passed upon them
    I won't even be alive for that
    How one can be a judge
    father used to say
    I ask myself how one can be a judge
    a curse hangs over this office
VERA: Oh Rudolf you are overtired
    You take your bath
    and everything will look quite different
    We'll have a good dinner tonight
    The champagne is chilled
    I've got everything ready for you
    the way you've always wanted it
    everything the way you're used to it
    everything brushed and ironed
    boots polished
    by me not by Olga
RUDOLF: Substitute commander he said
    substitute camp commander
    so young and already a judge
    In principle I never had anything against the Jews
    We always had our Jewish friends
VERA: Once you're in retirement
    I'll get slip covers for these chairs
    don't you think they're pretty shabby
    Our mother had them upholstered
    We changed absolutely nothing in here
    everything is the way we took it over from our parents
    Out of piety you always said
    we won't change anything
    And new curtains
    We should change everything just a bit
    once you're out of office

who cares about the money
for decades we never indulged
in any kind of luxury
always frugal
Everything for Clara
nothing for us
(Kneels down in front of him and starts massaging his feet.)
I wouldn't do this for anyone else
for no other man but you
The majority is on our side you know that
Her husband was with the Military SS
Mrs. Leupold said
and then she showed me her living room
Come on in it's all right she said
you see this is where my husband rejuvenates
this is his temple
nothing but memorabilia from his military days
Iron Crosses handwritten documents
by the highest dignitaries of our time
You are my hero my baby
you needn't be afraid
Afraid of what
(Looks at CLARA.*)*
If she could talk
if she could walk out of here
and talk
if she weren't dependent on us
she would betray us
if it didn't mean her death
this is how we all pay our dues
in order to maintain
the balance of our conspiracy
yes there was something else Mrs. Leupold had
she opened several drawers
and showed me this and that belonging to her husband
medals and pieces of clothing
several pieces of jewelry from Jews
She had known for a long time
that we shared the same views

but I mustn't tell anyone
what I had seen there
her husband made her swear
but she showed me everything
she even has a letter from the Führer
but that letter's locked up in a safe
Her husband has dealings with the Near East
Business isn't bad
One of his nieces fell off a horse
and for twenty years
she's been a paraplegic just like Clara
they put her in an institution in the Black Forest
she's doing well there
they have the best doctors
(The telephone rings in the adjoining room.)
RUDOLF: Who can that be
      No one calls on October seventh
VERA: Wait
      (Exits.)
RUDOLF: *(To* CLARA.*)* Who can that be
      *(*VERA *can be heard talking, but she can't be understood.)*
RUDOLF: I think it is Roesch
CLARA: That disgusting man
RUDOLF: He saved my life
CLARA: He saved your life
      If only he hadn't saved your life
      If only he hadn't saved you
      All our misery comes from him
      saving your life
      What a life
      If he hadn't dragged you out of the fire
      we too would have perished
      But this way you came back
      and caused all our misery
RUDOLF: The way you talk to me
      Too much
CLARA: He should have let you burn
RUDOLF: Is this the thanks
      for what I did for you
      which is everything I could possibly do

CLARA: For what you did
    did
    did
    It would have been so simple
    if you hadn't come back
    I was terrified
    when you appeared
    I sensed this was my tragedy
    That's why I hate that man
    your friend and partisan
    You two make me sick
    I hate you two
    I always hated the two of you
    Your ruthlessness
    your hypocrisy
    your viciousness
RUDOLF: I have to take this
    from a cripple
    who spends her time
    stuffing her head with printed garbage
    with demented freakish ideas
    with perverted literature
    which I abhor
CLARA: I abhor you
    you and everything you do
    everything you ever did
    and I abhor Vera
RUDOLF: We should have left you on your own
    then nothing would be left of you
    You would be dead gone finished
CLARA: That's your language all right
    that is the language of the judge
    the Chief of Justice
RUDOLF: Look who's talking
    in our time we simply put the likes of you
    under gas
CLARA: You oh yes your kind oh yes
    You constantly talk about the scum
    and what are you

VERA: *(Enters.* CLARA *pretends she is reading.)* Roesch
    it was him
    he is sorry he couldn't come
    I turned off the telephone
    He has a cold
    he wanted to call the doctor
    but then he changed his mind
    he is with us all the way he said
RUDOLF: He saved my life
    it would have been all over
    he pulled me out of the fire
    at the very last moment
VERA: What's the matter with you
    you're all upset
    What's going on
    (Looks at CLARA.*)*
    What is it with you two
RUDOLF: She turned into a beast
    in her wheelchair
    a filthy rotten beast
VERA: Rudolf
RUDOLF: One shouldn't pay that much attention to her words
    she's demented
    perverted and demented
    did we need this
    having saved her
    having kept her here
    *(*VERA *massages* RUDOLF's *neck.)*
    If I hadn't come back
    you may not have survived at all
VERA: What makes you say that
RUDOLF: For decades nothing but work just for her
    and for you
    day in day out
    I paid my dues
    If it weren't for you
    (Screams at CLARA.*)*
    What an insult
    what an insult

VERA: What's the matter with you two
RUDOLF: She keeps watching us
     and waits only for the opportunity
     to destroy us
     that's all she's preparing for
     (To CLARA.*)*
     but you won't make it
     people like you
     who squat in their wheelchairs for decades
     fall over suddenly and drop dead
     I don't hear of anyone getting very old
     That's not what we deserved
     I would be happy with Vera alone
     happy happy happy
     (Points at CLARA.*)*
     There squats our enemy
     and waits
     (Jumps up.)
     Let me tell you Clara
     I wish you'd drop dead
     and leave us alone
     you've tormented us for twenty years
     even longer than that you've tormented us
     But this is it now
     this is it
     Now it is
     (Sits down in the chair exhausted.)
VERA: Just leave her be
     it's always the same
     you two will never change
     (Kisses RUDOLF *on the forehead.)*
     You are cold all over
     come on get up
     your bath is ready
     everything is ready
     my dear Rudolf
     *(*RUDOLF *gets up again. She embraces and kisses him, then*
     VERA *to* CLARA *accusingly.)*
     We belong together

Rudolf and I
we won't let you come between us

Act 3

The adjoining room. Two hours later. A dining table, chairs, easy chairs, a sofa, a cabinet with guns and a bureau. RUDOLF *is slightly drunk, he is dressed in full uniform of an SS Obersturmbannführer with a gun in his belt and black knee-high boots.* VERA *across from him, with her hair braided, wearing a long brocade gown.* CLARA *in her wheelchair, as before, positioned between them. All three are eating and drinking champagne.*

VERA: And then you'll come with us
    to the symphony Rudolf
    Of course we'll take Clara along
    It'll do her good to get out again
    (Refills everybody's glasses.)
    If it weren't for these occasional cultural pleasures
    what would life be without music
    People with culture father used to say
    If you're out of touch with the arts for too long
    You're bound to deteriorate
    Now I have to check
    if everything is safely locked
    (Gets up and checks all doors and windows.)
    One never knows
    Suddenly someone pops up
    A spy
    (To RUDOLF.*)*
    You look so fine
    in that uniform
    it's a pity I always have to wait a whole year
    until you can put it on again
    nothing fits you quite so well
    Don't you think so Clara

(CLARA is silent.)
And those beautiful medals on your chest
you are the true German Rudolf
The ideal
And you have to hide to put on that uniform
and hide to wear those medals
(Sits down again.)
If only I could go out with you
the way you look now
out of this house into town
to the opera center box
Oh Rudolf will we live to see that day
I don't think it will take too long
until we can openly confess to what we are
until justice returns
to the world once again
you say it yourself we live in a time
that's filled with injustice
You as a judge as the Chief Justice
(She takes off RUDOLF's cap and puts it on the table.)
It's a shame
But the good and righteous shall prevail in the end
In this regard I trust father completely
(Lifts up her glass.)
Come Rudolf let's drink to your retirement
(To CLARA.)
You too lift up your glass to our future
(To RUDOLF.)
I am so looking forward to the day
you will be staying home for the very first time
(All three lift up their glasses and drink. VERA refills all glasses immediately.)
It's really admirable
the way you keep your oath
not letting them get to you
We must not be slaves
we must be free yes
You have my promise Rudolf
that I shall always be by your side

come what may
I've already proven it
in the darkest of times as you know
I paid my dues
as all of us did
To have an ideal and remain loyal to it
to always hold it dear and high
how beautiful
(To CLARA.*)*
Those fine fillets of veal
I picked them especially for you
and now you don't even touch them
(Holds a platter up for CLARA, *but* CLARA *doesn't take any-*
thing, puts the platter back on the table. To RUDOLF.*)*
The tragedy is as father used to say
that against all better judgment
mankind always chooses the wrong path
Mankind is a patient
swallowing whatever is prescribed for him
every deathly poison father said
Rudolf you've kept your figure
for ten or twelve years now
the uniform fits you like the very first day you wore it
absolutely perfect
I am proud of you
His Honor the Chief Justice
and State Representative
If only I could have been there
when you were giving your speech
against the plant
You are a good speaker Rudolf
You convince when you speak
so impressively so clearly so convincingly
My dear State Representative
(Gets up and adjusts the Iron Cross.)
I pinned it too high
There now see
now it's in its proper place
(Examines the Iron Cross and sits down again.)

If we had to leave this place
because of that plant
Corporations always win
For the first time you really showed them
you singlehandedly
against a huge corporation
If only this could set a trend
But the politicians and the industrialists
are in league with one another
and slowly they ruin everything
polluting the air and wrecking it all
Pretty soon you won't even find a place in the Alps
to catch a breath of fresh clean air
Perhaps in Greenland

RUDOLF: Perhaps in Greenland
you are absolutely right
Industry always controlled everything
I have nothing against industry

VERA: Of course not
but in this case
When I think
that they might have built a plant here
we would have had to move
and give up everything
everything we cherish
Oh no
as long as we live
we won't leave this place
Here is our life
Here were our parents
here we were children
here we've made it
here is where we want to stay

RUDOLF: And wait for the end

VERA: Now now Rudolf
why so gloomy
You have no reason at all
You should be the happiest person alive
Wait

(Gets up and gets a rather large photo album from the bureau. Sits down with it next to RUDOLF, *makes some room on the table for the album. To* CLARA.*)*
You don't mind do you
if we look through our album
Remembering
once a year
Nothing like memories
What a beautiful album this is
Mother gave it to me
Christmas of thirty-nine
(To RUDOLF.*)*
When you volunteered for the army
What a time
(Turns a page.)
Christmas thirty-nine
(To CLARA.*)*
That's when you wore the Swiss dress Clara
how well it fit you that Swiss dress
which father brought you from his trip to Zurich
He promised
he would take us to Switzerland
yes you my dear children he said
to lake Zug
It didn't work out of course
(Turns a page.)
Seebruck do you remember Rudolf
we just returned from picking raspberries
(To RUDOLF.*)*
You were always so ambitious
You always picked twice as many as I did
and Clara always ate them all
Uncle Rudolf took the picture
There you see the Kampen cliff
father climbed it to the top
He and his mountains
Father was a mountain man
Mother loved the sea the Adriatic sea
So they never vacationed together

because he always wanted the mountains
and she wanted the sea
(Turns a page.)
Uncle Rudolf went to the front
to Poland
terrible
(To CLARA.)
Do you remember when Uncle Rudolf was laid out
how afraid we were
terrified
we'd never seen a dead man before
Hardly half a year after he joined up
(To RUDOLF.)
You bear a great resemblance to Uncle Rudolf
The mouth the nose
from mother
The Poles were ruthless
always in ambush
At that time dead officers were still sent home
I cried for two days
(Turns a page.)
Pentecost in Vienna
Oh what a lovely time that was
the only trip we made with our parents
the only real trip
(To CLARA.)
They let us ride on the big Ferris wheel
You were afraid
and all of us went to the Hotel Sacher
and ate Sacher Torte
you didn't like it
(Turns a page.)
The first picture of you in your uniform
We were so proud of you
I kept bragging everywhere
that you are wearing the uniform now
Then off you were to Russia right away
a secret mission to the Russian front
for two months we didn't hear a thing

(Turns a page.)
The camp
how pretty those trees how pretty
And back there were your quarters right
What lovely countryside
And there you swam in the Weichsel river
(To CLARA.*)*
Rudolf didn't have his belly then
not even a trace of a belly
The picture of the sailors
that was in Zoppot
That's where you went on vacation
and there you met Himmler
(Turns a page.)
And that is the picture
Roesch took of you and Himmler
Yes
Surely he didn't have to kill himself
he could have disappeared into safety
An act of panic
See now he thought of you
he gave you the forged passport you and Roesch
RUDOLF: But of course it was also a consequence
he was basically a very sensitive human being
Nature simply does what it wants
father used to say
(Stretches his legs under the table.)
How nice it is
spending this day with you
quietly
without a sound coming through from outside
no noise nothing from outside
Being with you
joined in thoughts of our memories
(VERA goes to the bureau and pushes the button of a tape recorder on top of the bureau. Beethoven's "Fifth.")
RUDOLF: *(Closing his eyes.)* Not so loud
softer my dear
(VERA turns down the music.)

No one can determine the course of his life
You're born and you die
everything in between
is beyond your control
(VERA *goes back to the table, sits down and refills their glasses.*)
Suicide is nobody's privilege
Suicide is a crime
He who escapes into suicide
unquestionably commits a crime
(VERA *puts a fillet of veal on* CLARA's *plate.*)
Only man commits suicide
an animal doesn't
On the other hand
no reason exists for suicide
My dear Hoeller he said
I only hear the best about you
you do your work to our greatest satisfaction
Then we ate together
You can keep your father's house he said
the gas plant won't be built where it was planned
I have given the order
to build it in a lot
one hundred and eighty kilometers away
from your father's house
Then he jumped up quite suddenly
and said goodbye
Before I even realized what had happened
he was gone our Reichsführer SS
And I had lost my appetite
so I didn't bother to sit down again
There is nothing more depressing
than ending up alone
at a table set for two
I went outside and took a walk through the camp
The air was remarkably fresh that evening
no noises nothing
As if my lungs hadn't had fresh air in months
I walked through the camp and then around the camp

and I thought about my life
I had reached a turning point a turning point
He never even had himself announced
suddenly the door flew open
and there he stood escorted of course
and said he wanted to have lunch with me
he the Reichsführer SS
He'd just returned from the Führer's headquarters
Roesch wasn't there.
substitute commander you understand Vera
he only made that one visit to the camp
It made an impression
it certainly made an impression
(VERA *gets up, goes to the bureau and turns the music down
further.*)
We had the highest possible discipline
we were a model unit
we were always ready for inspection
(VERA *turns off the music completely, takes two bottles from
the bureau and sits down again.*)
We were executing a mission
for the welfare of the German people
You are executing your mission
for the welfare of the German people he said
without ever taking his eyes off me
It was impossible to escape him
there was no other choice
(VERA *opens another bottle and refills all glasses.*)
There is no way to falsify history
it can be smeared for a long time
much can be hushed up falsified
but then one day it will come to light
shining in its truest colors
that's when the smearers and the husher-uppers and the falsi-
fiers are
gone
It usually takes decades
(*Sits up and holds out his glass to* VERA *who refills it.*)
The devil must be exorcised by the devil

(Empties his glass and holds it up to VERA *who refills it.)*
Shame
who knew thee not
(Gets up suddenly and lifts up his glass. VERA *gets up too.)*
RUDOLF: *(With a glance at Himmler's picture on the bureau.)* I lift
up my glass
to this man
to this idea
(To CLARA.*)*
And you
Of course you are unable to get up
it would only mean a desecration of this moment anyway
Nature knew
What she was doing
(To VERA.*)*
Come Vera let us drink to this idea
we shall drink to this idea
to this one idea only
(Empties his glass. VERA *drinks.)*
RUDOLF *(With his glass held up high.):* I feel no shame
not the least bit of shame
(Sits down again.)
My dear Vera
*(*VERA *sits down.)*
My dear kind Vera
my dearly beloved sister
we must stick together
we must be one one one
Play something
don't just sit there
play something
a nice piece of music
*(*VERA *gets up and exits.)*
If it weren't for Vera
(To CLARA.*)*
You understand don't you
don't you understand everything
you aren't as bad as you pretend to be
not as bad as not to see

how kind my sister Vera is
(From the adjoining room VERA *can be heard playing a Bee-*
thoven fantasy.)
My dear sister Vera
she always understood everything
she is the best
because of her we are alive
without her we would be gone
gone gone gone
Everything is an act of providence
an act of providence
And you aren't really all that bad
you can thank the Americans for your fate
you are our bombing victim
a living reminder
of what the Americans did to us
Millions of dead Germans millions
Munich Dresden Cologne
everything razed to the ground
You can thank the Americans for all of it
(Looks into the adjoining room.)
The Americans destroyed our culture
not only did they destroy all our cities
they also destroyed our entire culture
but you don't understand that
you'll never get that into your head
it won't fit into your stubborn leftist head
You of course enjoy the privilege of fools
otherwise we'd have already liquidated you
The privilege of fools
there are always people
who have the privilege of fools
they can do as they please
nobody takes them seriously
if one would take them seriously
one would surely have to kill them
But we aren't killing you
you're here that's all there is to it
and what it comes down to

you are our sister
the next of kin the blood relation
from the same father and mother as I and Vera
That sweet girl
You can thank God that we have her
If one day we shouldn't have her anymore
but she is the strongest of us all
the one who won't quit
how many times would I have quit already
Vera prevented it
my Vera girl my beloved Vera girl
We wouldn't have made it the two of us
we have a good sister
always had a good sister through the worst of times
you should remember this
you should remember it when you wake up
and when you go to sleep
(With his right hand he points to the adjoining room.)
that we owe it all to her
that we are even alive today
(VERA has stopped playing and enters.)
How well you played
it makes such a difference right away
Music makes everything bearable
If we make our own
A civilized nation can make its own music
Come on Vera sit down
(Opens a bottle and pours VERA a drink.)
I told Clara
that you saved us
your courage
that you always held your own
in the worst of times
when I still was dwelling in the cellar
Vera my brave girl
(Drinks.)
We must never forget it
*(Gets up, goes to the cabinet with the guns, opens it and turns
toward his sister.)*

Vera who made us possible
(Takes out a rifle.)
I always was a soldier
I always will be a soldier
for our cause
no matter what's coming coming coming
(Aims the rifle at the chandelier.)
I could shoot her down
I could knock her off gun her down
should I shoot her down
tell me Vera should I knock her off
VERA: Rudolf please
RUDOLF: Of course not
    it would be crazy
    shooting down the chandelier
    (Aims again at the chandelier.)
    But I do know how to shoot
    I didn't forget
    if I shoot it'll drop
    right on the table
    right on the table
    all I have to do is pull the trigger
VERA: You didn't forget
RUDOLF: A soldier never forgets how to use his gun
    never his gun
    his gun
    never
    (Puts down the rifle.)
    I only have to hold it in my hand
    and I'm a soldier again
VERA: A soldier yes
RUDOLF: The soldier inside the soldier never dies
    (Goes to the cabinet and puts the rifle back in its place.)
    You hid it for me
    you got it safely across
    I owe this to you Vera
    They all surrendered their weapons they threw them away
    You kept my rifle for me
    I feel like shooting out the window

(Turns toward his sister.)
but I mustn't
not yet
not yet my girl
(Goes back to the table and sits down.)
I could think of a few
I'd love to gun down

VERA: *(Puts a fillet of veal on his plate.)* You must eat something
you just drink and you don't eat at all
you drink so much and you don't eat at all

RUDOLF: Not used to it
I am no longer used to it
If I drink only once a year
always on October seventh
on Himmler's birthday
I can't help getting drunk
but I don't care don't care don't care
(To CLARA.)
Well Clara what do you say
I am still the same
Von Metternich isn't it Vera Von Metternich
the brand we drank at the camp
That's something I always paid the greatest attention to
that there was always enough Von Metternich at the camp
otherwise we'd have never been able to take it
He said my dear Hoeller
I can depend on you
on you and on Roesch
he emphasized you
not Roesch
that coward
Roesch really was a coward
I never was a coward not me

VERA: Not you Rudolf

RUDOLF: That man had too much imagination
My sense of order comes from father
and not too much of mother's softness

VERA: But Rudolf you do have your tender spots from mother

RUDOLF: I know what Roesch is all about
　　Suddenly he doesn't care to come here anymore
　　calling us
　　telling us that he is sick
　　I am convinced he isn't sick
　　Roesch always lied
　　But that also caused his downfall in the end
　　I always mistrusted Roesch
　　not for a moment did I trust him out of my sight
　　But he can't give us away
　　he'd be finished himself
　　Most probably he's sitting at home
　　warming his kneecaps at the fireplace
　　Roesch what a milksop
　　But then those are always the most unscrupulous ones
　　it didn't bother him at all
　　to send thousands and thousands into the gas
　　it didn't bother him at all
　　for me it was an effort
　　Vera my good girl
　　I am a bit worried about my retirement
　　just a tiny bit
　　I'm afraid I might start brooding
　　The court distracted me
　　all these years I've been distracted by the court
　　suddenly I won't have anything to distract me
VERA: Retirement will be good for you
　　you can take walks
　　and do the things that you enjoy
　　that's what retirement is for
　　retirement
　　really Rudolf
　　you're not one to retire
　　you've always been an active man
　　you never get bored
　　We'll make our music again
　　you'll play the violin
　　I'll play the piano
　　Beethoven Mozart Chopin

And we'll go to the opera
now that you'll finally have the time
life will be better than ever

RUDOLF: But maybe that's just when I won't have any peace

VERA: It'll pass with time Rudolf
everything has always passed with time
(Pats his hand.)
It's there to enjoy
old age

RUDOLF: Maybe

VERA: *(Sits down in a way she can easily turn the pages in the album and turns a page.)* Look here our happy Rudolf
who is proud of himself
Rudolf our ideal
Where was this now

RUDOLF: In front of the Sukenitza
in front of the market

VERA: Are those Poles behind you

RUDOLF: Yes Poles
they looked on and they laughed
How they laughed when this picture was taken
well it was a beautiful day

VERA: *(Turns a page.)* That looks like a big hangover to me

RUDOLF: That's when we drank to the surrender of Paris

VERA: Where father always wanted to take mother
Have you ever been to Paris

RUDOLF: I never managed

VERA: I never understood
why everyone gets so excited by Paris
(Turns a page.)

RUDOLF: That's when I got a new uniform made
by a tailor in Litzmannstadt

VERA: Sturmbannführer Hoeller

RUDOLF: Shortly after that
I became Obersturmbannführer

VERA: Didn't you conduct
your first trials in Litzmannstadt

RUDOLF: Yes of course
that's why I was there
The youngest judge on the entire Eastern front

VERA: *(Turns a page.)* Awful
    those faces
    utter decay
RUDOLF: That's a snapshot of the Jews
    they sent us from Hungary
VERA: And they were put into the labor camp
RUDOLF: Yes and no
    only those who were fit enough of course
    not the others
    The Jews of Hungary were a tricky case
    we couldn't really use them
VERA: *(Turns a page.)* Bruges right
RUDOLF: That's when we made a trip to the Ardennes
    and went to Bruges
    and to Brussels
    you see that's where we lived
    I marked it with an arrow
    That was some hotel
    Deluxe
    they cleared the entire first floor for us
    we drank champagne day and night
    real champagne
    the Belgians were decent people
VERA: Was that when you took a course in Law
RUDOLF: Yes
VERA: *(Turns a page.)* And this is me
    all dressed in white
    it must have been a Sunday
    when we were always dressed in white
    Where was Clara at that time
    (To CLARA.*)*
    I know you were in boarding school
    our brain child
    the beautiful hair you had then
    that's when I learned English
    that's when we had a tutor from Holland
    a nice man
    Whatever happened to him
RUDOLF: *(Turns a page.)* There you see nothing but Ukranians
    We took care of them quickly
    traitors all of them nothing but traitors

VERA: They really look dangerous

RUDOLF: *(Pointing to it.)* That was the execution
    Those three I shot myself
    There was no one else around
    That was the first time
    I shot people
    (Turns a page.)
    There we were in an old villa
    at the outskirts of Leningrad
    it was an excursion we made in forty two
    I took the picture myself
    from there you could see way into the Inner City

VERA: Who is that at the window

RUDOLF: A medical assistant
    a woman from Austria from Graz
    she was shot later
    because she protected some Jews

VERA: *(Turns a page.)* A jolly group

RUDOLF: We went skiing in Zakopane
    for a whole week
    we had Russian caviar
    but I caught a cold
    (VERA turns a page.)
    The Führer
    I took it myself
    with a flash bulb
    as he passed
    that's why he's so blurred
    my only snapshot of the Führer
    He made an inspection in Kattowitz
    that's Himmler next to him
    you can't recognize him but it's him
    the Silesians were cowards
    traitors bastards all of them
    (VERA turns a page.)
    It was a dangerous atmosphere
    You could trust no one
    not even your own people

VERA: *(Turning a page.)* Berlin Kurfürstendamm

RUDOLF: Yes I with Roesch
    shortly before he was wounded
    If I hadn't been there
    he wouldn't have made it
    he would have bled to death
VERA: And he saved your life
RUDOLF: We made a very good team
    (Empties his glass and VERA *refills it.)*
    But even Roesch could not be trusted
    *(*VERA *turns a page.)*
RUDOLF: These were the shelters
    the Ukranians built before Radom
    (VERA *turns a page.)*
RUDOLF: The Dutch Circus
    which we saw in Luettich
    a terrific shot isn't it
    *(*VERA *gets up and goes with the open album to* CLARA, *showing her the picture.)*
VERA: There you are
    that's you there in the back
    sitting next to Rudolf who's laughing his head off
CLARA: Yes
VERA: *(Goes back, sits down and turns a page.)* How old were you
    then
    you really don't look well at all
RUDOLF: That was in Schitomir
    that's when I had bronchitis
VERA: *(Looks* RUDOLF *in the face and then back into the album.)*
    Your face looks entirely different here
    as if it were someone else
RUDOLF: I don't even know
    who took the picture
    maybe it was Roesch
    but he wasn't in Schitomir then
    he was in Danzig at that time
    Who could have made it
    maybe Dejaco
VERA: The one who poisoned his seven children
RUDOLF: He went to his death with all of them

VERA: *(Turns a page.)* Father
His only picture in uniform
He always had an aversion
to being photographed
And mother
in her dirndl
that was in Schwaz in Tirol
She was angry with father

RUDOLF: Sometimes I wonder
if it wasn't the right time she killed herself
She didn't live to go through
(Drinks.)
Clara all naked
Clara our little nudie
at the brook

VERA: Father in the back can you see
he caught some fish what do you call them

RUDOLF: Miller's thumbs
the same Miller's thumbs we caught as boys

VERA: What a shy child
(To CLARA.)
Don't you want to see this picture
You really are stark naked here
so free and open as never again
(Turns a page.)
At Count Uiberacker's estate
We used to go there as children
The only place where father could really relax
Poor Countess
she shot herself
when the Americans came
Do you remember
how she accused you
of pushing her nephew into the pond
You Rudolf of all people oh God
you pushing the Countess's nephew into the pond

RUDOLF: He jumped all by himself
and then he said
I pushed him

VERA: After that we weren't allowed to come anymore
    we never saw those aristocrats again
RUDOLF: He
    the count
    he was a real Nazi hater
    she denounced her brother
    for listening to enemy stations
    but nothing happened to him
    A few months Mauthausen that's all
VERA: *(Turns a page.)* Who are they
RUDOLF: That was our elite assault group
    none of them alive anymore
    (Drinks.)
    they drove through a forest near Litzmannstadt
    and hit a mine field
    laid by the Polacks
VERA: Such beautiful men
    can you understand that Rudolf
    how can one kill such beautiful men
    their poor parents
RUDOLF: During the war you can't give in
    to feelings
    during war
    feelings don't exist
VERA: *(Turns a page.)* That's our President
    can you see
    what a sweet boy
    in his Hitler Youth uniform
    who's that behind him
RUDOLF: No idea *(Looks closer.)*
    I can't tell
VERA: There you see
    what becomes of sweet little boys
    if they're capable *(Turns a page.)*
RUDOLF: That's Roesch
VERA: With a Polish woman
RUDOLF: Well naturally
    there were no others
VERA: What gorgeous black hair that woman had

RUDOLF: That one was from Warsaw
    she was gassed right away
    (VERA turns a page.)
    That's Auschwitz
    That's when we visited Höss
    Himmler was to be there too
    but then he didn't come
    Back there was the ramp
    that's where the trains came in
    that's where they drove them through
VERA: Terrible
RUDOLF: During war you can't have any feelings
    and you actually don't have them
VERA: Luckily you weren't in Auschwitz
RUDOLF: It wasn't meant to be
    (Points at the picture.)
    That's where they
    drove them in
    and that's where they
    were gassed
VERA: How many were actually gassed in Auschwitz
RUDOLF: Two and a half million
    that's what Eichmann said
VERA: Two and a half million
RUDOLF: That's what Eichmann said to Gluecks
VERA: *(Turns a page.)* I'm glad you weren't in Auschwitz
    I don't know but I'm glad
    Where you were
    that was different altogether
    And here's Ludwig our uncle Ludwig
    when he took the apprentice's final exam
    He was so proud of you
    you in your uniform next to him
    What a pity he had to die
    That's when we always got such excellent meat
    and those delicious sausages
    (Turns a page.)
    That's the Academy concert
    and you in the first row

RUDOLF: And you next to me
VERA: We got the tickets from Roesch
  didn't we
  Yes because his daughter passed the academy exam
  Beethoven's "Fifth" remember
  And that's Elli Ney sitting there
  (Turns a page.)
  How good these pictures are
  don't you think
  if one looks at them only once a year
  and doesn't expose them to light
  Schwarzbach
  Reichenall
  Piding
  we were happy then weren't we Rudolf
  oh come on I have to give you a kiss
  (Moves closer to RUDOLF *and kisses him on the forehead.)*
  Nobody can take these memories away from us
  our memories
  We can't lose them
  (Turns a page.)
  Father always said that too
  The Valley of Roses
  I never saw it again
  Maria Saal the church
  there you stand with the flowers
  you picked for me
  (Turns a page.)
  Oh that's when you were wounded
  but I was proud of you
  everybody admired me
  because you were wounded
  I went through town with my head up high
  and I could feel
  how they admired me
  because you were wounded
  luckily nothing serious
  (Turns a page.)
  Berlin after the first attack
  (To RUDOLF.*)*

Did you take this picture
Is that one dead
RUDOLF: Yes and behind him another one see
VERA: Terrible
   (Turns a page.)
   That's when our parents took Clara out of boarding school
   and sent her to Tirol
   (To CLARA.*)*
   To Reverend Langthaler
   Why are you so quiet
   instead of enjoying these pictures
   You'd love to ruin our evening
   (Turns a page.)
   The Giant Mountains
   In Alsace you wrote underneath
   What a lovely handwriting you had
   to this day your handwriting is beautiful
   (Turns a page.) Verdun *(After a pause.)*
   Oh Rudolf that we have to hide
   and look at this so secretly
   that's really terrible
   And yet the majority thinks just like us
   the majority hides that's what's so terrible
   it's really absurd
   The majority thinks like us and must do so secretly
   Even if they insist on the contrary
   they still are National Socialists all of them
   it's written all over their faces
   but they don't admit it
   I don't know anyone who doesn't think like us
   Except for the doctor and a few others
   but they are too few to count
   That is the horror Rudolf
   that we don't show the world who we are
   we don't show it
   instead of showing it quite openly
   just showing it
RUDOLF: Just wait and see
   the time will come for us to show it again

Everything indicates that we will show it again
and not only show it
VERA: Then again we do have a President now
who was a National Socialist
RUDOLF: There you are
this is proof of how far we've already come
no need to worry
don't you worry Vera
everything is going our way
it is no longer a question of waiting
and furthermore don't we have a whole bunch
of other leading politicians
who were National Socialists
VERA: *(Closes the album.)* Yes that is true
(To CLARA.*)*
We will be back in power soon
Then the likes of you won't have a chance
Just like you all these crazies ran amok
undermining our country violating its ideals
I'm really angry with you
sitting here silently all evening
but you won't manage to ruin our evening
And Rudolf really controlled himself
Last year he forced you to put on
the concentration camp jacket not today
And I had to shave your head last year remember
he kept referring to you as a camp inmate
he didn't do it today
Spoil sport
(Opens the album again, looks through it.)
Freiburg im Breisgau
we still saw it before they wrecked it
those Americans *(Turns a page.)*
Würzburg
All those beautiful cities they completely ruined them for us
Those Americans
(Closes the album.)
Good God how beautiful Germany once was

(Rudolf has tried for a while to pull the pistol from his belt, he's just succeeded and is flaunting it now in Vera's face.)

VERA: *(Frightened.)* Rudolf please
I ask you please

RUDOLF: I could blast you down if I wanted to
I could blast them all
I'm out of practice of course
but I could blast you all just like you are
(Gets up.)

VERA: Rudolf please
you drank too much

RUDOLF: If I feel like it
I can blow your guts out
(Vera jumps up.)

RUDOLF: Back to your seat
that's an order
back to your seat
(Vera sits down again.)

RUDOLF: Let me tell you
if I wanted to I'd blast you away

VERA: Rudolf that's going too far

RUDOLF: I decide
what's going too far

VERA: If anyone hears you
(Looks to the windows.)

RUDOLF: There's no one to hear me
nobody can hear me
if I just felt like it
*(Goes to Clara and puts the pistol to her neck.
After a pause.)*
But I don't feel like it
and the pistol isn't even loaded
(Proves it with one motion of his hand.)
There are no bullets in this pistol

VERA: You're pushing your luck
Rudolf
please

RUDOLF: It always comes down to
whether one does it or does not

it's not a question of character
(Sits down and puts the pistol on the table.)
VERA: You're drunk Rudolf
(Reproachfully to both.)
Because you didn't eat my delicious dinner
you ate nothing
(To CLARA.*)*
You didn't touch anything
(To RUDOLF.*)*
and neither did you
(To RUDOLF *referring to* CLARA.*)*
How she hates us
do you see how she hates us
*(*RUDOLF *takes his glass and empties it.)*
VERA: Rudolf I beg you
RUDOLF: You can't tell me what to do
not even you
nobody
(Takes the pistol and points it around wildly.)
I give you one more chance
one more chance is all I give you
one more chance
(Holds his chest and falls over onto the table.)
VERA: *(Has jumped up and exclaims pathetically.)* Oh my God
(She rushes to him and takes his pulse.)
He's had an attack
Clara an attack
His heart Clara
his heart
(Gets up and goes to the doors and windows, turns Beethoven's Fifth Symphony *back on exactly where it was interrupted before.*
Comes back to the table.)
Now what
what do we do now
(Drags RUDOLF *from the chair and tries to pull him over to the sofa; she succeeds.* RUDOLF *appears to be conscious, but he can't articulate anymore, he can only groan.)*

VERA: *(Kneels down in front of him.)* Rudolf
  can you hear me Rudolf
  my dear Rudolf
  my sweet dear Rudolf
  (Starts to take off his SS uniform.)
  Terrible just terrible
  (To CLARA.*)*
  What are you sitting there staring at me
  how terrible
  (Takes off his jacket.)
  That it had to come to this
  Such a beautiful day
  (Pulls off his boots and tries to take off his trousers as CLARA
  is watching her.)
  It's a tragedy
  a tragedy
  *(Grabs the uniform pieces, runs out with them, returns imme-
  diately to remove Himmler's picture. On her way out she re-
  members the pistol, which lies on the table; takes the pistol,
  leaves and returns immediately. She tries to put her brother in
  his civilian jacket.*
  Bends over RUDOLF, *kisses him, then to* CLARA.*)*
  It's your fault
  you and your silence
  you and your endless silence
  *(Goes to the telephone and calls the doctor. Lights fade. As
  the curtain is coming down)*
  Doctor Fromm please

CURTAIN

Translated by Gitta Honegger

BOTHO STRAUSS

Big and Little

Contents

Morocco   155
Nightwatch   166
Ten Rooms   176
Big and Little   203
Way Station   219
Family in a Garden   220
Wrong Number   230
Dictation   236
The Filthy Angel   243
In Society   249

Morocco

LOTTE, *middle thirties, alone. Noticeably dressed up, a tourist in the evening on the Mediterranean. Light pantsuit, very colorful blouse, hairpiece in a knot at her neck, large earrings, false eyelashes and fingernails. She sits at a table in the dining room. Behind her is a set of outsized venetian blinds, not entirely closed, so that moonlight comes through them, along with the shadows of two men who are taking a walk outside on the terrace.*

LOTTE: Can you hear?
   Two men are walking up and down outside.
   Forever.
   Deep voices. Can you hear?
   Crazy
   (She rubs her ear. In a disguised voice she mimics a picked-up sentence)
   "Real wonders were accomplished . . ."
   Crazy.

What deep voices these guys have!
They're not from our Siesta Tour.
They come from somewhere else.
Lord have mercy, in the heat of the night.
That sounds good! Boy, oh boy . . .
They don't belong to us, those guys.
I've never heard
such . . . such . . .
har-mony!
It would be healthier not to listen.
But what can you do?
You just can't sleep
with these supervoices outside—
The first one says:
"Why not think everything through again
from the beginning, Floyd?"
Yep. Floyd. That's the other one.
Floyd says: "This isn't getting us
any further and further's
where we've got to get.
So I suggest
we think ahead regardless of the consequences,
not think it through again from the beginning."

Yep. Peace. Now they're quiet.
Walking up and down again.
Logicians, that's what they are . . . !

Morocco, crazy!
You'd have to have seen it.
At the beginning we were a good tourist party.
We got along together. But in the meantime.
The infernal heat. Now it's sort of all against one
and one against all.

Did you hear?
The first one calls the other one Floyd
but Floyd doesn't call him anything.
This has been going on for hours, crazy.

Floyd never calls Non–Floyd by his name.
I'm just waiting around to finally find out
what Non–Floyd's called.
I'm just waiting around for Floyd
to finally let it slip out,
what Non-Floyd's called.
At least a little Ha— or
Bi— or To—, Chr—, Ro—, Ri—, Jo—
Crazy.
Logicians.
I wish I had that kind of peace of mind.
(She drinks a glass of mineral water)
The whole house full of wicked people.
There are two strangers outside
and there's solace in their voices.
As long as they keep walking
there's still hope
that they'll look in here later.
They'll notice: here in the dining room
there's still light, at least that much
presumably they'll notice.
Only when I start to hear them starting
to leave the terrace
then I'll know
they're going through the main entrance
up to their rooms,
not coming by here as expected,
where they would presumably, last but not least,
invite me to have a drink with them,
seeing that I'm not getting any younger,
sitting here like this.
Only when they're actually lying in their beds,
not till then will I be certain
that again today, the whole live-long day,
there's been nothing new for me, there's been nothing.

Eleven more days in Agadir.
Time passes.
All I've done so far is gain weight.

Everything is very simple: nothing's right.
Time passes, but not the way it should.

I feel, like when there's mail at home in the mailbox.
I see a big envelope.
I see the address, handwritten:
Number 8, Street of January 13, Saarbrücken 66. Crazy.
Who can be writing me there?
The book club announces its annual selections.
Oh. Well. I'm happy. Better than nothing.
Another close call, just missed having no mail.
There!
Can you hear? The first one . . .
A doctor's voice.
It's Non–Floyd who's speaking.
He's saying . . . just a sec! . . . sounds like . . .
He just said something like . . .
It's hard. Something like "the elements,"
"the elemental." Crazy.
I can't understand a thing with that
supervoice . . . that voice . . . music, music!
Just now he said: "warning . . ."
You have to have heard it: "warning."
Fabulist!
Logicians, that's what they are.
And Germans!
Of the two of them Floyd presumably the guiding light.
This can be seen in that
Non–Floyd constantly calls Floyd
by his name,
but Floyd never utters the name of Non–Floyd, although you'd
think he could let it slip out at least once, as I said before.
What were they just saying?
What did they mean?
It had to do with the one.
The one elemental.
After that it was "the elements" . . .
The elements, hm-hm-hm

(She tries to find the word)
What did they mean?
So then . . . so then . . .
Someone crossed the Rubicon.
So-and-so crossed the Rubicon.
A name fell.
Didn't sound like all that much.
Small vocabulary. Tiny little word.
Such a little word, it doesn't resonate in the chest,
and without the chest Floyd makes it sound,
and Non–Floyd too,
like a little mouse shooing across a kettle drum.

Wait a minute! Floyd . . .
(She smiles; fast, staccato)
"radiant with joy" . . .
(Amused)
"by all means," "by all means."
Non–Floyd: "admitted," "frankly" . . .
(Becoming faster and more intense)
Floyd: "Abuses are . . . centered in . . . drinking and a
craving for . . ."
What? I don't understand . . .
Non–Floyd: "Greed . . . hustling, a fangs-bared
ego— . . ."
Floyd: "Unsatisfactory!"
Non–Floyd: "Greed . . . difference between those who . . .
greedalone?
And those
(Becoming slower)
in spite of greed . . . spiteofgreed."
The End. Greed.
Crazy. So fast!
The logicians are leading, I can tell you that.
Now first they're going to make their
two or three little rounds, first they're going to think
it over, what they just said in such a rush.
Nice voices.
Wonderful sound.
Like I said, smooth as fudge.

But what were they talking about just now, dearie?
God, what were they talking about . . . ?
What can I say?
About drinking.
About avarice.
Don't ask me.
I'm not the kind who recollects everything.
I'm not a remembering kind of person. I never was.
Did I just hear myself say "Greed"?

As long as they keep walking
it's possible after all
that they'll take a look in here,
have a drink,
and get into a conversation with me,
as long as they don't decide
to go down to the beach and then up through the main entrance.
In this infernal heat no one
can find the sleep of the just.
Only those who undertook something today,
who went on the excursion to Marrakesh
and only got back late in the evening,
they're sleeping now, sound as rats.
I didn't do.
Completely at odds, our group is.
I like to sit all day long in the lounge,
where there's always a cool breeze.
The women yell at the men,
one after the other they drop their masks,
the men yell at the women
in the middle of the desert.
I haven't done any extras.
None from the beginning.
I didn't even book any extras.
(She drinks)

Greed, envy, disinterest,
avarice, and zeal—
these are the passions
that have afflicted our Siesta Tour the worst.
And drinking.

And—
you forget it every time,
Floyd,
as soon as we start to talk about this
there's a logical step missing
at this point
and it is: the distance
between the well-to-do,
who can afford quite simply everything, and the
less well-to-do, who can afford, down the line,
only the most essential of the best the promoter's organization
has to offer, that is, no extras of any kind.
That's how they talk. Crazy. Just like that.
That's just about the way they talk.
Of course with a different touch mentally.
They talk about completely different problems.
I mean only, the way they talk is just about the same.
Such deep voices, Lord have mercy.

Everywhere there's confusion, for years
confusion and bad luck,
lies and running around—
like Paul in Saarbrücken—
a life of separation,
and then men like Floyd and Non–Floyd,
what friendship!
What logic!
What voices!
You learn so quickly . . .
Can you hear?
It's starting again.
Floyd: . . . sounds like . . .
"vale of tears" . . .
Nice. So nice!
(Sings a little)
Vaaale-of-tears.
Crazy.
Non–Floyd:
(Repeats quickly)

"The earth aches" or "quakes" . . .
"Man has lost his picture of mankind . . ."
The earth aches or quakes.
"Hold on," says Floyd.
"We can't go on without thinking this through!"

(Unsatisfied)
The earth aches or quakes.
Not much there. They're already quiet again.
Sounded like . . .
a man had lost a picture.
Or package?
Package or picture, I could be wrong.
Wasn't anything earthshaking.
A picture, oh, well.
Lost, yeah, yeah.
But that's *it!*
That's *it!*
He almost let it slip,
what Non–Floyd's called, almost!
Hold on, Floyd said, like that!
That's what he said: Hold on . . .
(Tries to find the name from the rhythm)
hm-hm . . . hm-hm-hm . . .
Tip of my tongue! Ha—!
Her—! Raaal—! Bar—!
Or Carr—!?
It *must* have slipped out of him.
Shit.

Eleven more days in Agadir.
(Sings loudly)
Vaale-of-tears.
Two men, crazy.
Up and back, back and forth.
Not exactly light on their feet, I must say.
Men in full manhood,
on leather soles, in good shoes,
going their rounds and, listen: a distinct crunching

out there on the terrace,
sand, leather, and stone—
under a certain weight,
under the press of stature,
they're no sandal-wearers, inaudible,
no cloth-shoe strollers.
Probably light evening suits,
cream-colored the one and lilac the other,
with a maroon tie, and behind the knot
the collar is open a little,
for that throat, for that voice!
Inaudible, too, the slap of the trouser legs.
The one is jingling a lighter and change
in his jacket pocket:
Non–Floyd, I guess, while he thinks.
Floyd, the guiding light, doesn't need any jingling
to think.
Oh, I wish I were Floyd
or Non–Floyd and were walking up and down
next to Floyd or Non–Floyd
out there tonight, step for step . . .

No, no. I don't want anything.
Who do I think I am.
I'd just like to hear you speak,
my blessed pair!
Oh, speak, my indivisible voices . . . !

One day in Marrakesh
should cost me seventy-one dollars
in additional pocket money.
On top of this, visits to the market,
that means purchases, without them why go to Marrakesh?
On top of this, countless mobs of beggars,
fruits, drinks, and lunch on the side.
On top of this, the heat,
and that I can't always take riding in a bus,
and there's constantly the fear,
will I be able to stand it today or is today a day I can't,

the constant cold sweat, worrying whether the bus will make
it to
a stop
before I get sick,
when anyway we're all
mortal enemies, one against all.
There!
Floyd . . . !
(She jumps up; laughs happily, tries to understand)
What?—What?—What?
*(Moved by the voice, she advances a few steps—away from
the direction in which she is listening)*

Yes! . . . Yes!
A fraid
A fraid fraid fraid
(She speaks in high spirits)

Behold, man will
depart from this earth
and be done in all his works.
After him the earth will redden with
shame and fruitfulness.
The gardens and the fields will
enter into the empty cities;
the antelopes will browse in the rooms
and the wind will gently leaf through open books.
The earth will be unmanned and will bloom.
Freed from all its prophets, fettered hope
will be redeemed and will grow rich in the silence.
Freightless, the sea lulls itself,
the land wanders untrodden and the air plays in tall flowers.
And it will be so for one thousand two hundred and sixty
days . . .

(To herself again)
One thousand two hundred and sixty days . . .
what does that mean? How did I arrive at
one thousand two hundred and sixty days?

That adds up to about four years.
Four years, not quite. Four years of what?

(She listens)
The men have stopped!
The men aren't walking any more!
Merciful heaven, what have I said?
They've stopped—!
I'm listening: they're standing, they're swallowing!
They're listening! They're hearing me . . .
Dear God, make them go on walking . . .
They're hearing me!
(She holds her mouth closed)
Non–Floyd: "It seemed to me
that someone cried out inside."
Floyd: "I thought that someone
cried out, too. Though at the moment no one is shouting.
Either the need has passed—"
Non–Floyd: "or the joy—"
Floyd: "or there will be another cry" . . .
They are quiet. They look at the tips of their shoes.
They raise their heads, inaudible, they shake their heads.
Crazy.
They're walking! Almighty God, they're walking again!
(In the course of the final sentences, piece by piece she removes the hairpiece, the earrings, the eyelashes, etc., and puts them all on the table in front of her)
I suppose—
I suppose I did get a little too loud.
How stupid of me.
How stupid.
It isn't easy for me
to spend my vacation
without—
without even a chat,
sometimes days without a single hello.
So that evenings
one little word
can easily slip out and I don't even notice it.

I'm talking up a storm and I'm positive that
I'm only thinking. What can you do?
You just have to get it straight once and for all
and then it's all right.
(She falls silent and listens)
Nice voices.
Can you hear?
Forever.
Better now than then.
(She smiles)
Crazy.
(Darkness)

Nightwatch

Lotte
The Man
The Woman

WOMAN's *bedroom in the morning. Window with drawn curtains.
The* WOMAN *sleeping in her bed. The* MAN *sits next to the bed on
a chair. Suit jacket over the back of the chair, open shirt, untied
shoelaces.*

WOMAN *(Is startled from her sleep)*: What is it?
MAN: Quiet, darling. Sleep.
    It's nothing.
WOMAN: Didn't you just call?
MAN: No.
WOMAN: What are you doing in my room?
MAN: I'm sitting here.
WOMAN: Since when?
MAN: All night.
WOMAN: All night?
    Don't you have to get ready?
MAN: I'm not going to work today.
WOMAN: Is something the matter?
MAN: No.

WOMAN: Why aren't you sleeping in your own room?
MAN: I didn't feel like it.
WOMAN: I have to pick up the children today.
   What's the weather like outside?
MAN: Foggy. I think it's foggy.
WOMAN: Damn. I don't like to drive in the fog.
MAN: I could drive.
WOMAN: Do you want to pick up the children?
MAN: We could go together.
WOMAN: Rosa didn't take her coat.
   (She lifts the blanket off and sits up)
   What time is it exactly?
MAN: Eight-forty.
WOMAN: You should have left a long time ago.
   Did I say something?
   Did I talk in my sleep?
MAN: No.
WOMAN: Were you trying to eavesdrop or what?
MAN: No.
WOMAN: Is there something we should talk about? Hey!
MAN: No. We could pick up the children together.
WOMAN: You know, I mean, you're sitting here in my room
   and eavesdropping while I'm asleep, somehow I don't
   think that's so great, now what do you think?
   (When he doesn't answer, she turns around to face him)
   Hm?
   (He shrugs his shoulders)
   What does that mean?
   (She imitates his shrug)
   Don't be so thick-skinned! Just tell me
   what it's supposed to mean, why you've been sitting here
   all night and eavesdropping?
MAN: I didn't want to eavesdrop. I didn't—
   mean it like that.
WOMAN: Now I can spend the whole day racking my brains,
   what's this supposed to mean, sitting here and eavesdropping
   while I'm asleep. You always come up with something new to
   make everything even more complicated, more complicated!
MAN: Actually—

WOMAN: Listen: what do you really want from me?

MAN: Look, what is so complicated about all this?

WOMAN: Everything. You just make everything even more complicated.

MAN: Actually it's a very simple thing,
    a perfectly simple thing for someone to sit near you
    and for someone to be awake near you while you're sleeping.
    It's actually something—something comforting.

WOMAN: It *could* be nice if someone *said* he would watch over you.
    It *could* be nice if you *knew,* when you fell asleep, that
    someone was watching. But you, you sneak into my room
    at night and I feel it, unconsciously I feel it, there is
    someone in the room, something's breathing, and I tell
    you that it's down and upright weird, it's weird!

MAN: How could I tell you in advance I was coming to watch over
    you?
    No one does that in advance.
    You're looking for an argument.

WOMAN: No one does that, no one does that,
    better for me to have bad dreams. And how I'm
    supposed to come out of them, that's not your business.
    How am I supposed to come out of them, huh?!

The whole town fell down off the slope, plunged down
into the river and I, little, over in old Birkholz's
living room . . .
(The MAN *has risen, he goes to the window)*

MAN: By and large you slept peacefully.
    Until the early morning, when it got light outside.
    (He busies himself with the curtains at great length; the
    WOMAN *watches him)*
    The curtains are much too thin.
    They let the early light come in.
    We used to have these thick drapes . . .
    We should maybe—either shutters outside,
    Or inside more than just curtains . . .

WOMAN: Worm.

MAN: You need darkness as long as possible in the morning.

WOMAN: Worm.
MAN: God, you know . . .
>*(The* WOMAN *tries to get up, falls back on the bed)*
WOMAN: How on earth can I get out of this nightmare?
>I feel totally destroyed.
>God, that was really a shitty thing to do!
>I'm sure there'll be some damage.
>*(She rises, goes next door into the bathroom. The* MAN *draws the curtains, opens the window)*
MAN: *(To himself)* She can say that, she *has* to say that
>simply because she is such a beautiful woman.
>She can't afford to have a bad night,
>I'll never do that again.
>*(He sits in a chair)*
>The sun is even breaking through the fog.
>She'll be pleased.
>I know above all she wants to be cheerful and
>she's determined to be in a good mood, to have high hopes.
>With every breath she takes now, she's looking for the blue-
>bird of happiness,
>and as a result she's become so terribly nervous
>that if the bluebird flew in singing
>she could hardly bear the noise.
>With others, in company, it's inevitable: there's
>a burst of laughter from the far corner and suddenly
>she jumps up, shaking, and runs out, furious as a cat.
>It's because she doesn't know what her friends in there
>were laughing about and so she hears them laughing at
>her, hears the vultures crying overhead. She says so herself.
>Then I have to hold on to her. With the greatest care
>I take her to her room and let the fear
>and the curses, vulgar and blind, rain down on me.
>Then she starts screaming. I sit there and she loses control of
>herself. I don't have to say anything and I still can help her.
>She admits that herself. Sometimes later she goes down again
>and joins the guests, sometimes not. Sometimes not.
>*(From the street,* LOTTE *leans in at the open window. She wears a somewhat out-of-fashion two-piece suit)*

Since I have known sorrow, I need neither joy nor longing.
Sorrow fills a man completely, joy can never do that.

LOTTE: Who are you talking to so nicely?

MAN: I was thinking of my wife.

LOTTE: I've seen her before.
Go on talking.

MAN: Nothing can separate me from this person,
not even the children and not the love for the children.
It's her I want to see with my last glance and be holding her hand
when one day the party's over.

(The WOMAN *comes out of the bathroom)*

WOMAN: *(To* LOTTE): Who are you?

LOTTE: I've seen you before.

WOMAN: You are?

LOTTE: I am Lotte.

WOMAN: And?

LOTTE: And nothing.

WOMAN: You're leaning in our window, because?

LOTTE: Because I heard your husband talking
and it sounded nice.

WOMAN: Talking, were you? About what?

MAN: Just talking.

WOMAN: Stayed up all night . . .

LOTTE: He stayed up all night?

(The WOMAN *takes clothes from the closet, lays them on the bed to choose among them)*

WOMAN: You don't happen to be a nurse in Professor Tischner's clinic?

LOTTE: No. I'm a graphic artist. Freelance though.
I used to be a physical therapist, so you weren't off base altogether. But in the city hospital, and back then
I was on the staff.

WOMAN: I was there once, too.

LOTTE: My husband is the freelance writer Paul Liga.
Familiar?

WOMAN: No.

LOTTE: He also writes under the name *Smoky.*
No idea?

WOMAN: I wouldn't know.

LOTTE: You're not only beautiful,
  you have extremely beautiful things to wear, too.

WOMAN: Joking aside.

LOTTE: I'm not joking.

WOMAN: You can believe me or not—
  I haven't bought anything new in months.

LOTTE: In the life of Saarbrücken you are, and always have been,
  someone to watch.

WOMAN: I don't want that any more.
  For years I did my best to bring some excitement
  back into this godforsaken dump.
  I don't want to any more, I can't any more.
  No one notices.

LOTTE: You're lucky—
  You have your style, a personal touch.

WOMAN: But I feel that's exactly what people hate.
  They hate my personal touch.
  They hate me from top to bottom: my face, my rouge, my
  whiteness.
  I can't stand in front of a shop window any more
  without constantly being afraid that from behind me
  someone will shove my skull into the glass.

MAN: It's probably only the tip of the iceberg of the general
  excitability of today's life—

LOTTE: The tip of the iceberg? Aha!

WOMAN: Such a profound observation, Edward!

LOTTE: The tip of the iceberg! Aha!
  That's an inspired comparison, Edward!

WOMAN: Careful!

LOTTE: Yes.
  I'd love to see you again in the quiet color
  that you wore two years ago to the state tennis finals.

WOMAN: The quiet color?
  You mean: three-quarter length and beige?

LOTTE: Yes.

WOMAN: The Chanel.
  (She goes to the closet, pulls out a dress)
  This?

LOTTE: No. That wasn't it.

WOMAN: *(Searches)* The quiet color from two years ago . . .
  This?

LOTTE: No. Not that either.
  Look, there next to the moss-green pleats . . .

WOMAN: This?

LOTTE: No. Back one.

WOMAN: This?

LOTTE: One more.

WOMAN: This?

LOTTE: Yes!
  That's it! That's it!

WOMAN: But it's not beige!

LOTTE: Please, put it on for a second, over,
  just for me . . .

WOMAN: The dark Missoni!
  I never in a million years had this on at the state finals.

LOTTE: Yes, you did. I swear it.
  The quiet color . . .

WOMAN: I could prove it to you. It's in my diary.
  I haven't worn this since Martina was born.

LOTTE: It doesn't matter. I want to experience it. Please!
  (The WOMAN *puts on the dress)*
  I thought back then: She's sitting there like a beautiful woman
  long ago, for whom knights battled in tournaments . . .
  Magnificent. It's magnificent. Perfect!
  Such a quiet color, completely from within,
  and soft and flowing!

WOMAN: Crepe de Chine
  Shot silk. A little somber.
  (She puts on stockings)

LOTTE: In the very middle of the Middle Ages stood unshaken
  the image of the beautiful woman.
  For back then, to man, she was the first step to God.

WOMAN: And still is. And still is today as she was then!

LOTTE: Only: no one wants to get to God any more.
  Who wants to go beyond the beautiful woman?
  For man, woman has become an end in itself.

WOMAN: *(Brushes her hair)* What can you do?

You don't happen to be someone from the church?

LOTTE: No.

WOMAN: Sure?

LOTTE: What I'd like to know is how you

can be satisfied with Saarbrücken.

WOMAN: I'm not satisfied with Saarbrücken.

You mustn't think that of me.

LOTTE: You ought to be seen. In great cities once in a while, too.

(The MAN, *looking back and forth from* LOTTE *to his wife like a tennis referee, chuckles softly and shakes his head)*

WOMAN: How? Put the children in a suitcase?

LOTTE: Once hidden, twice shy.

If you don't show yourself, you decay.

Walk across the room for me once.

Please.

WOMAN: I'd rather be looked at quietly from the front.

LOTTE: Are you hiding something not so beautiful?

WOMAN: No. Nothing.

The shoes that match are missing this early in the morning.

I don't know which.

Which ones do I have to wear today?

Edward, what are you going to wear today, outside the office?

MAN: Me? . . . I thought I'd just wear the pale stripes.

WOMAN: The tired old pale stripes?

That goes with . . . that goes with . . . No. Shit.

Well, I'll just have to get that old Pucci dress down from the attic.

MAN: No, no. Please, I'll take all my cues from you.

Maybe then I'll wear . . .

WOMAN: Maybe the indigo worsted?

MAN: If I have to.

WOMAN: *(Claps her hands)* Oh, yes! Fine! Just fine!

I'll finally get a chance to try that cute Brosoli

silk blazer to go with it.

LOTTE: Now do walk around a little.

Feel free to walk for me in just your stockings.

Please.

(The WOMAN *rises hesitantly)*

Yes! Walk! Go on! Get those feet going!
(The WOMAN *walks back and forth with growing allure)*

LOTTE: Don't dawdle, don't drag your feet, and now faster!
    Tip-top . . . tip-top . . . tip-top!
    Yes, now you're walking. Great!
    God, if I blink my eyes a little,
    I see you far away, an idol . . .
    Good for the memory, I thank you.
    It's made to be remembered.
    Walk! Walk! And turn around!
    What you're missing is the envy of thousands.
    What you're missing are runways, gala dinners, tête-à-têtes
    in the highest walks of life!

WOMAN: *(She sings)* How I am to blame!

LOTTE: I just can't help it!

WOMAN: I just can't help it!

MAN: *(Loud)* Crap!

WOMAN: It's very kind of you this morning.
    I feel better again.
    A few good words from an open window
    work even better than exercise.
    (She sits at her dressing table)

LOTTE: Now we should find the right shoes.

WOMAN: Edward's sulking.
    There are only three employees in his company. Four men
    to do all the exporting. We all get by. But he's fifteen years
    behind what's going on in the world.

LOTTE: Find the shoes. Try on the jewelry. Keep the vision!
    Hats, coats, capes, and shawls!

WOMAN: I have to ask you now to give up this hocus-pocus.

LOTTE: Well, hopefully we've grown a little closer.

WOMAN: Now there is one more face in Saarbrücken
    I have to remember.

LOTTE: What?
    Is that what you think?
    That I've made a fool of you? Played some game?

WOMAN: Who knows.

LOTTE: No, no! That's just the way I am . . . that's my way!

You're strangers, you're squirming around and soon you're
talking up a storm. Believe me, I want to get to know you.
WOMAN: What do I know how you are?
 I don't want to be taken in by someone.
 Your way, yes. Your way is fine.
 But a way like that passes so quickly.
LOTTE: I am simply a free-enough person
 that I somehow appeal to you inside . . .
WOMAN: And I am a family.
 I do not look for relationships among strange people.
LOTTE: Am I supposed to understand this?
WOMAN: It's exactly what you *have* to understand.
LOTTE: Anyway. There's always a lot to talk about
 with a new acquaintance.
WOMAN: We are not a new acquaintance.
 (She rises, goes to the window, tries to close it)
LOTTE: Hey! . . . No!
 The subjects I am interested in are:
 drawing, reading, languages, current events!
 No!
 Let's take a walk!
 Let me hear your child's voice just once!
WOMAN: *My children!* There are two. Rosa and Martina.
 (The WOMAN *shuts the window, draws the curtains. The* MAN
 begins to speak uneasily)
MAN: It's strange that no one from the firm has called to find out
 where I am. I wish Schönborn, Körner, and Berkenrath would
 do what I'm doing and stay home with their wives in the
 morning. We don't have to sell so many magnetic valves, we
 really don't. Progress in electronics, as you say so often, from
 deep in a magazine, has never given us any reason to worry.
 On the contrary, the turnover has even increased somewhat.
 The magnetic valve. Or the thingamajig, as you like to say.
 *(He takes a magnetic valve made of gold from his jacket
 pocket)* A thingamajig like this can forge an entire existence.
 My special, without it in Basel and in Bogota even today you
 can't build an aquarium ventilator. It's supplied through me
 from Germany to the entire world. Of all the magnificent
 goods traded by mankind on the open market, I offer this ugly

little thingamajig. It makes you want to laugh. And yet you gave it to me in gold for my fortieth birthday, because gold is what it's brought us to date. Yes. I'm the first to laugh at myself. But you see, my self-respect begins with you. You are my self-respect. Let the material world be just an act, leave it behind, down there, giggling and shrieking. Up here it should be solemn and still. Up here for us.

WOMAN: What are you thinking? What?
>   Don't sleep at night.
>   Talk out loud to yourself in the mornings
>   and attract the passers-by. Daydreaming!
>   Don't go to the office.
>   What's going to become of us?
MAN: *(Softly)* With two hearts beating as one, please, it'll be all right.
>   *(Darkness)*

Ten Rooms

Lotte
The Fat Woman
The Old Woman
The Old Man
Guitar Player
Research Assistant *(Boy)*
Research Assistant *(Girl)*
Woman *in zipped-up dress*
Paul, *Lotte's husband*
The Turk
The Tent

1

The room. Empty space. Along the rear wall on the right a door, on the left a window. Bright light. Window, door, the proportions of the room in general are enlarged so that grown men in the room appear surprisingly little. In the middle of the room on the floor is a crumpled, dirty plastic raincoat. One hears LOTTE *running on the stairs and along a landing. There is a knock at the door.* LOTTE *tries the door handle. A large key, hanging loosely from the lock, falls into the room. The door remains unopened.*

LOTTE: *(From outside)* Hey, old man!
  Open up!
  (She listens)
  It's me: Lotte . . .
  (She knocks more softly; quiet)
  Darling . . . ?
  (The lights dim)
  Darling?
  (Slowly, then more quickly, disappearing footsteps on the stairs)
  (Darkness)

2

Another / the same room. Empty space. Bright. A FAT WOMAN. *Her naked left arm is bound by a tourniquet with flowers pinned to it. She searches for a comfortable position in which to give herself an injection of morphine. She bends over, leans against the wall, squats, kneels, and finally sits on the floor.* LOTTE *opens the door and stands in sight of the woman. She is wearing an open coat over the grayish-blue suit. In her left hand is a small portable television, under her right arm a drawing portfolio.*

FAT WOMAN: In or out.
  (LOTTE closes the door very slowly. The woman gives herself the injection)
  (Darkness)

3

The room. Open window. A small one-man tent with a mitten hanging from the front tent pin. Like a piece of clothing, the side walls of the tent hug a body that is breathing heavily. LOTTE *comes in the door. Shocked, the tent jerks to one side.* LOTTE *slams the door and walks away.*

4

The room. An older married couple. In front of the open window the husband is massaging the bowed, naked back of his wife. LOTTE *knocks softly, enters without invitation. Both old people straighten and turn toward her.*

OLD WOMAN: *(Quietly)* Rose . . . !
　　Merciful God in heaven, the child!
LOTTE: Excuse me . . .
OLD MAN: Please, go, only for a minute,
　　just outside the door, please.
　　*(*LOTTE *backs up, closes the door)*
OLD MAN: That was not Rose, Mother.
　　Do you hear me?
OLD WOMAN: Now Rose is here at the door.
　　Oh, that makes me happy!
OLD MAN: Quiet, quiet.
OLD WOMAN: Just now I thought I saw the child standing in the door.
　　(He strokes her neck)
OLD MAN: Yes. It wasn't Rose.
OLD WOMAN: No.
　　How do you know?
OLD MAN: Good. Now I am going to get the young lady and bring her in again.
OLD WOMAN: At first glance, what she looked like!
　　God in heaven, that makes me happy!
OLD MAN: *(Opens the door)* She's not there any more. Gone away.
OLD WOMAN: Gone?
　　You shouldn't have sent her outside, for just that.
OLD MAN: *(Closes the door, comes back)* No. Perhaps.
　　On the other hand, she wouldn't have wanted much from us.
OLD WOMAN: Gone, just gone . . .
　　It's almost like it really was Rose.
OLD MAN: Think about it, how impossible it would be.
　　(She bends forward again; the OLD MAN *massages her shoulders)*

OLD WOMAN: With missing people, nothing is impossible.
OLD MAN: But, Rose, if Rose appeared here at the door one day, she would look much, much older now than back then. Now she would look maybe just as old as the woman on the first floor.
OLD WOMAN: As Inge?
　　I don't believe it.
　　(Darkness)

5

The room. On the floor, a young man leaning against the wall plays softly on a guitar. LOTTE *opens the door, listens a little. Then she closes the door very slowly.*

GUITAR PLAYER: Stay.
　　*(*LOTTE *opens the door again, only a crack)*
LOTTE: What?
GUITAR PLAYER: Stay, OK?
LOTTE: Beautiful. It sounds beautiful.
GUITAR PLAYER: Do you live here?
LOTTE: I am looking for someone.
　　(The GUITAR PLAYER *leans his head back, plays louder.* LOTTE *closes the door and goes away)*
　　(Darkness)

6

The room. A woman in a light one-piece dress, fastened up to her chin. It fits her torso tightly like a white uniform. She stands behind the door and listens to the footsteps that are approaching. Right before LOTTE *can knock she tears the door open.*

WOMAN IN ZIPPED-UP DRESS: What do you want?
LOTTE: Does Mister . . . Mister . . .
WOMAN: Manfred, right? Manny, right?
　　*(*LOTTE *shakes her head)*
　　He doesn't live here any more.

(She slams the door shut, goes to the window, opens it, and stands at the window with her arms crossed behind her back)

LOTTE: *(Carefully opening the door)* Mr. Paul Maria Ingrate . . .

WOMAN: *(Looks* LOTTE *over)* Come in.

LOTTE: *(In the room)* Alias Sebastian Deceit . . .
  (She moves next to the WOMAN *at the window)*
  Familiar?

WOMAN: *(Nods)* Alias Manfred Larceny.
  *(*LOTTE *nods. They stand for a while next to one another at the open window)*
  (Darkness)

7

The room. The RESEARCH ASSISTANTS *enter. Both are in warm-up suits and sneakers. She is wearing glasses, carrying a number of plastic supermarket bags overflowing with books from the library. He closes the window.*

BOY: Tired?

GIRL: *(Shakes her head)* You know me.

BOY: Put them down.

GIRL: Why am I carrying your books?

BOY: Gudrun, you don't *have* to carry my books.

GIRL: All right. But I carry them anyway. That's the main thing.

BOY: Tell me, sweetheart, what have you brought me today in those plump little grab bags?
  (She kneels on the floor, unpacks books, reads the titles)

GIRL: Bismarks . . . Bis-markin.

BOY: Read properly. *Bismarkian*—

GIRL: *The.*

BOY: What?

GIRL: *The Bismarkian.* Know it?

BOY: Go on! I didn't ask for that one. I can't use it.
  Go on!

GIRL: Hold your horses.
  (Reads)
  Storia degli—

BOY: *Storia degli salutationi cordiali alla corte di Federigo secondo!*
Finally! Finally! God in heaven, thank you!

GIRL: Finally! Thank you!
(He runs over to her, tears the glasses from her face, the book from her hands, and takes them to the window)

BOY: *The History of the Cordial Greeting* . . . Finally!

GIRL: *(Calmly)* Please don't tear the glasses off my face.
Please don't rip the *Storia* out of my hands.
(She takes more books, holds them under her nose, and reads the titles out loud)
The Psychoanalysis of Rin-Tin-Tin. Go ahead and ask. Or wait a minute. *Katharina Medusa.* I was just as pleased as you were about the *Storia. Intentions and Contentions. Walden. Wellington. Wilderness Diary.*
(She cries silently)
You, I mean, what's the use.
The Waves . . . The Waif of Bebra. They're all W's. Fucking W's.

BOY: Gudrun, what are these books for?

GIRL: You know, I think this is really shitty of you.

BOY: Why?

GIRL: Because I think it's just shitty.
(LOTTE half enters through the door. Both look around, but pay no further attention to her. After a while she closes the door again)

GIRL: *(Reads further, sniffling, dabs at her nose)* Luther, Prussia, Report.

BOY: Gudrun, what are these books for?
You selections today are very odd.

GIRL: Traces of the theme everywhere, traces everywhere.
The literature of the greeting.
(The BOY goes to her, hands her the glasses and the book. She puts on the glasses, opens the book. She takes the glasses off again, wipes tears from her eyes)

GIRL: Shitty glasses. You read.
(The BOY takes the glasses and the book back, returns to the window)

GIRL: *(Leafs through a paperback)* We have to search more systematically. The whole library, scour the place, traces of the theme everywhere . . .

BOY: If only the *Storia* is not a disappointment.
GIRL: What did you say? What?!
BOY: The foreword is drivel.
GIRL: The *Storia?* That's all we needed. Yeah, that's all we needed.
    I hope to God it gets back on its feet.
    Otherwise we'll be laughing on the wrong side of our faces,
    won't we, huh?
    (Darkness)

8

The room. Closed window. An older, powerfully built man paces back and forth in an open raincoat. LOTTE *comes in the door with the drawing portfolio and the portable television.*

LOTTE: Here you are! . . . Ooof!
    You could spend a lifetime looking.
    (She puts the television and the portfolio down. Takes off her coat, lays it carefully over her arm. The old man continues in his course without interruption)
    Do you work here?
    Did you hear my message on the radio?
    I requested they play Meyerbeer's "Torch Dance" and dedicate it to you. It was broadcasted, too. Broadcast.
    No?
    Are you doing all right, Paul?
    How do things look professionally?
    Trouble?
PAUL: *(Stops suddenly)* What do you want?
LOTTE: Money.
PAUL: Make do on what you've got.
LOTTE: Then I want to be divorced.
PAUL: We don't need a divorce.
LOTTE: I need one.
    I get an allowance from the state
    if I want to go back to school.
    I don't get anything from you.
    *(*PAUL *starts pacing again)*
    I want to study languages.

What's happening for you in politics?
No papers up here, huh?
I can still hear you saying: "It'll mean war . . . It'll mean war!"
Do you remember?
But somehow we've had peace all this time.
I still often hear you saying things, you know that?

Don't pace like that.

Why are you pacing so wildly?
What are you thinking?
Stand still!
You are an animal, Ingrate.
I feel like I'm in a cage when you pace.
Stop! . . . Stand still! . . . Stop!
(Very loud)
What time do you go to bed at night, huh?!
(PAUL stops, stares at her.
Quietly)
You never even wrote me.
You never even wrote me if I should come or not.
(Darkness)

9

The room with the little tent. LOTTE *is pushed into the room by* PAUL. *The door is slammed shut and locked from the outside. She is startled by* THE TENT, *which is creeping toward her. She takes refuge along the wall, head buried in one arm.* THE TENT *follows her. After a while . . .*

LOTTE: Bernard.
    (THE TENT comes to her feet. She turns around)
    Bernard, my brother, he had a tent too, just like you . . .
    Are you a boy or a girl?

    At our house—
    or was it later at the Roths' on the corner?—

he was allowed to put up his tent under the dining-room table. I used to say, "Bernard, I'm not going in there with you." "No," he would say. "You have to! This is an expedition. In there we're on the slopes of Mt. Everest, and you'll freeze if you stay outside."

"OK," I said—

but what comes now I can only tell you

if you're a girl.

You aren't, are you?

(She runs to the door, tries to open it. THE TENT follows her slowly)

Leave me alone! Go away!

You belong in the army, you!

Shove off!

(She kicks THE TENT, it backs away. LOTTE kneels on the floor, feels for the body inside the tent)

You're not getting any air in there . . .

Well, you're not so little, after all.

Not so little, after all, are you?

(The door is opened, INGE, the woman in the zipped-up dress, appears)

INGE: You can move in whenever you want.

　　The old man died yesterday.

LOTTE: Who?

INGE: The old man downstairs, who never knew whether to say hello or not. I think the only thing he wanted here was to leave all his shit behind for us. He only moved in so he could dump all his shit in the room.

LOTTE: You're speaking about a dead man!

INGE: An old stinker is an old stinker.

　　Death doesn't make him more interesting.

　　Come with me. I'll show you the room.

　　My name is Inge.

LOTTE: Inge . . . tell me: who's hiding in the tent?

INGE: Clarissa's daughter lives in the tent.

LOTTE: A girl!

INGE: Clarissa went to Holland with Peter Scheuer.

　　Just took off, pfft . . .

She left the child here because she knows of course we'll take
care of her.

But she's hiding. She is incredibly sad.

LOTTE: *(Wants to go to* THE TENT*)* The little one!

INGE: No. Leave her alone.

She's not so little.

She's seventeen: she's not so little any more.

(Exiting)

Now she's had a taste of life

and that's why she doesn't dare come out any more.

(Darkness)

10

*The room with the dirty plastic raincoat on the floor. The door
stands wide open.* LOTTE *(with coat, television and drawing portfolio) and* INGE *enter.*

INGE: So. You have the window looking onto the street.

In the summer the hedge will grow over.

All right?

LOTTE: Thanks.

*(*INGE *takes the plastic raincoat, drags it behind her. She goes
out, closes the door.* LOTTE *opens the window, looks out. She
sits on the floor, with her back against the wall. On her right
the television is on without sound. After a while the door
opens. The* FAT WOMAN, *who gave herself the morphine injection, enters and stands near the wall)*

LOTTE: What is it?

FAT WOMAN: Fear of Sunday.

LOTTE: Sit down.

(The FAT WOMAN *lets herself down next to* LOTTE *with a
groan. She begins to tremble.* LOTTE *puts her arm around her.
In the distance a game of tennis can be heard)*

Can you hear?

Tennis!

Plop. Plop. Plop. Plop. A quiet match. Wonderful!

Can you play tennis?

FAT WOMAN: It makes you feel like drowning yourself in the kitchen sink.
(The GUITAR PLAYER enters hesitantly, with his instrument. He greets them awkwardly)
LOTTE: Yes. Come in!
Would you please close the window?
GUITAR PLAYER: *(Does so)* You don't have to be so formal with me.
LOTTE: I live here now.
And you spend the whole day playing the guitar, right?
GUITAR PLAYER: No. I go to the institute every morning.
Does it bother you . . . ?
LOTTE: No.
What do you do at the institute?
GUITAR PLAYER: I am a crystallographer.
LOTTE: Crystallographer? Hm!
GUITAR PLAYER: Crystallographer, yeah. Sure. Physicist.
LOTTE: Tell me about it.
GUITAR PLAYER: Roughly speaking, we determine the atomic structure of solid objects; we make extremely refined measurements, you know.
LOTTE: Ah!
GUITAR PLAYER: And minerals and artificial crystals; we investigate them under different pressure and temperature conditions.
LOTTE: Give me an example!
GUITAR PLAYER: *(He draws back)* The layman today can best keep in touch with crystallography by finding out, for instance, how his or her quartz watch functions.
LOTTE: Are you going already?
GUITAR PLAYER: Yes. I must.
LOTTE: Come again!
(He goes out)
FAT WOMAN: *(Stands up)* I must also.
Whale of a misser like me.
I go to visit somebody next door, it's a sure thing I'm missing somebody visiting me. I've already missed a lot.
(She goes out. LOTTE alone. She turns the television toward her, begins to draw with a pencil that is attached to the portfolio. She copies something from the television screen. From above, in his room, one hears the GUITAR PLAYER. After a while . . .)

LOTTE: *(To the television)* Should I go?
    What?
    Should I go?
    (She lays the portfolio aside, leaves the room)
    (Darkness)

11

The room. Near-darkness. In the left corner INGE, *the woman in the zipped-up dress, and* PAUL, *the old man, are lying next to one another in an embrace. There is a knock on the door.* LOTTE *enters.*

LOTTE: I can't sleep.
INGE: Not now, Lotte.
    Another time. Later.
    There is someone with me.
    *(*LOTTE *backs up, closes the door)*
    (Darkness)

12

The room. The GUITAR PLAYER *is with the* RESEARCH ASSISTANTS.

GIRL: So, Jürgen, that's it. That's all of it.
    The Children's Children. Contributions to the Social History of the Third Generation of the Southern German Merchant Families of the 14th Century. Source material. Bibliography. Documents. Edited by Jürgen Binder in collaboration with Gudrun Leibolt . . . That's all of it, three long years! What was it all about, do you know any more? Cologne and Munich, 1976. Approx. 250 pages. 30 facsimile reproductions. Clothbound $15.00.
    Is this the one and only thing we've been
    living for, for the last three years? Is it?
    God and the devil, what have we done!?

BOY: So. Well. That's the very worst thought—
    The worst thought there is. You thought it.
    (After a while)

GUITAR PLAYER: NASA, back then, sent us a little packet of moon rocks and we made a fuss about it, like a band of pirates finding the treasure of Captain Kidd. But there was nothing there. Nothing new. No trace. The old optics, the old structures, everything the same in the moon rocks. At the beginning though, the greed, the hands flying . . . ! You weren't there though, you don't know what it was like.

GIRL: Why did we write the book, why?

BOY: The book deserved to be written.
And so we wrote it.

GIRL: You know, I think you're really off your rocker!
Why did we, the two of us, write a book together? I'm asking you!

BOY: But, Gudrun, that's just not a reasonable question.

GIRL: Listen, don't you have any idea
what's going on between us?

BOY: And you think it has to do with the book?

GIRL: The book, fuck the book.
The book means absolutely nothing.
That's just it, you read it and you have the feeling
that two people wrote this book, a man and a woman,
two people who belong together too!

BOY: I think I see this somewhat differently.

GIRL: What? What? What?!

BOY: I think that we are standing at the very beginning of a long common task, a long scientific journey that may stretch out perhaps over decades.
Currently, in a somewhat critical phase—

GIRL: And how do you picture it, this love, huh?!

BOY: Gudrun—

BOY: *(He is silent)*

GIRL: *(Nods, as if she knows the answer)* Hmm . . . hmm.
(Silence)

GUITAR PLAYER: Do you still need me?

GIRL: Sören, please, stay.
Play something. Why didn't you play something long ago?
(The GUITAR PLAYER plays. All three begin at once to sing one or two verses of country music together in harmony. In the middle the GIRL breaks off and turns again to the quarrel)

One thing I want to say to you, Jürgen: you are and always
will be the mama's boy of the family. A creature from
Hanover. A human desert. A token product from the middlest
middle of the middle class . . .

BOY: How imaginative.
GIRL: Imaginative? Listen, you, I mean, you have to try to picture
this: You fix yourself up—! You literally comb your hair
before you telephone your mother on Saturday afternoon. Try
to picture that some time! That's how much damage has been
done.
BOY: Idiocy.
GIRL: Yes, you do. Unconsciously. Unconsciously you do it.
You don't dare talk to your mother uncombed,
just like you are.
I swear it! Of course you're unaware of it. Of course.
That's exactly how much damage has been done.
Unconsciously!
BOY: You shut up now, all right?!
(After a while)
GUITAR PLAYER: Okay? Finished?
BOY: Wait another moment, Sören.
GUITAR PLAYER: In physics the real aces, the guys with the big
perspective, there are only a few of them, fewer and fewer, as
usual, like a little prison yard full of experts, walking around
restlessly and pushing against the dark walls of the silence
of the masses. Of course you can have bad luck and be
assigned an institute director like ours, a Japanese who has
been doing research all alone along the wrong lines for the
last twenty-five years. All of us in the institute have to go
along with him, under his thumb, in the wrong direction,
while 90 percent of his colleagues reject his theories and have
proven to him often enough that he is doing research along
the wrong lines and that for decades he has been wallowing
in error . . . The Tashi Superstructure model . . . another
abandoned focus of world history.

GIRL: Sören, what you do, it's only a job!
Only a job! But me, with me I am a whole existence!

. . I am a twenty-four-hour person . . . I am the book . . . I am our one and all . . . I am Jürgen and I!

(She grows quieter)

I'd just like to know why both of you have to smirk all the time?

I'd like to know, for what fucking reason you assholes . . .

(She is leaning against the wall, breathing with exhaustion)

BOY: If you'd like to lie down a little . . .

Because we've got to be in the seminar in a little while.

(He gives her the glasses, leads her to the door)

GIRL: *(She turns back into the room)* It was the devil . . . this time it was the devil.

He came and went and came again and went again and came again and went again.

BOY: Oh, it's normal, it's perfectly normal, my love.

Everybody has to let go sometimes.

We've got a good grip on it.

GIRL: No. The devil.

Have you any idea what a powerful guy the devil is?

(The three of them go out)

(Darkness)

13

The room. LOTTE *alone. She leans against the door frame, goes out onto the landing. She comes back, looks at her watch, leafs through her drawing portfolio, opens the window, closes it again. She practices for an upcoming conversation.*

LOTTE: There is no reason to make fun of . . .

You don't need to make light of your being so late . . .

try to make light?

We don't want to make fun, do we?

Just don't try to make light of it!

Is that supposed to be a joke?

Oh, goose chase. He won't make jokes.

I don't think he'll try and make any jokes.

Where do you stem from?

Stem? Uh!

Where were you born, if I may ask?
No, other way around. He asks first.
Where was I born?
I come from Rhineland . . . from the Rhineland.
Lennep. And you?
Remscheid-Lennep. And you?
You play the guitar and I like to draw.
Do you like it?
You don't like it?
No: perhaps you would like a sketch . . . ?
I can do nothing for hours.
Doing nothing takes practice.
Free time is *the* problem of today's life . . .
In our society. *The* problem of the hour . . . the
future?
Ouch, this is getting off base.
But "Doing nothing takes practice," I have to remember that.
*(She goes to the window, looks out of it for a moment, then
turns around enticingly, as if someone were standing in front
of her)*
I almost died of . . . of . . .
Of what? Hm?
Of fright? Of "dreaded anticipation"?
Nuts.
(She turns again to the window, and back immediately.)
No. I am separated.
I mean, I have been dying of . . . of . . .
Shit.
(The GUITAR PLAYER *has entered, without his instrument)*

GUITAR PLAYER: Who are you talking to?
LOTTE: Just talking.
  (They stand facing one another)
  What's your name?
GUITAR PLAYER: Sören. Sören like in Kierkegaard.
LOTTE: You needn't make fun of it.
GUITAR PLAYER: Look, I only wanted to tell you,
  I think you're making a few maybe typical mistakes around
  here.

LOTTE: Oh?

GUITAR PLAYER: You seem to think there should always be someone here for you, when things don't happen to be going especially well, when you can't sleep or something.

LOTTE: *(Lowers her head, nods, agrees uneasily)* Hm . . . hm.

GUITAR PLAYER: But then you yourself are incredibly fast on the draw, you concern yourself maybe a little too much with the others.

LOTTE: Hm . . . hm.

GUITAR PLAYER: For example, the tent on the first floor.

You definitely made a mistake there.

LOTTE: Hm . . . hm.

GUITAR PLAYER: You know, the tent, we all take care of it.

I mean, it's probably not good

if you do more than the others.

You probably shouldn't go there any more often than the others.

LOTTE: Hm . . . hm.

GUITAR PLAYER: In theory, every room here is responsible for itself.

That's a kind of silent house rule.

LOTTE: Right, yes, right.

GUITAR PLAYER: I have to say, naturally there'll be times,

when something just isn't working at all,

that you can call on someone for help.

Only: not so much fuss. No fuss.

LOTTE: No, no.

GUITAR PLAYER: You understand, I have to tell you this, otherwise—

LOTTE: Right, Sören. It's good that you told me.

GUITAR PLAYER: Do you paint?

LOTTE: I draw.

(He takes a look at the portfolio)

GUITAR PLAYER: You even paint from the television, eh?

LOTTE: You play the guitar and I like to draw.

GUITAR PLAYER: I just wanted to tell you that. But otherwise—

I think it's great that you're here.

LOTTE: Yeah?

(He nods several times and goes out)

(Darkness)

14

LOTTE *stands at the open window. The door opens a crack. Someone is listening.*

LOTTE: Four floors above the Esso station
one morning a woman in a dressing gown steps out of her
little apartment . . .
A man leads her carefully to the railing of the balcony.
With a stiff neck she leans forward and asks to see the void
over which she lives.
Now you've seen it, says the man.
Yes.
Right here it's about thirty feet down.
Yes.
They turn around and go back into the apartment.
Down in the carwash music cassettes are playing.
Tunes full of pride and full of broken pride.
In the sky there's color and light.
In the sky today there's summer.
(The door opens. The OLD WOMAN *comes forward)*
OLD WOMAN: Someone moved out.
LOTTE: Who?
OLD WOMAN: Don't know.
I only wanted to see whether—
(She listens)
LOTTE: Whether?
OLD WOMAN: Psst!
Wanted to see in whose room it's empty.
A familiar sound's missing in the house.
Your husband is the old man upstairs, right?
LOTTE: Hm.
OLD WOMAN: *(Draws back into the half-open door)* A young
woman like you . . .
(The door shuts to just a crack)
LOTTE: Do you have something against older men with younger
women?
OLD WOMAN: He's a liar.

LOTTE: Yes. He is.

OLD WOMAN: *(From the crack of the door)* Rose . . . ?
Rose . . . ?

LOTTE: What is the matter?

OLD WOMAN: You can get a better fellow anytime
than the old man upstairs, dearest.

LOTTE: Don't whisper, Mrs. . . .
Do come in. There's good light in here. The television's on.
There's fresh air. The walls are standing still . . .
I knew he would start lying and lying.
And I would go on believing and believing.
(PAUL, LOTTE's husband, suddenly enters the room. LOTTE, sitting against the wall, turns her head back and forth)
Oh, no . . . oh, no . . .

PAUL: Get out of here, Lotte.

LOTTE: I don't want to.

PAUL: Stand up, I tell you. Don't lie around on the floor.

LOTTE: *(Slides her back up the wall)* Yes . . . always have to stand.

PAUL: You get out of here!
How dare you?
Move in here—upstairs my work is at a standstill.
I can't do it, I'm not getting anywhere.

LOTTE: I want to help you . . .

PAUL: Not another word!

LOTTE: I—

PAUL: Not another word!

LOTTE: *(Pause)* I simply have to get it off my chest—

PAUL: You, shut your mouth!

LOTTE: *(Almost shouting)* Don't you want me to clip the newspapers for you again?!)

PAUL: Get out!
(LOTTE takes the portfolio and the television in both hands, stands with her back against the wall)
Clip the newspapers, sure!
Then everything would go wrong! You're a jinx!
You would bring me your newspaper clippings again.
You'd say in that way of yours: "Isn't this some kind of special story?"
Like that? Yeah? I can still hear it, you mother hen.

It makes me sick, your voice, it's poison to my ears.

A freelance writer, you think that's someone who works sort of on call, right? Like a mental wizard in vaudeville.

Someone says, "Tramway crash," and zip!, I write a touching sketch. Someone says, "Buying slump," zip-a-dee-zip!

Someone must be doing all right in the seventies.

LOTTE: You are such a tender person, so much more tender than you think . . .

PAUL: Try writing these up-to-date comments!

"More and more toys are being produced for fewer and fewer children. This is one side effect of the pill that cannot be ignored . . ." Try writing that!

LOTTE: I could help you.

The smaller papers would be happy to accept your humorous sketches, too.

(The OLD WOMAN *appears in the half-open door)*

OLD WOMAN: We are going to show some slides.

Please come on time.

(She remains standing in the door)

LOTTE: Oh, I can't help remembering!

Please, Paul, let's go on, stay together.

Otherwise I'll die from too many memories!

PAUL: Not another sound.

Pest . . .

Shut your mouth.

I tried to teach you how to speak correctly.

(He gives her a slap on the back of the head)

And don't think that I feel embarrassed in front of other people.

(He picks up the suit jacket that she has let slide to the floor)

Don't you want to put your jacket on?

(He lays it over her shoulders. The OLD WOMAN *comes over and also starts to clean up and fuss over* LOTTE*)*

OLD WOMAN: Now there . . . now there . . . you can't walk around like that, not quite so untidy. Bangs out of your face!

(To PAUL*)*

She's not a bad little thing, is she?

PAUL: *(Pushes* LOTTE's *hair off her forehead)* No. Of course not. Not a bad little thing.

Just once in a while a little too much mouth, huh?
(PAUL *leads* LOTTE *to the door. The* OLD WOMAN *takes* LOT-
TE'*s raincoat, follows them*)
LOTTE: One more thing: don't forget me!
(*Darkness*)

15

The room, INGE'*s, the woman in the zipped-up dress.* PAUL *stands
facing her, holding her hand loosely.* LOTTE *comes in wearing a
coat, pushing the door open with the portfolio and the television.
She sees the two of them and stops.* PAUL *goes to the window and
looks out.*

LOTTE: I just wanted to say good-bye to you.
I . . .I have to get out of here.
INGE: Yes.
Do you know where?
Where you're going?
(LOTTE *looks at* INGE *for a long moment, slowly shakes her
head.*
She hands INGE *the television set*)
LOTTE: Will you take it?
INGE: Sure, I'll take it, thank you, thanks.
Be glad to.
LOTTE: Can't drag it around everywhere with me.
INGE: No, you shouldn't have to.
I'll keep it for you
You're not taking the car, right?
LOTTE: You can hold on to it.
INGE: Yeah?
All right, I'll hold on to it, then.
(*She puts the television down, it stays on the whole time with-
out the sound*)
This still works really well. You can see fine.
You're not taking the car, right?
LOTTE: Don't have one. But I can drive a car. But don't have one.
(*She looks toward* PAUL *at the window*)
What's he doing?
Paul!

INGE: Don't. Leave him alone.

He can't work, he's not getting anywhere.

(Under the gaze of the two women, PAUL *slowly leaves the room)*

LOTTE: So. Can't work. Hm.

Well, don't you know why?

That's the reason I'm going. The wise man gives way.

You know why?

Paul and I, it's simply too much for him,

something too unique, too unforgettable—

he just can't concentrate on anything else

when I'm around, yes!

(Strangely angered, INGE *suddenly unzips her dress from her chin to her navel and rips it open. She reveals a T-shirt with a big photo-portrait of* PAUL *printed on the fabric)*

LOTTE: Oh, well.

Zip up, Inge.

I have to go. Take care.

INGE: I'll show you to the door downstairs.

(Darkness)

16

The room in semidarkness. The old married couple. A slide projector beams white light onto a projection screen on the rear wall. Eight chairs. A MAN *sits on one of them.*

OLD MAN: No one's coming.

Did you let everyone know?

OLD WOMAN: I let everyone know.

Except the tent.

The tent won't come, anyway.

OLD MAN: The tent shouldn't even have to know

that anything's going on up here.

OLD WOMAN: Only the Turk is here so far.

OLD MAN: I want to begin.

I'm curious.

OLD WOMAN: And someone moved out.

OLD MAN: Yes. I know. The freelance writer.

OLD WOMAN: No! Why? Not him.
> The floor below. The one who never visited us.
> The freelance writer is not about to move out!

OLD MAN: And the little one next door?

OLD WOMAN: Which little one?

OLD MAN: You know, the little one next door.

OLD WOMAN: Don't know.

OLD MAN: Is she coming?

OLD WOMAN: She's coming, yes.
> *(Pause)*
> No, Father. She won't be coming any more.

OLD MAN: I don't care.
> If no one comes we'll just show the slides to the Turk.
> I'm starting now.
> *(He goes to the door, calls into the stairway)*
> We're starting!
> Let's go, first slide!
> *(There follows a series of slides in which can be seen what the OLD MAN and his wife do in their room, empty and bright as usual, and how they pass their day. The two of them stand right and left of the projector and accompany the slides with a prepared text. Gradually the inhabitants of the ten rooms appear—the GUITAR PLAYER, the RESEARCH ASSISTANTS, the FAT WOMAN, INGE, and PAUL. They sit in the chairs; one remains empty. It doesn't take long before someone stands up, goes out again, comes back later, leans against the wall, etc., so that there is continually a slight movement among the people.*
> *The first slide shows the OLD MAN hugging his wife to him, one hand on the crown of her head)*

OLD MAN: Good morning.

OLD WOMAN: Good morning.
> *(Second slide: the two at some distance. The WOMAN's head is lowered, the MAN offers his open left hand)*

OLD MAN: Come here.
> *(Third slide: the two together; medium shot; the MAN points to the camera)*

OLD MAN: Do you remember?
> *(Fourth slide: the MAN has put his arm around his wife's shoulders, he looks at her)*

Do you remember?
Our famous contemporaries.
Bugatti.
OLD WOMAN: Oh, yes, Bugatti.
(Fifth slide: both close up, the same shot)
OLD MAN: Maria Meneghini Callas.
OLD WOMAN: Oh yes, Callas.
OLD MAN: Rudolf Steiner.
OLD WOMAN: Oh yes, Dr. Steiner.
(Sixth and seventh slides: similar to the fifth)
OLD MAN: Madame Blavatsky.
OLD WOMAN: Oh, yes, Madame Blavatsky.
(Eighth slide: similar to the preceding ones)
OLD MAN: Emmeline Pankhurst.
(OLD WOMAN is silent)
Emmeline Pankhurst!
OLD WOMAN: Oh, yes . . .
(Ninth slide: the two kneel in front of a large shopping bag and place the purchased goods around them)
OLD MAN: We went shopping in the morning.
OLD WOMAN: We can shop wherever we want—
we get good discounts everywhere.
GUITAR PLAYER: Who took these pictures of you?
OLD MAN: You'll see him! You'll see him!
(Tenth slide: medium shot: the MAN lets a stream of oil run from a can of vegetable oil into his mouth)
OLD MAN: Oh, most lovely oil,
ave sanctum oleum!
(Eleventh slide: both of them. The WOMAN opens a box of sugar cubes)
OLD WOMAN: Sugar, you world traveler!
Welcome! Let me look at you!
FAT WOMAN: Good photos. Lively.
(Twelfth slide: the MAN washes his face with oil)
OLD MAN: Oil, wash me clean and bring me peace.
Have mercy on me.
(Thirteenth slide: the MAN hands the WOMAN a package of brightly colored drinking straws)

OLD MAN: One should pay more attention to objects.
One should put oneself in the service of objects.
The objects will outlive us.
With so many straws we'll easily have enough until
the end of the month.
(Fourteenth slide: the MAN *lets rice run through his hands
back into the box)*
OLD MAN: Rice.
(Fifteenth slide: the WOMAN *takes a slice of dark bread out of
the wrapper)*
OLD WOMAN: Bread.
(Sixteenth slide: the MAN *points to an apple)*
OLD MAN: Apple.
Here you see an object that has gone far.
It is a symbol. Almost more a symbol than an object.
(Seventeenth to nineteenth slides: the MAN *and the* WOMAN
*pack the goods back into the bag. At one point they bashfully
look up into the camera, as if they were being called from that
direction)*
OLD WOMAN: How long it's been since I've eaten till I'm stuffed!
OLD MAN: But you're not supposed to eat till you're stuffed.
OLD WOMAN: Yesterday, for instance: two little slices of
dark bread, two tangerines, a yogurt and in the evening,
a plate of pancakes.
And that's after the meager start the day before—

OLD MAN: Pssst!
OLD WOMAN: . . . two slices of dark bread, an apple, turkey with-
out any trimmings . . .
OLD MAN: Don't you hear?
The Lord is speaking . . .
Don't keep interrupting Him.
OLD WOMAN: Yes, yes. He's speaking.
Every year it's getting harder for me to believe in Him.
OLD MAN: Quiet!
OLD WOMAN: I've lost the thread, anyway.
*(Twentieth slide: Christ figure in foreground, viewed from the
rear. Bleeding wounds between the shoulder blades. Crown*

of thorns, the blessing right hand. The MAN *and* WOMAN
kneeling with lowered heads)

GIRL: Who is that?

TURK: It's me, it's me!

With automatic release we did.

OLD MAN: Lord, at the heart of everything we do
your slumber reigns . . .

OLD WOMAN: Lord, at the heart of everything we do and say
it reigns and watches over us, your sightless eye.

TURK: Good job, I act.

Really, huh? Good act.

(Twenty-first slide: the MAN *and* WOMAN *at the window in
half profile)*

OLD WOMAN: *(Hums a tune)*

OLD MAN: Who is singing in our house and hasn't been good for
the Lord?

(Twenty-second slide: the WOMAN *looks at the ground, the*
MAN *reproaches her)*

OLD MAN: Cross the street on a red light!

You crossed yourself and then you went across the street on a
red light. That wasn't right this morning, Mother.

OLD WOMAN: No.

There was a woman on the other side standing with the
others.

She gave me a secret sign.

OLD MAN: You imagined it.

OLD WOMAN: Yes, but it was clear as could be.

(Twenty-third slide: the MAN *and* WOMAN *on the back wall
of the room. She looks sideways up at him)*

OLD WOMAN: What I can't remember any more is,
did Jesus actually have brothers and sisters or—
and if so, what happened to them?

OLD MAN: *(Reciting)* "Is not this the carpenter, the son of Mary,
the brother of James, and Joses, and of Juda, and Simon?
and are not his sisters here with us?"

OLD WOMAN: Aha.

OLD MAN: That's because you used to be Catholic.

Catholics don't believe in the brothers and sisters of Jesus.

(Twenty-fourth slide: both look straight ahead.

Twenty-fifth slide: the WOMAN *again looks sideways up at the* MAN.

Twenty-sixth slide: the WOMAN *stands against the wall, the* MAN *walks in front of her from left to right)*

OLD WOMAN: And when did I actually become a Protestant? Nineteen hundred what?

Question after question.

GUITAR PLAYER: Where's Lotte?

(Twenty-seventh slide: the MAN's *neck is being massaged by the* WOMAN)*

OLD MAN: How nice that there are two of us.

(Twenty-eighth slide: the laughing face of the WOMAN)*

OLD MAN: Why are you laughing?

Don't laugh like that.

(Twenty-ninth slide: both of them. The WOMAN *laughs, the* MAN *with his back to the camera looks over his shoulder at the camera)*

OLD WOMAN: You did something naughty.

OLD MAN: Come on. Silly goose.

(Thirtieth slide: both are leaning in the open window)

OLD MAN: Again today, I don't want to leave the house.

(Thirty-first slide: the WOMAN *touches the hair on the back of the* MAN's *head)*

OLD WOMAN: Tomorrow you go to the barbershop.

OLD MAN: I wouldn't think of it.

OLD WOMAN: You need to badly.

The freelance writer wears his hair very short, too.

OLD MAN: He's not anything for me to go by.

OLD WOMAN: I'm not going to be seen any longer with you like this.

(Thirty-second slide: the WOMAN *at the door, tries to leave without being noticed. The* MAN *is still at the window)*

OLD MAN: Where to?

OLD WOMAN: I'm going to see what the little one's doing.

OLD MAN: You stay here, please.

(Thirty-third slide: the WOMAN *turns away from the door. Hands behind his back, the* MAN *comes toward her)*

OLD WOMAN: All right. I'll stay here, then.

(Thirty-fourth slide: horrified, the WOMAN *stares into the camera. The* MAN *stands next to her on one side, tries to turn her around by the shoulders)*

OLD MAN: Don't look over there!

(Thirty-fifth slide: the MAN *and* WOMAN *walk next to each other along the length of the room)*

OLD WOMAN: I want to take off my street shoes.

(Thirty-sixth slide: the MAN *kneels and takes her shoes off. Thirty-seventh slide: the* MAN *kneels and in his open hand, held out in front of him, shows a coin)*

OLD MAN: You've been walking around the whole time on a dime!

OLD WOMAN: That brings good luck.

That really brings good luck!

(Thirty-eighth slide: the MAN *and* WOMAN, *hands behind their backs, lean on the rear wall. In the middle of the room is the overturned shoe)*

OLD WOMAN: You're not talking to me any more, right?

OLD MAN: Nonsense.

FAT WOMAN: Lovely photos. Lively.

(Darkness)

Big and Little

Lotte
Meggy
The Turk
His Wife
A Young Man
The Boy
The Girl
Building Inhabitants

In front of the glass door of an apartment house. An intercom over a buzzer panel. LOTTE *in a raincoat with the drawing portfolio under her arm.*

LOTTE: *(Looks for a name on the buzzer panel)* Niedschlager . . .
It's not on here. It's got to be on here.

85 Virchow Street. Right.

Tillmann, Karnap, Karnovsky, von Roel . . .

The son of the man who ran the movie house. Controversial child.

Niedschlager becomes von Roel through a later marriage with her first love. To see *Quo Vadis?* once for free she French-kissed with him, and God knows he had a wet mouth . . .

Victor Mature had a wet mouth, too! . . . Oh, Meggy, you sure do have a lot to say.

(She presses a buzzer. A crackling in the loudspeaker of the intercom)

LOTTE: *(Speaks into the intercom)* Yes, this is Lotte-Kotte from Lennep . . .

(No reply. Renewed crackling in the intercom)

LOTTE: Hello?

Whoops!

Whoops! Said the porcupine, that was no lady, that was a clothes brush.

(She presses another buzzer)

INTERCOM: *(Male Voice)* Who's there?

LOTTE: Lotte.

INTERCOM: *(Joyful)* Dotty!?

LOTTE: No. Lotte.

INTERCOM: Dotty? Well, you're still alive?

LOTTE: No, no. I am someone else.

You're confusing me with someone else. I am looking for Margaret Niedschlager . . .

INTERCOM: Oh . . .

(Crackling in the intercom. LOTTE presses another buzzer. No one replies. She presses the next . . .)

INTERCOM: *(Voice of an Old WOMAN)* Yes?

LOTTE: Excuse me, please,

I am looking for Miss Niedschlager—

INTERCOM: No.

LOTTE: Or Mrs.—Mrs.!

INTERCOM: No.

What's her name?

LOTTE: I don't know exactly. It could be—
   in case of marriage.
INTERCOM: You know, my husband and I, we come from the East.
   We know practically no one here.
   Our daughter is a district court lawyer,
   but unfortunately she isn't here right now.
   Ask at the Heinzes'.
   They generally know about everything.
LOTTE: Thanks . . . Heinz, thanks.
   (She looks for the name and presses the buzzer)
INTERCOM: (WOMAN's *Voice)* Yes, please!
LOTTE: Mrs. Heinz?
INTERCOM: Yes. Which one?
LOTTE: Please excuse the interruption—
   do you know Niedschlager, Meggy? Margaret.
INTERCOM: *(The* WOMAN *calls to her sister in the apartment.)*
   Gunilla!
   (To LOTTE*)*
   Wait a moment.
LOTTE: Thanks.
INTERCOM: *(Another* WOMAN's *Voice)* Yes?
LOTTE: Please . . . there must be a woman here
   living in this house with the maiden name Niedschlager.
   But it seems, maybe she did get married and I can't
   find her. Do know she lives here from her father's letter!
   (She puts her ear to the intercom)
   At the Brauns' they told me you know about everyone.
INTERCOM: Just one moment, please.
   (She calls into the apartment)
   Laura! Laura!
   (After a while)
   Did we understand correctly: Tannsieder, right?
LOTTE: Nied-schlager. Nied like neatness.
INTERCOM: Oh, that's a whole other name.
   Wait a moment, please.
   (After a while the voice of the FIRST WOMAN*)*
   Are you listening?
LOTTE: Yes . . .

INTERCOM: We don't know.

As much as we'd like to help, we don't know.

Even though we know almost all the women in the house well, we only know a very few of them by their maiden names.

Please believe us!

LOTTE: Oh. Thank you. Many thanks.

I'll try it at random.

(She presses a buzzer, reads the name over it)

INTERCOM: *(Jovial Male Voice)* Yes?

LOTTE: Mr. Schneider?

INTERCOM: Hmmm.

LOTTE: Excuse the interruption . . .

I am Dotty, uh, Lotte—

INTERCOM: That's OK, that's OK.

LOTTE: Maiden name Niedschlager: by any chance do you know anyone with that name in this building?

INTERCOM: So what's the rush, girl?

Why don't you come up for a minute?

(The door opener buzzes several times. LOTTE hesitantly opens the door. She enters, but comes back out immediately. The door shuts behind her. She presses another buzzer)

INTERCOM: *(Voice of a Little Girl).* Who's there?

LOTTE: *(Shouting)* Meggy!

(Pause)

Meggy?

INTERCOM: Who do you want to speak to?

LOTTE: Aren't you Meggy?

INTERCOM: Nope.

(Giggles.

LOTTE *waits, her back leaning on the door)*

INTERCOM: *(Voice of the Jovial Man)* Hello, Lotte!

LOTTE: *(Goes to intercom)* Yes?

INTERCOM: Well, come on up!

No one's going to bite you. My tiger just finished his Alpo.

(The door opener buzzes)

LOTTE: You are . . . who are you now?

INTERCOM: Schneider.

LOTTE: Oh, Mr. Schneider.

No, Mr. Schneider.

INTERCOM: Now don't be a cold fish, girl.

(The door opener buzzes several times)

LOTTE: *(With a stretched-out index finger she presses a buzzer)* No!

INTERCOM: *(The Lazy Voice of a Woman)* Yeah?

LOTTE: *(Tired)* Good evening. Excuse the interruption.

I am looking for a Niedschlager, Mrs., however
possibly no longer Niedschlager . . .

INTERCOM: Yeah.

And?

LOTTE: And . . . and . . .

Lives in number 85, but where?

INTERCOM: Yeah, yeah.

That's me.

LOTTE: *(Joyfully)* Meggy! Meggy!

Well, Meggy, you know . . . now that your name is finally . . .
what?

(She looks at the buzzer panel)

Well, what? . . . Wittich. Wittich!

INTERCOM: Who are you?

LOTTE: It's Lotte-Kotte . . .

(She is silent, listens, no answer)

You remember: the pencil snitcher . . . the crazy nut . . .
who dropped the stick in the two-hundred-yard relay . . .
Laughty-Notte!
Naughty-Lotte, Naughty-Lotte!

INTERCOM: Oh—yes.

LOTTE: Oh, Meggy . . .

INTERCOM: Lotte-Kotte.

LOTTE: Of course! How are you, how are you?

INTERCOM: *(Monotonous, lazy)* Oh, all right.

Are you here for a visit?

LOTTE: Yes. No. I came right through Essen
and I thought, take a look, see how Meggy's doing.

INTERCOM: Hm.

LOTTE: So, I'll come on up, OK?

INTERCOM: I'm not doing especially well.

LOTTE: Are you sick?

INTERCOM: Who knows.

LOTTE: Just a little word with you, just a little word.

INTERCOM: I don't know . . .

LOTTE: There's so much to talk about!

    Meggy! Think of it!

INTERCOM: To talk about . . . hm.

    So much?

LOTTE: Well, sure. Lots.

    (An older married couple come by. LOTTE greets them po-
    litely. The man unlocks the door; both disappear into the
    building)

INTERCOM: Lotte-Kotte?

LOTTE: Yes.

INTERCOM: What's going on down there?

LOTTE: Nothing. Some people went into the building.

INTERCOM: Foreigners?

LOTTE: No, I don't think so.

INTERCOM: Tell me exactly.

LOTTE: Two older people, around medium height, a man and a
    woman in a transparent rain cape.

INTERCOM: Both of them in rain capes? OK, OK.

LOTTE: I thought, but you know them, so I said good evening.

    Once again they looked exactly like people I know.

    I am so dog-tired, I see friends everywhere.

INTERCOM: If you're tired

    you should first get some sleep.

LOTTE: Look. I thought you'd be pleased;

    we'd talk to each other, you'd be pleased.

INTERCOM: Talk, talk.

    And afterward?

    Afterward you'll fall asleep on me up here, right?

LOTTE: Meggy, listen!

INTERCOM: I can't sleep a wink

    when somebody's sleeping in my room.

LOTTE: Meggy, listen: then let's not!

INTERCOM: Even Wittich doesn't sleep here any more.

LOTTE: Then let's not.

    'Bye, good-bye.

INTERCOM: No. Wait.

> *(Pause)*

Come on up.

> *(The door opener buzzes.* LOTTE *disappears into the building. Shortly afterward a* YOUNG MAN *in a festive parade uniform comes out of the door with a clarinet in his hand. He moves quickly around to the right at the rear of the stage. After a while a* BOY *enters from the left with his girlfriend. The* GIRL *follows him at some distance; she walks slowly because of bladder pains)*

GIRL: Ou . . . ouuch.

> *(The* BOY *stops, turns around. The* GIRL *stops)*

BOY: What is it? Wanna go home?

> That with the bladder, you're doin' that cause ya wanna spoil my fuckin' parade.
>
> Wanna go home?

GIRL: Nah.

BOY: What's the matter, then?

> Can't pee right, in the john, or what is it?

GIRL: I can't go.

BOY: This ain't happenin', this ain't happenin'.

> Is somethin' stopped up in the bladder, the stopper, or ya got stones in the bladder or what else?
>
> Wanna go home?

GIRL: Nah.

BOY: But ya can't march along on this parade like that.

> You're always fallin' behind and stayin' back.

GIRL: All right. I'm comin'.

> *(They continue, exiting right at the rear of the stage.* LOTTE *comes back out of the house, leans against the door. She looks as if she has been crying)*

INTERCOM: *(*MEGGY'S *Voice)* Lotte-Kotte!

> Can you hear me?
>
> Lotte-Kotte?
>
> *(*LOTTE *goes to the intercom)*

LOTTE: What . . . ?

INTERCOM: You are so—

LOTTE: What are you doing to me? What?

INTERCOM: You are so—
    restless.
LOTTE: God, I make it a point—
INTERCOM: So restless.
    You're restless when you walk and
    restless when you come in
    and restless when you sit down and
    restless sitting on my footstool . . .
LOTTE: I tell you something and you say
    I'm restless. I make it a point
    not to fall asleep up there
    and you say I'm restless.
    How little friendship, Meggy!
    I make it a point and tell you a story,
    I sit down on that awful footstool,
    no ass could get a wink of sleep there
    because it wobbles every which way,
    and I tell you a story without once faltering,
    as calm as a Persian
    and without falling asleep.
INTERCOM: But it looked like
    you would have rather fallen asleep.
LOTTE: Where? Where?
    (Music from the parade band softly in the background)
INTERCOM: But your drawings are nice.
LOTTE: Yes.
    (She looks in the portfolio)
INTERCOM: The picture of Paul is nice.
LOTTE: Yes.
INTERCOM: In school you were number one in crafts.
LOTTE: I'm talented with my hands.
INTERCOM: Yes. Very.
LOTTE: I want to study languages now.
INTERCOM: Languages, oh pooh!
LOTTE: When I'm divorced I'll get money from the state.
INTERCOM: Allowance . . .
LOTTE: Yes. An allowance . . .
    Can I come up, Meggy?
INTERCOM: *(After a pause)* I'm not doing especially well.

LOTTE: Yeah, right, I can understand.

INTERCOM: Are you going to be staying in Essen?

LOTTE: I'm on my way to Sylt.

INTERCOM: To Sylt? Are you going on vacation?

LOTTE: No. I'm visiting my brother in Hörnum
    Bernard.

INTERCOM: Oh, Bernard. The little one.

LOTTE: Well, he's been a dentist for ages and he's been married
    for ages to a dentist's daughter in Hörnum.

INTERCOM: How little you must have been,
    seven years old, when I swore
    eternal friendship to you, how little,
    my hand on your heart,
    how little I!

LOTTE: Oh, Meggy, tiny, tiny!

INTERCOM: The outing to the Burg Castle . . . eternal friendship!

LOTTE: Yes! Yes!
    The outing. Yes, that's what I mean. Exactly!
    Finally you've remembered, finally.
    Go on, go on, don't forget anything!

INTERCOM: Today you have a fatty breast
    on the same spot where I once lay my little hand to swear.

LOTTE: I do not.

INTERCOM: Yes, you do.

LOTTE: You too.

INTERCOM: Not quite, you.

LOTTE: Meggy . . .

INTERCOM: Fatty breasts, fitful slumber.

LOTTE: Long arms—

INTERCOM: God, how you must pant when you sleep!

LOTTE: Long arms—
    I do not pant!

INTERCOM: Long arms: what?
    Not easy to make fun of me, huh?
    Long arms! Godlet . . .
    Don't trust yourself to take a nibble, huh?
    Don't trust yourself to say
    what you really saw, up here,
    what kind of a person, sitting here in my chair?

(In the background hats, jackets, paper streamers from the parade fly into the air)

INTERCOM: It's not so easy to make fun of me, huh?

LOTTE: No.

INTERCOM: Try it.

LOTTE: No.

INTERCOM: Make a mock of me
   and I'll let you up.

LOTTE: I can't do it.

INTERCOM: Make a mock, put some effort into it.
   And if it's a good one, then you get my very own bed
   to sleep in.

LOTTE: *(After a pause)* There's no face like your face
   though your face's like no face.

INTERCOM: That was no mock.

LOTTE: Yes, it was.

INTERCOM: I didn't know there was anything wrong with my face.
   My *face?*

LOTTE: It's just that I'm too tired to make a good mock.

INTERCOM: Too bad. It isn't easy either.

LOTTE: *(Last try)* Who is it?
   Got a mug like a slug,
   Ties her shoes on her knees,
   A hunk of her trunk's
   Sunk where no one ever sees.
   Who is it?

INTERCOM: Me?

LOTTE: Yes.

INTERCOM: I think something's wrong with you!
   (An old man appears with three shirts from the cleaners. He unlocks the door. LOTTE follows him into the house. From inside she presses her face against the glass door, squints at the intercom)

INTERCOM: Pig.
   Hardhearted.
   Animal.
   Dirt.
   Has-been.
   Monster.

Big and Little · 213

Bitch.
Scum.
(Pause)
Lotte-Kotte?
Lotte?
(The intercom is silent. A WOMAN *enters from the left with her husband, a* TURK. *She has her arm through his. After they have passed the apartment-house door, the* TURK *stops suddenly, turns toward the rear of the stage, and begins to utter short cries. He bellows one-syllable words: "Bite." Then after a pause: "Door." They sound like military commands. From behind the glass door* LOTTE *watches the two of them. Interrupted by gradually longer pauses, the* TURK *bellows: "Shit." "Make." "Beer." The* WOMAN *frees herself from her husband, moves to the side, and observes him like a stranger.* LOTTE *comes out of the building, presses a buzzer, watches the two uninterruptedly . . .)*
Yes?
LOTTE: It's me.
INTERCOM: Oh, Lotte, I thought you had left already . . .
LOTTE: No. I'm here.
INTERCOM: Come on up!
(The door opener buzzes for a long time. The TURK *continues to shout: "One," "Jerk." "But." "When."* LOTTE *goes over to them)*
LOTTE: What's the matter?
WOMAN: Don't know.
LOTTE: Your husband?
WOMAN: I'm scared, huh.
LOTTE: But you don't have to be scared of your husband.
WOMAN: He never was like this before. Screaming bloody murder. Don't know him like this, huh.
LOTTE: He's just drunk.
WOMAN: Can't hold nothin', huh. Got him drunk as a skunk. Have a drink, come on, drink up. The skunks, huh. I send him down to the corner for two packs of cigarettes and he don't come home. Just can't hold nothing', huh.
(The women watch the drunken man, who calls out at intervals: "Shit." "Fritz." "Cunt." "Pants." "Nope." "Come."

Every so often a call still comes from the intercom: "Lotte"
"Lotte-Kotte . . .")

Standin' like the number one. Don't fall down, that guy, huh.
Ya can see for yourself, standin' like nothin', huh.

LOTTE: Yeah. Great!

Keeps his balance to the end. Like a sergeant!

Drunks aren't all alike.

(The TURK *throws his right leg out so forcefully that his shoe*
flies high in the air)

WOMAN: Only in his head everything's stirred up.

LOTTE: What is he? Turkish?

WOMAN: Yes. Turkish.

LOTTE: I'll ask him what he wants.

WOMAN: He can't talk, huh.

*(*LOTTE *picks up the shoe that has fallen on the street. She*
goes to the drunk, bends over, and puts the shoe on him)

LOTTE: Calm yourself. Your wife is frightened.

Tell me what it is you really want.

Don't yell any more. Come along.

(She puts her arm through his)

I don't mind if you speak in Turkish. I'll understand.

(The drunk moves from his stationary position and goes with
LOTTE*)*

WOMAN: Where are you goin'? Hey! Where?

LOTTE: Wait here.

I'm going once around the block with him.

Wait here.

*(*LOTTE *and the* TURK *go off to the right. The* WOMAN *goes*
to the entrance to the building and squeezes into the corner
opposite the intercom. After a while a YOUNG MAN *comes in*
from the right, shabbily dressed. He stops in the vicinity of
the door, whistles "Some Enchanted Evening . . ." The
WOMAN *turns away, hides her face in her elbows, which are*
propped on the edge of the door)

YOUNG MAN: What's up, buttercup . . .

Listen, Rita, we've known each other long enough by now.

You know that I don't try to talk to strange broads on the
street.

I'm much too shy . . .

WOMAN: *(Peeks out of her hiding place)* I've never seen you before.
YOUNG MAN: You see,
    all I got to do is say Rita in a loud voice
    and already it comes out who you really are.
    It comes out, namely, that in the end
    you're nobody else than good old
    Ingeborg—
WOMAN: Oh, man, huh!
YOUNG MAN: . . . Leo's baby.
WOMAN: Chatterbox? Go on!
    Keep moving!
YOUNG MAN: What kind of bees give milk?
    (Admonishing finger)
    Boobies!
WOMAN: Ha. Ha. Ha.
YOUNG MAN; Yep, it's pressin' in Essen.
    Too bad, so sad.
WOMAN: Lucky I already know that Abraham Lincoln is dead, huh.
YOUNG MAN: Come into the corner with me, Regine.
    down into the corner with me,
    I'll show you a trick!
    We can turn a cold beer
    Into a warm surprise.
WOMAN; Into the corner! What else, huh!
    All those skunks hangin' around the corner,
    they made the Turk go crazy, huh.
YOUNG MAN: What Turk?
WOMAN: The Turk, my husband.
YOUNG MAN: I thought you said berserk.
WOMAN: My husband, man, huh. He's walking around the block
    with what's-her-name.
YOUNG MAN: Look, I just know what I read in the papers.
    Turks and what's-her-name are like Trygve Lie and Syngman
    Rhee. Heard of them, but don't ask me what.
WOMAN: You're nuts! Gaga.
    Man, what do you do, with a chatterbox like that in your
    mouth?
YOUNG MAN: Me? Traveling companion.
WOMAN: Traveling companion . . .

YOUNG MAN: Yourself?

WOMAN: We have two stores, huh. One is ours and one is Arslan's brother's.

One on Mevissen Street near the parking garage and one in Erlenbruch.

YOUNG MAN: Stores with everything?

WOMAN: Stores for fresh fruit, fresh vegetables.

You should know that, huh.

In Essen people know that.

(Pause)

Traveling companion. For who?

(The TURK *enters from the left, alone)*

YOUNG MAN: It depends. Race horses, political candidates, works of art, old ladies, blind men. Anything that doesn't like to travel alone, from a newborn to a corpse.

WOMAN: Arslan!

Come here!

Where is the woman, Arslan?

TURK: Bilmem, gitti.

YOUNG MAN: What did he say?

WOMAN: He doesn't know. She left.

TURK: Kim bu adam?

WOMAN: No one. We both just happened to be standing here.

YOUNG MAN: What did he say?

WOMAN: Who you are.

TURK: Defolsun, gitsin.

WOMAN: No, Arslan.

YOUNG MAN: What?

WOMAN: He's saying I should send you away.

YOUNG MAN: Yeah. Do that.

WOMAN: No. Wait, huh.

TURK: Gitsin istemiyormusun, Karin?

WOMAN: No, Arslan.

YOUNG MAN: Well?

TURK: Iyi, kalsin, öyleyse.

WOMAN: You can stay.

TURK: Ismi ne?

WOMAN: Your name.

YOUNG MAN: Jürgen.

WOMAN: Jürgen what?

YOUNG MAN: Jürgen Jürgen.

WOMAN: *(Laughs)* Wisecracker. The front's like the back, huh.

YOUNG MAN: Yes. So it seems.

WOMAN: Jürgen—does that mean anything?

YOUNG MAN: Mean anything? Don't know.
What's Hitler mean? Hitler doesn't mean anything, either.

WOMAN: I'm named after something: Damla.
Damla means water drop, water droplet.

YOUNG MAN: Karin Water Droplet.

WOMAN: Yes. Karin Damla.

TURK: Sen benim karımsın, bir tanem . . .

YOUNG MAN: What did he say?

WOMAN: You are my wife and my darling.

TURK: Bir tanem!

WOMAN: My beloved.

TURK: Hayat merdivenin binlerce taş basamaklarından aşağı be-nimle beraber in.

WOMAN: You follow me . . . down the stairs, or what was that?

TURK: Binlerce taş basamaktan . . .

WOMAN: The thousand stony steps . . .

TURK: Hayat merdivenin basamaklarından aşağı.

WOMAN: . . . down the staircase of life.

YOUNG MAN: So ask yourself, when you tie the knot,
if the married state's really all that hot.

WOMAN: You'd be better off with your mouth shut, huh.
That's how they talk, it's really beautiful.

TURK: Haydi gidelim.

YOUNG MAN: What?

WOMAN: Let's go.

YOUNG MAN: Yeah. I'm going.

WOMAN: No. We're going together. You stay.

TURK: *(Goes a step closer to his wife)* Sen benim karımsın, bir tanem.

YOUNG MAN: What's the matter?

WOMAN: *(Fast)* You are my wife and my beloved.
(She seizes the YOUNG MAN*'s hand)*
Stay!

TURK: Sus, tercüme etme.

WOMAN: Quiet. Don't translate.

TURK: Tercüme etme.

WOMAN: Don't translate.

TURK: Ağzını kapa!

WOMAN: Shut up.

TURK: Orospu.

WOMAN: You are a streetwalker, call girl, woman of easy virtue.

TURK: Sus! Sus! Sus!

WOMAN: Quiet, quiet, quiet.

> *(The* TURK *turns around on the spot and begins again to bellow one-syllable words like commands)*

TURK: Shit! . . . Door! . . . Jerk! . . . Come!

> *(The* YOUNG MAN *tears himself loose and runs off to the right)*

WOMAN: Stay here! Just stay here!

> Oh, no! . . . Oh, no . . . !

> *(She sits down on the step in front of the building entrance. The* BOY *and his girlfriend enter from the right. He has been drinking)*

TURK: One! . . . One!

BOY: *(Stops)* Hey! Drunk, eh, buddy?

GIRL: Leave 'im alone.

BOY: *(To the* WOMAN*)* Is he drunk, that guy, or what?

> He's got a wet wick, ya won't get him burnin'.

> What's he doin' there?

WOMAN: Countin', huh.

BOY: Countin'. What's he countin'?

> Count yourself, buddy.

> The whole city, ya know . . .

> Just go home . . .

> Malsberg and Siebing, ya know it?

> Chemical pilot plant . . . the warehouse . . . I, ya know,

> I used t'work like a fuckin' slave there,

> poison gas, cans this big. Monsters.

> One day, ya know, the whole city, ya know . . . Bang! Bang!

GIRL: *(Uninterested)* Don't worry, the worst is yet to come.

BOY: Hey, you, just go on home . . .

> The whole city, you know, down into the bunker . . .

> Bang!

GIRL: Come on.
TURK: One!
BOY: Bang!
> (*The two go off to the left. The* TURK *and* HIS WIFE *alone. Silence. Darkness*)

Way Station

An illuminated telephone booth on the edge of a rural highway. In it is LOTTE. *It is comfortably furnished with objects she has picked up: a curtain made from a handkerchief along the front, a kind of bar stool, on which she is sitting, next to a rubber tree. A glass of milk on the telephone box, a broken shaving mirror. A strip of fly-paper hangs from the ceiling; a drawing of Paul is on the rear wall. Off and on* LOTTE *puts a coin in the telephone, dials, always the same number, hangs up after a while. During this, one can hear her voice over the sound system.*

LOTTE: Dear Paul,
> I hope this letter finds you healthy and hard at work. I am already far away from you now. (But only in body!) I made it hitchhiking past Lüneberg without any problems, then right from there I started hiking back toward Lüneberg.
> The memories of our first years in Saarbrücken will always be for me the most beautiful ones of my life. Now sometimes I dial our phone number on the Street of January 13 and let it ring in the emptiness.
> We could have talked about everything in good time. I want to study languages.
> I stopped over in Essen too, to visit my best friend from school, Margaret Niedschlager (married name Wittich), but unfortunately both physically and mentally she has turned into a real drip and she's not interested in anything any more.
> Tomorrow I'll see if I can't find a pillow or a cushion in one of the old cars. My rear end hurts.
> In the woods nearby there is a wreck from two cars strewn about that's almost completely grown over.
> Once again. Just like after the last war. Some-

times I think: maybe something has happened that I
know nothing about. The people from this region are all
up and gone, there's just no one to be seen.
The borders have shifted and I'm sitting here
long since in another country.
Excuse my momentary panic. Deep down I'm
strong and in time it will dawn on me how I can become
a little happier again.
Now to you, dear Paul.
I only want to tell you that I know that you are in love
with the woman in the zipped-up dress and that she is
in love with you. Now that I know it I feel somewhat
relieved about you. That's how it is and I
have to accept it. But I only hope that one day you too
will discover that you're far happier
and feel things far stronger when you
really love someone than when you just let someone love you.
Please don't throw this letter away after just one
glance or just at the sight of my handwriting!
That would hurt me very much.
Dear Paul, I will always search for you. (I mean:
figuratively speaking—don't worry!)
God is simple. God doesn't change and He
deceives no one.
Love, Lotte.

P.S. Say hello to everyone from me. Especially the girl in the
tent. Are you taking good care of her?
(*Darkness*)

Family in a Garden

Lotte
Bernard, *her brother*
Wilhelm
Josephine, *his daughter*
Albert, *his son*

*A barbecue patio in a garden. In the foreground a low table with
five patio chairs. On the right a barbecue, next to it a bar cart. A
column with a madonna figure on it. Chairs, table, barbecue are
cemented into the ground at their bases. All movable objects are on
narrow chains. Sitting at the empty table are:* ALBERT; WILHELM,
his father; JOSEPHINE, *his sister; across from them:* LOTTE, *next to
her brother* BERNARD. *The people frequently change position in
their chairs, since they have nothing, such as eating or drinking, to
divert their attention from each other.* LOTTE *wears her two-piece
suit. Each time it appears more colorless and bleached-out. She
draws a sketch of* ALBERT, *the young man.*

LOTTE: Don't you recognize me, Albert?
ALBERT: Yes, I do.
LOTTE: I know you. But you don't know me any more.
    Big as you've gotten.
ALBERT: Yes, I do.
    (Pause)
WILHELM: *(Leaning forward, rubbing his folded hands together)*
    So you want to take an interest in my only son?
LOTTE: Well, yes.
WILHELM: What do you think of that, son-in-law?
BERNARD: *(Looks nervously at his watch)* I mean: what do you
    have in mind for him?
    You're married, aren't you, sister?
LOTTE: We're separated.
BERNARD: Love? Kindness? A desire to educate?
WILHELM: See here, my boy needs a little support more than he
    needs any further excitement.
LOTTE: *(To* BERNARD*)* Fiddler. Don't fiddle around with your watch
    all the time.
WILHELM: Three full years this boy's been waiting to get into
    dentistry school. Three years' delay. Two years in the military
    at the outset. Duty for our *welfare* state. It means that now
    he's in his mid-twenties. And he's still parked in theology.
    The best years of his life are passing, his calling
    remains undecided. He's going to come to nothing. Sits
    at home in Hörnum and gives us crazy lectures.

BERNARD: The war generation didn't have it any easier.

WILHELM: War generation? Are you the war generation?
Good grief, Bernard! In the sixties everything just fell
into your laps. From school straight into an internship,
with a few connections—

LOTTE: We had absolutely no connections.
Our father wasn't rich! He was only a
little man at the gas works and when my brother
was a student he always had a job on the side.
It's not fair to say something like that. And my brother
didn't have a practice right in front of his nose, that he only
had to grow into, sooner or later, like Albert.
Otherwise today my brother would have his own
practice and he wouldn't be your assistant!

WILHELM: *(Together with* BERNARD*)* He's not my assistant.

BERNARD: I am not an assistant.

LOTTE: Or something like it. Married dependent.

WILHELM: Yes, yes. Doom and gloom.
A state, a *welfare* state . . . but one can't talk about things like
this with you people.
(Pause. LOTTE *draws)*

JOSEPHINE: Thirteen thousand dollars.

LOTTE: *(Leans toward* ALBERT, *tries to move her chair forward)*
Before I met you, Albert—
Why am I so tied down, damn it!?
Everything's walled in, everything's chained up!

WILHELM: And what do you think would be left in the garden
tomorrow
if we didn't wall everything in, chain everything up?

LOTTE: Before I met you, Albert,
I was numb from such grief,
like the figure there on the little column . . .

WILHELM: *(Approvingly)* Yes, yes—right, right.
(No reduction from ALBERT. LOTTE *leans back again. On the
next sentence she slides to the edge of the chair)*

LOTTE: A thousand thoughts
fly through my head,
a thousand unthought-of things . . .

WILHELM: Yes, yes—right, right.
   (She leans back again)
LOTTE: Say a little something precious to me in French.
   To be able to speak as well as you can . . . !
WILHELM: Yes, right!
ALBERT: But I can hardly speak it . . .
LOTTE: Come now, of course you can speak French,
   and you can speak Italian, too . . .
ALBERT: *(Laughs)* I can't speak Italian at all . . .
   (Both laugh)
   No, really!
   *(JOSEPHINE tries to stand up, but her knees crack and she sits
   down again)*
JOSEPHINE: *(Addresses her leg)* Leg, if you do that—!
   It will never be the same.
BERNARD: It's just 2:50, Feeny.
   It's not even 3 o'clock yet, darling. Perhaps
   you should wait at least another half an hour.
JOSEPHINE: *(Stands up)* You, Bernard, quiet!
   Where are my thirteen thousand dollars?
   *(She goes to the bar cart, looks slowly up and down at the
   row of bottles. Her father follows her, concerned. He stands
   at her side)*
WILHELM: Nothing hard, Josephine. Nothing hard!
JOSEPHINE: What should I have . . . ?
WILHELM: Let me beg you, my child . . .
JOSEPHINE: Where should I start . . . ?
WILHELM: You have the whole day ahead of you . . .
   *(She finally takes a bottle of vodka or gin, pours a big glassful.
   The father attempts to be helpful on one hand and on the
   other hand to hinder her. He gives her the glass, only to take
   it immediately from her lips. As she is drinking he strokes her
   hair. He accompanies her back to her seat)*
ALBERT: What you're wearing, Lotte, that suit—
   is that the new grandmother look on the Continent?
   You look right out of last year's Easter parade.
LOTTE: I thought I was dressed halfway decently, halfway.
ALBERT: I hope you didn't forget to put a mothball in your gusset.
LOTTE: A monkey, you're a monkey!

ALBERT: I would love to see what you look like when someone talks
about sex in front of you.

WILHELM: Turn back, Albert!
Turn back!

ALBERT: I bet you get a whole different expression on your face
when someone talks about certain sexual specifics in front of
you.

LOTTE: Just don't talk so much about it!

ALBERT: Don't want to just talk sex with me, right?

LOTTE: I will. But—

ALBERT: But?
You know, Lotte, there are loving mothers
who masturbate their babies when they cry . . .

LOTTE: No more sexual . . . please!

ALBERT: Look at the wonderful face she's making!
With so few words! Dot-dot-dash, the face of sex
in a flash.

WILHELM: Now hear me, Lotte.
Back there the sea hisses, it hisses and roars,
and at high tide my son here spews out his worst jibberish.
But if the sea grows silent, the ebb tide comes, then—
(He has to get up, as JOSEPHINE *has stolen over to the bar
cart. He overtakes her and guides her carefully back)*

ALBERT: And there are other mothers, or there used to be,
less loving, who attach an apparatus
to their son's flesh that announces each erection of the child
in the parental bedroom by means of an electric bell.
My father had such a mother.

WILHELM: I'll catch both my children
in my arms,
I'll take Albert under the left and Josephine under the right,
and then I will flee, down from the North,
where I wasn't born,
where my children weren't born,
down from the North Sea and out of the North Sea air,
poisoned with iodine.
I'll leave what's ours standing here, lying,
catch you both, you trembling little birds,
if you don't stop up your evil at last!

You your stupidity.
You your madness.
You your silence.
You your silliness.
You your staring.
You the gleam in your eye . . .

JOSEPHINE: Listen to that, he's moping about us kids!

LOTTE: He's moping? No. He's concerned.
You torment him.

JOSEPHINE: Now I'm going to tell you something: your brother Bernard robbed me.

LOTTE: Robbed?
(To BERNARD*)*
Don't fiddle with yourself all the time. Leave that!

JOSEPHINE: Yes, robbed.
Thirteen thousand dollars in gold ingots and paper money.
Behind the wall paneling in the bedroom.
My most private money, huh!

WILHELM: You should never have hidden so much money in one spot.

JOSEPHINE: But money that isn't safe from your own
husband, who would believe that.
Never in a million years should I have shown him
the hiding place.

LOTTE: Bernard, say something.

BERNARD: Approximately one year ago I took thirteen thousand dollars from behind the wall paneling in the bedroom and put it on my person.

WILHELM: Well, then.
For weeks we've been discussing nothing else.
Does it have to be brought up again just now?

JOSEPHINE: She is the sister. She belongs to the family.
She should know about it.

LOTTE: Why do you steal?

JOSEPHINE: No one knew about the hiding place. Except him.
Even I almost forgot all about it.

WILHELM: But he admitted he did it, he admits it.

JOSEPHINE: He probably thought: she never looks behind the wall paneling; who knows when she's going to look back there again . . .

LOTTE: Why do you steal?
    You never stole before.
    Why? Here it belongs to you, anyway,
    more or less, sooner or later—everything.
BERNARD: Not all to me.
LOTTE: Did you give the money back?
BERNARD: No.
LOTTE: No?!
BERNARD: At the moment I'm not in a position . . .
LOTTE: What have you done with thirteen thousand dollars?
BERNARD: I don't want to talk about it.
LOTTE: All right.
JOSEPHINE: The gentleman doesn't discuss that with us.
WILHELM: *(Quietly)* Unfortunately. Up to today, unfortunately, we
    haven't been able to find out.
    (To BERNARD*)*
    You know, a touch of information in the meantime wouldn't
    kill us, a spark of enlightenment!
LOTTE: Did you speculate with it? Gamble?
    Did you have gambling debts?
BERNARD: No . . .
    (He reflects)
    I don't want to talk about it.
LOTTE: Robbed your own wife . . .
    My God! Bernard! Crazy!
    At least tell us, why?!
    And stop that awful tugging at your pants!
WILHELM: What should I do? What should I do?
    This reaches down into the very depths, what?
    Right?
    (He stands up suddenly)
    Leave my garden and leave
    my house and my practice.
    Go away from us.
JOSEPHINE: Hey! Heeeeey!
WILHELM: *(Sits down again)* You see.
JOSEPHINE: Think about what you are saying, Father.
    Don't fart around all over the place.

WILHELM: You see.

    In which forum shall we hold the trial?

    The family? The family cites a thousand other factors;

    to the perpetrator the family is a sheltering jungle,

    he is submerged and he can't be found.

    (BERNARD stands up)

JOSEPHINE: *(Together with LOTTE)* Where are you going?

LOTTE: Where are you going?

BERNARD: I'm not running away.

    (He goes over to a pile of newspapers standing near the barbe-
    cue, and slowly spreads pages from the paper on the ground
    so he can clean parts of the grill)

LOTTE: I'd like to say that I love my brother and

    that I feel responsible for him,

    because I am his older sister, and in the past I

    always took good care of him.

JOSEPHINE: Oh, well. That's just how it turned out.

    Last year I had a store in Keitum

    for arts and crafts. This year for a change

    I haven't undertaken anything . . .

    I could have always had a child.

LOTTE: Josephine, what are you thinking?

    Are you thinking about a divorce?

JOSEPHINE: I don't know.

    I still love him, too.

    He should be ashamed of himself.

WILHELM: But he's not ashamed of himself. Now stop it!

LOTTE: No! Be fair!

    Here, please, he's there on the ground,

    he's ashamed. Be fair!

    Albert, you look over here, too!

ALBERT: Just don't wet your pants, eh?

    I don't care one way or the other.

JOSEPHINE: Apathetic, typical!

    Apathy is just apathy, for everything.

ALBERT: I do need to meddle in your sex, Feeny!

    Theft and shame? Oh, you poor little church mouse!

    Robbery, that's something very deep, something immensely

    sexual, it's very rare, an insane cry, an insane surge!

And you're jabbering away, cold and sweaty,
like a tour guide. You usually don't talk
about sex. This whole time now you've been talking about
your sex life and you don't even know it!

JOSEPHINE: Sex! . . . What's supposed to be sexual about that?
Maybe if he had cheated on me, yes.
But a robbery victim senses it differently.

ALBERT: Because sexually you can't count from one to ten.

JOSEPHINE: Albert, I can't say I'm familiar with your philosophy.
That's enough.

LOTTE: *(To* BERNARD*)* Don't you want to join us again?

BERNARD: I'm just about to clean the grill.

LOTTE: *(Almost cheerful)* What in the world did you do with
all that money?
(No answer. BERNARD *continues spreading out papers)*

LOTTE: *(Serious)* Bernard, you are a man who has changed
radically.

BERNARD: Well.
I'm a pessimist.

LOTTE: Pessimist? You're a thief!
Don't try and talk your way out of it.

JOSEPHINE: I'm convinced he had secret debts . . .

LOTTE: Did you have secret debts?

BERNARD: To be a pessimist . . .

LOTTE: *(To* JOSEPHINE*)* Obviously.

BERNARD: . . . is not so easy in today's world.
The belief in the goodness of man
holds people together everywhere. It unites.
But once you're a skeptic, once you see a dark future
for mankind, in general, then you
experience bit by bit how your best friends
draw away from you. Though you haven't offended
anyone personally. People are afraid of a pessimistic
thought in and of itself, the truth, finally.
Personally you can be the nicest guy in the world,
a pessimist is always left alone. Too bad. It is
conceivable one could be a pessimist without being a
misanthrope at the same time. One should be allowed
to be a pessimist and to be socially desirable, too.

(JOSEPHINE has risen and, on her way to the bar cart, has turned aside to stand next to BERNARD. WILHELM *follows her)*

JOSEPHINE: Perhaps it was just some kind of sudden attack
out of the thick of life . . .
After all, your nerves do whatever they want.
A man steals from his wife.
Something like this doesn't even happen in war.
Instead of war we've got this.
We've got bad luck.
(She goes over to the drinks.)

WILHELM: *(Whispers to* BERNARD*)* By the way, you're still behind
with the rent . . .
I only wanted to mention it.
(He follows behind JOSEPHINE.
LOTTE *leans over the back of the chair to* BERNARD*)*

LOTTE: Where to now?

BERNARD: What do you mean?

LOTTE: We can't stay here, Bernard.

BERNARD: Why not?

LOTTE: I thought, here at last, I could stay for a little while.

BERNARD: Just wait a little, have some tea.

LOTTE: You never stole as a child . . .
But you used to flex your biceps when you were praying,
that's what you were like! Don't do that, Mother used to say,
don't do that, or else the angel won't carve a dimple on your
chin, like you wanted so badly. When you grew up you
wanted so much to have a little thing like that on your chin.

BERNARD: You see. And now I've got one.

LOTTE: I don't see anything.

BERNARD: It's much worse to be afraid when it's not dark . . .

LOTTE: I'd like to live on a river again.
The best years I lived right across from a river.
The dirty old Saar in Saarbrücken. But how it flowed.

BERNARD: Here we have the sea.
The sea's nice, too.

LOTTE: But we can't stay here.

BERNARD: Why not?

(JOSEPHINE and WILHELM *come back to the table. This time,*
JOSEPHINE *has taken a tall, full glass with her)*

ALBERT: Listen to me!
   What are you doing to me!?
WILHELM: But if the sea grows silent, the ebb tide comes, then—!
LOTTE: You don't always have to be the center of things, Albert.
WILHELM: The ebb tide is coming, he's afraid.
   (He holds ALBERT's *hand)*
   Nature is a vindictive thing.
   It'll be over soon, my boy.
   This little family . . . This littlest family . . .
   above all, don't hurt each other, watch out! . . . Above all,
   don't hurt one another . . .
JOSEPHINE: This must be pretty much the same as the time he was
   sleepwalking.
WILHELM: Right at the changing of the tides . . .
JOSEPHINE: Neglected sleepwalking, is there such a thing?
   God, I don't really know, either.
   (She drinks)
LOTTE: You like to drink, don't you?
   I'm sure you need that, to be able to sleep at night?
JOSEPHINE: *(Smiles)* That too.
LOTTE: Can you get to sleep without it?
JOSEPHINE: *(Laughs kindly)* With it, it's easier.
   (Darkness)

Wrong Number

Empty stage. LOTTE *on a chair. Very pale face, smeared mascara
under her eyes. A gigantic book lies open on the floor in front
of her.*

LOTTE: Where
   now?

   No answer.

   Sitting here like this—
   I should have left long ago.
   I can't forget:

the spirit moves me to go
sitting here like this.

Floyd has left
and Non–Floyd has left.
Edward has left
and Inge has left.
Sören and the Turk have left.
And Wilhelm, Meggy, Pechstein,
and Karin.
At the end Paul left, too.

North south
east west
far wide
northeast
north northeast
a distance unthought through.
One degree one minute
no one's there
then two degrees one minute
passed away
then heaven or hell
ocean or book—
I wouldn't know
where else they could be hiding.
The wind rose
and the windless rose, too:
there's nothing more.
That is the whole round of the earth.
Or oval.

Paul didn't stay.
The room didn't stay.
Bernard and Sister Annegret
didn't stay
De Soto, Father, and Clown Grock
didn't stay.
Here in the book

even the guests' script didn't stay.
The script didn't stay.
I'm sitting completely, utterly in the open!
But I can't become
as white as the book.
Not me!
When the blank pages start to come at us again
it's in God's hands, my misbeloved.

Where
now?
Each step could be the wrong one.
Where next in this everywhere?
Utterly free, utterly free.
Completely.
Given: I go to look for Paul.
Given: I knew where to begin . . .
No. I won't be able to get up if I think like this.
Thinking like this, no man alive could
get to his feet.
Careful, misbeloved, careful!
Thought is thought.
Something like that can't be blacked out
like a forbidden line in a book.
As long as it's me who's thinking,
it can only be wrong.
Or in Paul's words:
Sit here quietly,
never talk out loud.
We'll all be back soon.
OK, OK.
Then I'll say to everything that I'm thinking,
No!

Once before, when I just
couldn't forget things,
Emily gave me moral support.
Emily left Carl.
Carl left Dorothy.

Dorothy left John.
And at the end Paul left, too.

It's you I love.
It's you I love!

Could he hear me?
It depends.
In the West perhaps.
In the West it's,
from where I'm standing,
not more than about five thousand miles
to the end of the West,
where America ends and the East begins.
In the West a Paul could hear me,
could! However faintly, however barely.
Perhaps he'd notice a wisple-pisple
and think it was his inner voice.
His own little squeaky voice,
which he never listens to, anyway.
Yes, that's what they say.
What it's really like,
no one knows.

Of course no one will return.
It's a figure of speech.
All this time.
Not one.
How could they?
Going is going and going.
Things are dissolving.
We know that from science.
Or, if you will, the guest book.
Book losing script!
Or the mouth.
Mouth losing rouge.
Things are dissolving.

The soil is losing its seed.
Death is losing its dead.

Things that belong together
are sick of each other and fly apart.
Just like the cosmos in general.
It's exploding slowly endlessly outward.
We don't fall, as often dreamed,
we fly upward, away from each other.
Seen like this, things now for the first time
take on their actual weight.
Cosmos and supercosmos, upward,
and away!
Why take a stand against the turn of events?

Are you listening? Chair!
Wake up! Lazy old thing!
Just you and me, we're still here sitting tight.
You're on the ground, I'm on you.
The turn of events has just rolled over us, you say?
That's no reason at all to get yourself go, you!
A person has to always want something!
The clock has to always strike something!
(She stands up)
Ding dong Gloria.
Oh, the beautiful sky, unique each time!
And clouds, wet bellies, air shows!
Ding dong Gloria.
Today heaven lies round us like a cave,
a womb, a garden,
and soon we, the little earth, will come into the world.
Ding dong Gloria.

Doesn't Lotte know
what Lotte's saying?
(To the chair)
No, Gracious Lord, oh . . .
Your bride, the misbeloved, doesn't know any more.

You call yourself my bride?

I say it only out of courtesy,
Almighty Father.

I didn't know that you happened to be so close by.
(Suddenly, as if she were in her apartment)
Oh, God, my house is a chaos . . .
No, please, leave me alone!
I'm not the one you think I am.
I was just babbling away.
What of it? And I didn't mean anything by it.
I swear it, nothing to it and nothing behind it.
But please don't come any closer to me,
Heavenly Father, I beg you.
I cannot be your cup or your chalice
or any other vessel.
Then you would will me to break
and I should burst at the seams.
I cannot endure it with you, too!
I am not strong enough for that . . .
Oh, not this yellow!
I am terrified of yellow!
Not this yellow light!
Take Josephine or Meggy,
she can read palms,
but not me!
I am unworthy!
Lord, is this to be my punishment?
Just because I talked out loud to myself a little?
What am I supposed to do?
Why did you send all the others away?
Why?
What?! . . . I don't get it.
Leave me alone! Get away! It's a mistake! Wrong number!
No! . . . Help, help!
(She lifts up the book)
The book, the book . . .
The emptier it is, the heavier it is.
Don't touch me! Get out!
(She hoists the book above her head)
Don't touch me!
(She strikes the chair with the book, smashing the chair and, doing so, falls to the ground. She stands the book upright, so that it

*screens her from the wreckage of the chair. She squats with her
back to the binding of the open book)*

I don't think
I could have shaken Him off.
He can get in wherever He wants to.
He's probably already in, where He wanted to get.
(She scratches her back, looks at a bloodstained hand)
Blood! . . . What's bleeding on my back?
There was nothing on my back . . .
*(She tries to look at her back, turns around, squatting in front of
the book. There is blood running down from a small slit on the
right page. She reads aloud, as if trying to make out writing that
has just come into being)*
Faith Hope Love
Faithhopelove: No!
*(She slams the book shut. Blood continues to run from the front
edge. She rips scraps from her clothing, tries to clean the book)*
He makes me feel so little . . . !
I can see it coming. He'll get me to where I'm nothing.
Oh, why wasn't I watching out!
To send everyone away
and then start in on me . . .
To send everyone away
and then slowly start His witch work on me . . .
(She cleans and embraces the book)
Oh, no . . . Oh, no.
(Darkness)

Dictation

Lotte
Alf

ALF, *a young administrative employee, at his desk. He is using a
pocket calculator. In the rear, from the next room, one can hear the
sound of an electric typewriter.*

ALF *(Speaks into a dictaphone):* Dear Miss Dommermuth, at the Planning Commission

Monday morning until one. Please prepare memorandum for public bids: inner city beautification project. Await your call, recess around ten-forty. Letter to Wollhagen follows later in dictation.

(He uses the calculator again. Stands up, walks to the rear, comes back, speaks into the dictaphone)

Dear Miss Dommermuth, please don't be alarmed:

Monday morning possibly strange woman in office. Friend of mine. Wants to learn a little about our operation. Get her started on one job or another. She—

(He clears his throat)

means well . . .

(LOTTE enters from the rear with a sheaf of papers. She wears a long, light dress, almost summery)

LOTTE: Just take a look at what I've spent the whole day writing.

(ALF looks straight ahead, doesn't look at the pages)

Aren't you interested?

ALF: You didn't write it yourself, Lotte.

You only copied it.

LOTTE: Copied? . . . Hm.

Yes—but isn't that something?

When I'm copying it, I'm really fully

involved in what I'm doing. I'm your girlfriend!

ALF: Yes, you copied it very well.

A good job.

LOTTE: Read it!

ALF: No.

(LOTTE groans angrily)

ALF: If you like, next we could practice a correct

letter dictation with all the ins and outs.

LOTTE: Yes. I want to. Now. Begin.

(She takes paper and pencil, sits on the edge of the desk)

It's my ambition to be as good as old

Dommermuth in steno.

ALF: You know Dommermuth is no slouch.

In three decades of civil-service employment she has

progressed to the rank of a full-fledged right-hand man.

LOTTE: I'll get there, too.

ALF: Sometimes, Lotte—
in all kindness—
sometimes it seems to me
you are clawing your away a little hurriedly
into my daily life—

LOTTE: I want to help you, Alf.

ALF: Into my daily life,
you know, with the claws of a bear!
When you think that we've only known each other for fourteen
days and have hardly gone beyond a first acquaintance.

LOTTE: No, no, Alf. Don't worry. I want to help you.

ALF: Please don't forget how to stand on your own two feet.
A woman, today, gains noticeably with a sense of inner
independence. Yes, even coolness. A little coolness.

LOTTE: Right, I know. That's why I'm learning office skills.
Dictate!

ALF: Take a letter . . . Dr. Neuffer. Dear Dr. Neuffer . . .

LOTTE: Upper left full name, exact address.

ALF: Dear Dr. Neuffer . . .

LOTTE: Full name, exact address!

ALF: You find it in the file, Lotte . . . Dear Dr. Neuffer, All
things come to him who waits. After delicate negotiations with
my colleagues in the Parks Department, I find myself today in
the enviable position of being able to extend to you and your
friends the permit to put into operation a dog obedience school
on your acreage on the Deutsch mill pond. Accordingly, from
the State Parks Department—
Please don't read aloud with the text!
Accordingly, with regards to this, the obligations
previously quoted that pertain to you on the part of the State
Parks Department—in parenthesis: safety fences, the erection
of a parking lot, etc.—will be forwarded to you shortly
in a summarized statement from the State Director, Mr. Bels—
B E L S

LOTTE: The erection of a parking lot and so on?

ALF: Yes. And so on.

LOTTE: No: and so on instead of "etc."?

ALF: Dearest—don't ask me . . .
   As regards to the noise safety regulations you mentioned, I
   cannot see that you have anything to worry about out there.
   We are not, after all, located in the immediate vicinity of a
   residential area. Of course one should not, above all weekend-
   wise, begin training at too ungodly an hour. I remain then
   today, with all best wishes . . .

LOTTE: Weekend-wise? Can one say that?
ALF: Why not?
LOTTE: Weekend-wise, huh!
ALF: Write whatever you want.
LOTTE: Weekend-wise, it makes my hair stand on end . . .
   Now, was that serious? Or was that just a practice letter?
ALF: Serious, yes, serious.
LOTTE: Good. I'll type it immediately.
   (She exits at the back, types on the machine in the next room)
ALF: *(Into the dictaphone)* Dommermuth. Horrible. What's going
   to happen . . .
   This friend of mine, as I said. Hardly know her, just two
   weeks.
   We meet at Johnny's, we have a few laughs, she comes back
   to the house and once in the house she sits tight. Won't
   go away. A burden. What's going to happen? Afraid.
   *(LOTTE enters in a motorcycle helmet and motorcycle jacket,
   pulling a little sled behind her. On it lies a letter. ALF stands
   up, stares at her, moves to the side of the desk)*
LOTTE: I'm taking the letter to the post office.
ALF: There's no snow on the ground.
LOTTE: I'm taking my Honda.
ALF: You know how to drive a motorcycle, Lotte?
LOTTE: Yes.
ALF: And where is your motorcycle?
LOTTE: *(Tugs briefly on the sled rope)* There. I always have it with
   me.
ALF: You *don't* know how to drive a motorcycle.
LOTTE: Yes. I do.
ALF: Where did you get that outfit and the sled?
LOTTE: Well, I always have these things with me.

ALF: Not true. You're lying.
　　You stole it. Where? From the janitor?
LOTTE: Yes. I always have it with me.
ALF: Show me the letter, Lotte.
LOTTE: *(Hands over the letter)* Here is the letter.
ALF: Dear Paul . . .
　　It's a sunny day in June and the birds are all in tune.
　　I loveling the mayor. I loveling him with my whole
　　heart. This year is just another year. And so my calling
　　is still undecided. Am I at fault for having done out
　　the greenery in our living room? Yes. I myself
　　am a climbing vine, climbing back down again. I
　　myself have always been your Lotte Philodendron . . .
LOTTE: Instead of heart one could also say unicorn.
　　With all my unicorn.
ALF: *(Looks at the letter, nods)* Hm, hm . . .
LOTTE: The heart has always been the unicorn
　　that no one's ever seen.
ALF: And who is the mayor?
LOTTE: You are.
ALF: Why do you call me mayor?
LOTTE: You govern the people.
ALF: But that's not what I do at all.
LOTTE: Yes, you do, I already found out that you're
　　the mayor.
ALF: And how did you find out?
LOTTE: We're in Saarbrücken and you can also hear it
　　in your voice.
ALF: I am not the mayor.
　　You are here in the State Parks Department.
　　I am an employee of the State Parks Department.
　　I am not on the Parks Department Governing Board, do you
　　understand?
LOTTE: Yes.
ALF: *Not* on the Parks Department Governing Board.
LOTTE: Yes.
ALF: Now can we be reasonable again?
LOTTE: Yes.

ALF: The letter . . . The letter is horrible.

This can't go on. Horrible.

You will write this whole thing over again.

Figure out first exactly what you want to say.

What do you want to say?

LOTTE: I want my divorce.

ALF: But that's not anywhere in the letter.

LOTTE: Paul will know.

ALF: And what does "loveling" mean!?

What kind of a word is that?

"Loveling"—there's no such word, no such word in the whole language. Goddamned crap! Do you hear?

Either you say: Love him with my whole heart,

or you say: Darling, with my whole heart . . .

Maybe you meant darling?

LOTTE: No. Loveling. Paul knows what I mean.

ALF: And then it's got to read: done *in* the greenery!

LOTTE: Done out the greenery.

ALF: Done out! Done out! There's no such word, no such word.

Horrible. Not to be able to write a word of sense

and writing pleading letters all the same!

Now you will write this whole thing over again.

And figure out first exactly what you want to say.

LOTTE: *(Takes the letter back)* Yes.

I don't know how to write my letters any more . . .

ALF: Now you can get out of that silly uniform, too.

Come here . . .

(While he is in the process of trying to help her, with an awkward movement LOTTE's *helmet abruptly strikes his chin. He yells "Ow!" and smashes his hand on the helmet in a fit of rage.* LOTTE *stands dumbfounded. He grabs a ruler from the desk and smashes it over the helmet until the ruler breaks.* LOTTE *turns around and walks toward the back, pulling her sled behind her)*

I won't go out with you—

I can't be seen with you like this!

LOTTE: You won't have to, either.

I don't let anyone hit me.

(She goes into the next room, begins typing again immediately on the machine. ALF *rushes to the dictaphone)*

ALF: Dommermuth. Just hit Lotte. My God. Horrible. Frenzy.
Lotte suddenly changed mentally. Must help her.
But lost control. Am too high-tuned. Should approach her with more humor. Extremely talented when all's said. Draws beautifully. Goes to the window. Talks to the potted plants. Horrible.
(Pause)
Dommermuth. It's impossible for me to function here in our corner with such a mentally unstable woman. We have to help her. But gently, gently!
*(*LOTTE *comes back in, without the jacket and helmet, walking normally again. Her face is unreadable. She hands* ALF *a page from a letter)*

ALF: *(Reads)* Dear Dr. Neuffer . . .
(Trying to find a joke)
Oh! The letter to the puppy president, to Dr. Dog . . .
to the hound's gigolo, the four-legged general,
(More and more intense)
stud master, jack-boot instigator, race-dog breeder,
the dog gauleiter with his sic-him bite-him S.S.!

LOTTE: *(Doesn't react)* Read.

ALF: *(Scans the letter)* Dear Dr. Neuffer,
All things come to him who waits . . .
Well. You typed that perfectly, Lotte.

LOTTE: Not one mistake.

ALF: Yes.
(She takes the letter and starts toward the rear again)

LOTTE: Stamp it and send it off.

ALF: Leave it. It can wait until Monday.

LOTTE: *(Ill-tempered)* Even Dommermuth can't do better than not one mistake.

ALF: Stay here.
(She stops, without turning around)

ALF: What's the matter? Why won't you look me in the face?
What are you thinking, hm?
Lotte baby, we're not man and wife. We're not a married couple, not a match made in heaven. Now, we won't sulk. We'll always find a way to clear things up—

Now, what kind of a bad mistake was all this: sleds, Paul, and
the crash helmet? What am I to make of it? Tell me!
I have to know. Otherwise there'll always be the suspicion . . .
Were you able to correct this crazy person's letter?

LOTTE: Well—I tried . . .

ALF: Tried, Lotte? What does tried mean?

LOTTE: Well, then . . . if you think I should.

(She starts to go)

ALF: No, no, I don't think anything. I'm only asking . . .
Is the letter really worth it? Is it really worth it,
the divorce and staying here with me?
To my mind you're a kind of free spirit, everything about you,
and now you're off again to look for new horizons . . .
I'd have to do a lot of thinking if it were different.

LOTTE: *(Looks at him openly)* You're beginning to seem
strange to me, Alf.
*(She exits quickly to the rear. One can hear her typing on the
machine again)*
(Darkness)

The Filthy Angel

Lotte
Man *in a secondhand army jacket*

A bus stop, a full trash container. A young MAN *in a secondhand
army jacket is waiting. In the background* LOTTE *walks past several
times: short light hair, very pale face, again in the old, still extremely bleached-out suit, sneakers on her feet, a large shopping
bag on one arm. She walks with hurried tripping steps, stops sometimes abruptly, looks at her feet as if she didn't trust them, sets
them parallel to one another. It looks as though the rhythm of her
own steps disturbs her. Finally she approaches the young* MAN *from
the rear.*

LOTTE: Be not afraid!
I only want to stand next to you for a moment.

(She places herself next to him)
There.

MAN: Well, now what?

LOTTE: Better. I feel better.

Just a little bit longer.
(She suddenly begins breathing, opening her mouth wide each time, swallowing air)

MAN: What are you doing?

What's the matter with your mouth?

LOTTE: Don't know.

MAN: Can't you get enough air?

LOTTE: Yes, yes . . .

It's over now.

I've been sneaking around behind you the whole time.

MAN: I noticed.

Don't you have anything better to do?

LOTTE: I'm happy to be here.

MAN: Huh! Well, I'm drinking Löwenbrau:

'cause my computer graduated from high school today.

LOTTE: Ah, a joke, a joke!

Men always have to make jokes, right?

I bet you're one of those people
who puts on your seat belt when you see a movie
at the drive-in.

That's an American joke.

MAN: I wouldn't want to run into you at the breakfast table.

With *that* face . . .

LOTTE: You get used to it, young man.

MAN: Probably. Bad enough.

(Pause)

LOTTE: God is simple. He is true in word and deed.

He doesn't change and He deceives no one.

MAN: Get out of here.

LOTTE: Don't want to.

MAN: Jehovah's Witness, huh?

LOTTE: *(Shakes her head)* I'd like to stay, up until
you get on the bus.

MAN: What are you? What kind of person?

Not old, not young.

Chalk-white from head to toe.
In moonlight, couldn't even see you,
white as you are now.
Lily white or hoar-white?

LOTTE: Can't you see what I am?
Didn't I part my hair straight?
Don't you like me at all?

MAN: What else, huh?

LOTTE: *(Whispers in his ear)* I am one of the righteous . . .

MAN: Lily white or hoar-white?

LOTTE: I am one of the righteous.

MAN: Jehovah's Witness, oh, fuck, shit.

LOTTE: No. A righteous person is—
Look: in the whole word there are only thirty-six righteous men.
Only thirty-six in the whole world! The number is fixed.
It was put in writing by the ancient Jews. Each generation receives from God thirty-six righteous men, who hold the world together but who live in hiding.
No one knows them, everyone knows that they exist.
It could be your neighbor!
Thirty-six righteous men, whom no one knows,
and the world depends on them.

MAN: And of them, you're one.

LOTTE: Yes. Coincidence. I can't help it. Coincidence.

MAN: And what does one do as one of the righteous?

LOTTE: Goeth one's way. Get to know people.
Help, wherever you can. Just help always.
Make life difficult for the Antichrist.

MAN: Does that take up your whole day or—?

LOTTE: Whole day, yes.

MAN: And job-wise nothing else?

LOTTE: On the job, too. Where I work, too. Everywhere.
I used to be a physical therapist, a graphic artist, and soon an interpreter. I'm going to be. And yourself?

MAN: My name is Bob Fechter
and I work in broadcasting.

LOTTE: In broadcasting . . .
What exactly in broadcasting?

MAN: Computer programmer.

LOTTE: What are the fine points of that? Tell me!

MAN: Well, as you can perhaps imagine, such a big operation
has got to have x-million facts in the data bank
at all times!

LOTTE: Yes.

MAN: Well.

> *(Pause)*

LOTTE: Protestant or Catholic?

MAN: Nothing.

LOTTE: *A*-the-ist?

MAN: Not even.

LOTTE: Not even an . . . atheist—

> *(Suddenly in a rage)*
>
> Who on earth, who do you think is up there
> sending the light shimmering down on us?!
> Man, Bob! Watch out, watch out . . .
> You don't know what's going on . . .

MAN: You sure do have a lot to say.

> *(Again* LOTTE *is seized with shortness of breath)*
>
> Stop that!
> Stop your mouth from opening and closing.
> Do you have some kind of illness?
> Are you going to sweat it out here next to me?

LOTTE: It's better already.

> It just happens to me.
> It's not a cough.
> You don't know what's going on . . .

MAN: How long have you had this?

LOTTE: It just started here.

MAN: You are not healthy.

LOTTE: Everything's still so new to me . . .

MAN: Just don't die on me here.

LOTTE: No. I won't die.

> *(He takes a package of lozenges from his jacket pocket. He
> holds it out to her)*
>
> What is that?

MAN: Multivitamins.

LOTTE: That doesn't do anything, that stuff.

MAN: If Farrah takes them, they can't be too bad.
LOTTE: Does she take them?
MAN: Yes. Everyone knows that.
LOTTE: Only on TV.
MAN: I'm sure she takes them otherwise, too.
  It's not too bad, this stuff.
  (LOTTE *walks slowly to the trash container which is fastened to the bus-stop sign*)
MAN: Where are you going?
LOTTE: I just want to see something back there.
  Turn around!
  (*She rummages in the garbage, collects paper in her bag*)
MAN: (*To himself*) A woman. . . .
  Not old, not young.
  A woman . . . this too, hm?
  If one had a question at home, say,
  she would answer.
  What do you mean "question"?
  Well. That's true, too.

  With two people you laugh better watching TV
  than with only one.
  (*In doubt, he raises and lowers his shoulders*)
  She knows how to play chess . . .
  But that's exactly what you can do better at the club.
  She doesn't know how to play chess . . .
  Handicap.
  (*He glances at* LOTTE)
  What are you doing over there?!
  You little piglet . . . !
  Phooey! . . . Ugh!
  Get your hands out of that shit! Ugh!
LOTTE: Coming, coming . . .
  Turn around! I'm coming . . .
MAN: Ugh! . . . Nasty! Nasty!
LOTTE: Don't say anything. Quiet. I'm coming.
  (*She comes back and again stands next to him*)
MAN: How can you let yourself go like this. Phooey!
LOTTE: I'm not.

MAN: I saw you. Rooting around in other people's shit.

LOTTE: I was only looking for the papers.

　　If there was anything in them about Paul.

　　Just papers. Dry stuff . . .

MAN: Nowadays here nobody has to eat

　　anyone else's shit.

LOTTE: No.

MAN: You could look halfway decent.

　　You have an occupation, you could help.

　　There's no reason to let yourself go.

LOTTE: I'm not. I was just taking a quick look at what was

　　published.

MAN: Only the mentally ill put their hands in there, vagrants put

　　their hands in there. Greedy, greedy like hyenas . . .

LOTTE: *(Quietly)* I am one of the righteous . . .God has come back.

MAN: You are a woman. Not old, not young.

　　You could look halfway decent.

　　Find a group of friends you like.

　　Start to work on your problems together.

　　You could look like a woman everyone likes.

LOTTE: Me? Well. I don't know.

　　Make a vision for me.

MAN: Maybe tomorrow, maybe only day after tomorrow—

　　what are you going to do when the leisure culture arrives?

　　The leisure culture is coming as sure as an amen in church.

LOTTE: Right. Go on!

MAN: The people who don't have a good grip

　　on themselves, who don't know how to keep themselves busy,

　　in other words, who let themselves go—!

LOTTE: I'm not, I'm not!

MAN: For example: I belong to a chess club.

　　Twice a week. Always the same respectable

　　faces. First of all: the quiet. That alone is enough

　　to put you at ease. Then the games with other clubs.

　　The enjoyable trips—

　　(He falls silent)

LOTTE: Lovely. Go on.

MAN: What are you going to do when the bus comes

　　and I have to get in?

LOTTE: I won't go back in the trash, Bob!
MAN: But what are you going to *do?*
LOTTE: Well. What to do . . . ?
    What to do, what to do,
    when the music's over . . .
MAN: Do you know how to play chess?
LOTTE: No.
MAN: Do you want to learn?
    (She looks at him, shakes her head slowly)
LOTTE: No . . . No.
    (Pause)
MAN: The players take their places.
    One offers one's hand but one doesn't shake . . .
    Among themselves the men call each other Korchnoi and Karpov,
    Polugaevsky and Portisch. Or Spassky and Fischer.
    Or—
    (Darkness)

In Society

Lotte
Doctor
Patients

Waiting room of an internist. On the walls are antismoking posters designed to shock. LOTTE *waits with six other patients. They leaf through magazines, solve crossword puzzles, stare straight ahead. A* FAT WOMAN *is knitting, a* TURK *moves restlessly in his chair. Above the door to the consulting room, which is covered in white leather, a loudspeaker calls out the names of the patients. It is summer.* LOTTE *(in her faded suit) sits in the vicinity of a half-open window. Street noise and children's cries come from a schoolyard. The* DOCTOR *takes one to two minutes with each patient. Sometimes, when there is only a prescription to renew, it goes even faster. At intervals are called: "Miss Quadt, please" . . . "Mr. Werner Schmid, please" . . . "Mrs. Melchior, please." The patients who have been treated come back into the waiting room only if they have to pick up a piece of clothing or a package. They are able to leave the offices from the consulting room as well. After the third call—Mrs. Melchior, for whom it takes somewhat longer—an* OLD WOMAN *enters the room and greets everyone politely. The people waiting answer with an indistinct murmur. Suddenly from the circle of hushed people,* LOTTE *speaks up loudly.*

LOTTE: Perhaps it might interest you that my husband
    received a high honor not long ago . . .
    My husband is the freelance writer Paul Liga.
    He also writes under the name Smoky.
    He—
    (All the PATIENTS *look at* LOTTE *with astonishment. She falls silent and stares at the floor. Mrs. Melchior comes back out of the examining room and takes a light coat from the coat rack. As she leaves she says "Good-bye" loudly and clearly. Everyone responds. "Mr. Uranuz, please" is called. The* TURK *stands hurriedly and goes into the consulting room. A* YOUNG WOMAN *enters and says "Good day" so quietly that no one answers. Everyone eyes her. "Mrs. Pentowski, please" is called. The* FAT WOMAN *rises, leaves her knitting on the chair, goes to the door, turns around, takes her purse with her, goes into the consulting room.*
    It gets dark and immediately afterward light again. LOTTE *sits alone in the waiting room. The* DOCTOR *enters, throws the latest issue of* Der Spiegel *on the reading table. He sees* LOTTE . . .)

DOCTOR: Haven't you been called?
LOTTE: No.
    I'm just sitting here.
DOCTOR: Did you have an appointment for this morning?
LOTTE: No. I'm just sitting here.
    There's nothing wrong with me.
DOCTOR: Please leave.
LOTTE: Yes.
    *(*LOTTE *exits slowly. The* DOCTOR *closes the door behind her. He goes into the consulting room, closes the door)*
    (Darkness)

Translated by Anne Cattaneo

Acknowledgments

Every reasonable effort has been made to locate the owners of rights to previously published works and translations printed here. We gratefully acknowledge permission to reprint the following material:

Rosica Colin Ltd. for permission to publish *Stallerhof* by Franz Xaver Kroetz. Translation reprinted by permission of Michael Roloff.

"Offending the Audience" from KASPER AND OTHER PLAYS by Peter Handke, translated by Michael Roloff. Translation copyright © 1970 by Farrar, Straus and Giroux, LLC. Reprinted by permission of Farrar, Straus and Giroux, LLC.

Eve of Retirement By Thomas Bernhard, published in *The President and Eve of Retirement* by Thomas Bernhard, translated by Gitta Honegger. New York: PAJ Publications, 1982. © copyright 1982 PAJ Publications, translation copyright by Gita Honegger. Reprinted by permission of PAJ Publications.

BIG AND LITTLE: SCENES by Botho Strauss, translated by Anne Cattaneo. Translation copyright © 1979 by Farrar, Straus and Giroux, Inc. Reprinted by permission of Farrar, Straus and Giroux, LLC.

Titles Available in
The German Library

All titles available from **Continuum** *International*
370 Lexington Avenue, New York, NY 10017
www.continuumbooks.com

Beginnings to 1750

Volume 1
GERMAN EPIC POETRY: THE
NIBELUNGENLIED, THE OLDER
LAY OF HILDEBRAND, AND
OTHER WORKS

Volume 2
Wolfram von Eschenbach
PARZIVAL

Volume 3
Gottfried von Strassburg
TRISTAN AND ISOLDE

Volume 4
Hartmann von Aue, Konrad
von Würzburg, Gartenaere, and
Others
GERMAN MEDIEVAL TALES

Volume 5
Hildegard of Bingen, Meister
Eckhart, Jakob Böhme,
Heinrich Seuse, Johannes
Tauler, and Angelus Silesius
GERMAN MYSTICAL WRITINGS

Volume 6
Erasmus, Luther, Müntzer,
Johann von Tepl, Sebastian
Brant, Conrad Celtis, Sebastian
Lotzer, Rubianus, von Hutten
GERMAN HUMANISM AND
REFORMATION

Volume 7
Grimmelshausen, Leibniz,
Opitz, Weise, and Others
SEVENTEENTH CENTURY
GERMAN PROSE

Volume 8
Sachs, Gryphius, Schlegel, and
Others
GERMAN THEATER BEFORE 1750

Titles Available in The German Library

Volume 9
Hartmann von Aue, Wolfram
von Eschenbach, Luther,
Gryphius, and Others
GERMAN POETRY FROM THE
BEGINNINGS TO 1750

Eighteenth Century

Volume 10
Heinse, La'Roche, Wieland, and
Others
EIGHTEENTH CENTURY GERMAN
PROSE

Volume 11
Herder, Lenz, Lessing, and
Others
EIGHTEENTH CENTURY GERMAN
CRITICISM

Volume 12
Gotthold Ephraim Lessing
NATHAN THE WISE, MINNA VON
BARNHELM, AND OTHER PLAYS
AND WRITINGS

Volume 13
Immanuel Kant
PHILOSOPHICAL WRITINGS

Volume 14
Lenz, Heinrich Wagner, Klinger,
and Schiller
STURM UND DRANG

Volume 15
Friedrich Schiller
PLAYS: INTRIGUE AND LOVE,
AND DON CARLOS

Volume 16
Friedrich Schiller
WALLENSTEIN AND MARY
STUART

Volume 17
Friedrich Schiller
ESSAYS: LETTERS ON THE
AESTHETIC EDUCATION OF MAN,
ON NAIVE AND SENTIMENTAL
POETRY, AND OTHERS

Volume 18
Johann Wolfgang von Goethe
FAUST PARTS ONE AND TWO

Volume 19
Johann Wolfgang von Goethe
THE SUFFERINGS OF YOUNG
WERTHER AND ELECTIVE
AFFINITIES

Volume 20
Johann Wolfgang von Goethe
PLAYS: EGMONT, IPHIGENIA IN
TAURIS, TORQUATO TASSO

Nineteenth Century

Volume 21
Novalis, Schlegel,
Schleiermacher, and Others
GERMAN ROMANTIC CRITICISM

Volume 22
Friedrich Hölderlin
HYPERION AND SELECTED
POEMS

Titles Available in The German Library

Volume 23
Fichte, Jacobi, and Schelling
PHILOSOPHY OF GERMAN
IDEALISM

Volume 24
Georg Wilhelm Friedrich Hegel
ENCYCLOPEDIA OF THE
PHILOSOPHICAL SCIENCES IN
OUTLINE AND CRITICAL
WRITINGS

Volume 25
Heinrich von Kleist
PLAYS: THE BROKEN PITCHER,
AMPHITRYON, AND OTHERS

Volume 26
E. T. A. Hoffmann
TALES

Volume 27
Arthur Schopenhauer
PHILOSOPHICAL WRITINGS

Volume 28
Georg Büchner
COMPLETE WORKS AND LETTERS

Volume 29
J. and W. Grimm and Others
GERMAN FAIRY TALES

Volume 30
Goethe, Brentano, Kafka, and
Others
GERMAN LITERARY FAIRY TALES

Volume 31
Grillparzer, Hebbel, Nestroy
NINETEENTH CENTURY GERMAN
PLAYS

Volume 32
Heinrich Heine
POETRY AND PROSE

Volume 33
Heinrich Heine
THE ROMANTIC SCHOOL AND
OTHER ESSAYS

Volume 34
Heinrich von Kleist and Jean
Paul
ROMANTIC NOVELLAS

Volume 35
Eichendorff, Brentano,
Chamisso, and Others
GERMAN ROMANTIC STORIES

Volume 36
Ehrlich, Gauss, Siemens, and
Others
GERMAN ESSAYS ON SCIENCE IN
THE NINETEENTH CENTURY

Volume 37
Stifter, Droste-Hülshoff,
Gotthelf, Grillparzer, and
Mörike
GERMAN NOVELLAS OF REALISM
VOLUME I

Titles Available in The German Library

Volume 38
Ebner-Eschenbach, Heyse,
Raabe, Storm, Meyer, and
Hauptmann
GERMAN NOVELLAS OF REALISM
VOLUME 2

Volume 39
Goethe, Hölderlin, Nietzsche,
and Others
GERMAN POETRY FROM 1750 TO
1900

Volume 40
Feuerbach, Marx, Engels
GERMAN SOCIALIST
PHILOSOPHY

Volume 41
Marx, Engels, Bebel, and
Others
GERMAN ESSAYS ON SOCIALISM
IN THE NINETEENTH CENTURY

Volume 42
Beethoven, Brahms, Mahler,
Schubert, and Others
GERMAN *LIEDER*

Volume 43
Adorno, Bloch, Mann, and
Others
GERMAN ESSAYS ON MUSIC

Volume 44
Gottfried Keller
STORIES: A VILLAGE ROMEO AND
JULIET, THE BANNER OF THE
UPRIGHT SEVEN, AND OTHERS

Volume 45
Wilhelm Raabe
NOVELS: HORACKER AND TUBBY
SCHAUMANN

Volume 46
Theodor Fontane
SHORT NOVELS AND OTHER
WRITINGS

Volume 47
Theodor Fontane
DELUSIONS, CONFUSIONS AND
THE POGGENPUHL FAMILY

Volume 48
Friedrich Nietzsche
PHILOSOPHICAL WRITINGS

Volume 49
Hegel, Ranke, Spengler, and
Others
GERMAN ESSAYS ON HISTORY

Volume 50
Wilhelm Busch and Others
GERMAN SATIRICAL WRITINGS

Volume 51
Bach, Mozart, R. Wagner,
Brahms, Mahler, Richard
Strauss, Weill, and Others
WRITINGS OF GERMAN
COMPOSERS

Volume 52
Mozart, Beethoven, R. Wagner,
Richard Strauss, and
Schoenberg
GERMAN OPERA LIBRETTI

Titles Available in The German Library

Volume 53
Luther, Heine, Brecht, and
Others
GERMAN SONGS

Volume 54
Barth, Buber, Rahner,
Schleiermacher, and Others
GERMAN ESSAYS ON RELIGION

Twentieth Century

Volume 55
Arthur Schnitzler
PLAYS AND OTHER STORIES

Volume 57
Gerhart Hauptmann
PLAYS: BEFORE DAYBREAK, THE
WEAVERS, THE BEAVER COAT

Volume 58
Frank Wedekind, Ödön von
Horváth, and Marieluise
Fleisser
EARLY TWENTIETH CENTURY
GERMAN PLAYS

Volume 59
Sigmund Freud
PSYCHOLOGICAL WRITINGS AND
LETTERS

Volume 60
Max Weber
SOCIOLOGICAL WRITINGS

Volume 61
T. W. Adorno, M. Horkheimer,
G. Simmel, M. Weber, and
Others
GERMAN SOCIOLOGY

Volume 62
A. Adler, A. Freud, C. G. Jung,
and Others
PSYCHOLOGY

Volume 63
Thomas Mann
TONIO KRÖGER, DEATH IN
VENICE AND OTHER STORIES

Volume 64
Heinrich Mann
THE LOYAL SUBJECT

Volume 66
Benn, Toller, Sternheim, Kaiser,
and Others
GERMAN EXPRESSIONIST PLAYS

Volume 69
GERMAN 20TH CENTURY POETRY

Volume 70
Rainer Maria Rilke
PROSE AND POETRY

Volume 71
Hermann Hesse
SIDDHARTHA, DEMIAN, AND
OTHER WRITINGS

Volume 72
Robert Musil
SELECTED WRITINGS: YOUNG
TÖRLESS, TONKA, AND OTHERS

Titles Available in The German Library

Volume 73
Gottfried Benn
PROSE, ESSAYS, POEMS

Volume 78
T. W. Adorno, W. Benjamin, M. Horkheimer, and Others
GERMAN TWENTIETH CENTURY PHILOSOPHY

Volume 79
Winckelmann, Burckhardt, Panofsky, and Others
GERMAN ESSAYS ON ART HISTORY

Volume 82
Einstein, Heisenberg, Planck, and Others
GERMAN ESSAYS ON SCIENCE IN THE TWENTIETH CENTURY

Volume 83
Lessing, Brecht, Dürrenmatt, and Others
ESSAYS ON GERMAN THEATER

Volume 86
GERMAN RADIO PLAYS

Volume 87
Plenzdorf, Kunert, and Others
NEW SUFFERINGS OF YOUNG W. AND OTHER STORIES FROM THE GERMAN DEMOCRATIC REPUBLIC

Volume 88
F. C. Delius, P. Schneider, M. Walser
THREE CONTEMPORARY GERMAN NOVELLAS

Volume 89
Friedrich Dürrenmatt
PLAYS AND ESSAYS

Volume 90
Max Frisch
NOVELS, PLAYS, ESSAYS

Volume 91
Uwe Johnson
SPECULATIONS ABOUT JAKOB AND OTHER WRITINGS

Volume 92
Peter Weiss
MARAT/SADE, THE INVESTIGATION, THE SHADOW OF THE BODY OF THE COACHMAN

Volume 93
Günter Grass
CAT AND MOUSE AND OTHER WRITINGS

Volume 94
Ingeborg Bachmann and Christa Wolf
SELECTED PROSE AND DRAMA

Volume 95
Hedwig Dohm, Rosa Luxemburg, and Others
GERMAN FEMINIST WRITINGS

Titles Available in The German Library

Volume 96
R. Hochhuth, H. Kipphardt,
H. Müller
CONTEMPORARY GERMAN PLAYS I

Volume 97
T. Bernhard, P. Handke, F. X.
Kroetz, and B. Strauss
CONTEMPORARY GERMAN PLAYS II

Volume 98
Hans Magnus Enzensberger
CRITICAL ESSAYS

Volume 99
I. Aichinger, H. Bender,
G. Köpf, G. Kunert, and
Others
CONTEMPORARY GERMAN
FICTION

Volume 100
P. Handke, F. Mayröcker, Uwe
Timm, and Others
CONTEMPORARY GERMAN
STORIES

Author Listing
in The German Library
by Volume Number

Abbe, Ernst 36
Adorno, Theodor W. 43, 61, 78
Aichinger, Ilse 99
Albert, Heinrich 9
Allmers, Hermann 42
Alte, Reinmar der 9
Anonymous: from Carmina Burana 9
Anonymous: Dr. Faust 4
Anonymous: Duke Ernst 4
Anonymous: Muspilli 9
Anonymous: from Theologia Germanica 5
Anschütz, Ernst 53
Arnim, Achim von 35
Arnim, Bettina von 43
Audorf, Jakob 53
Aue, Hartmann von 4, 9

Bach, Johann Sebastian 51
Bachofen, Johann Jakob 36
Bachmann, Ingeborg 86, 94
Balthasar, H. von 54
Barth, Karl 54
Baumbach, Rudolf, 53
Bebel, August 41
Becher, Johannes R. 53
Bechstein, Ludwig 29

Becker, Jürgen 86
Becker, Jurek 87, 99
Beer, Johann 7
Beethoven, Ludwig van 42, 51, 52
Bender, Hans 99
Bendix, Richard 61
Benn, Gottfried 66, 73
Berg, Alban 51
Bernstein, Eduard 41
Bichsel, Peter 99
Bierbaum, Otto Julius 42
Biermann, Wolf 53
Bingen, Hildegard von 5
Birken, Sigmund von 9
Blackenburg, Friedrich von 11
Bloch, Ernst 43
Bobrowski, Johannes 87
Böda-Löhner, Fritz 53
Böhme, Jakob 5
Boelitz, Martin 42
Börne, Ludwig, 33
Borchert, Wolfgang 86, 99
Bosch, Robert 82
Bräker, Ulrich 10
Bräunig, Werner 87
Brahms, Johannes 51
Brant, Sebastian 6
Brasch, Thomas 99
Braun, Volker 87

Brecht, Bertolt 43, 53, 83, 87
Brehm, Alfred E. 36
Brentano, Clemens, 30, 35, 39, 42
Breuer, Hans 43
Brežan, Jurij 87
Bruchmann, Franz Ritter von 42
Bruckner, Anton 51
de Bruyn, Günter 87
Buber, M. 54
Buch, Hans Christoph 99
Büchner, Georg 28, 83
Bürger, Gottfried August 11, 39
Bultmann, R. 54
Burckhardt, Jacob 36, 49, 79
Busch, Wilhelm 50
Busoni, Ferruccio 51
Butenandt, Adolf 82

Campe, Johann Heinrich 42
Celtis, Conrad 6
Chamisso, Adelbert von 35, 36, 42
Chezy, Helmina von 42
Claudius, Hermann 53
Claudius, Matthias 39, 42, 53
Clausewitz, Carl von 36
Collin, Matthäus von 42
Craigher de Jachelutta, Jakob N. 42
Czerny, Carl 51

Dach, Simon 9, 53
Dahlhaus, Carl 43
Dahrendorf, Ralf 61
Dahn, Daniela 87
Daimler, Gottfried 36
Daumer, Georg Friedrich 42
Degenhardt, Franz Josef 53
Dehmel, Richard 42, 53
Des Knaben Wunderhorn 42
Dessau, Paul 51
Dietzgen, Joseph 41
Dilthey, Wilhelm 49, 62
Disselhoff, August 53

Ditters von Dittersdorf, Karl 51
Döblin, Alfred 68
Dorst, Tankred 83
Drach, Hans 53
Droste-Hülshoff, Annette von 37, 39
Droysen, Johann Gustav 49
Dürrenmatt, Friedrich 83, 89
Dvořák, Max 79

Ebel, Edward 53
Ebner-Eschenbach, Marie von 38
Eckhart, Meister 5
Egk, Werner 51
Ehrlich, Paul 36
Eich, Günter 86
Eichendorff, Joseph Freiherr von 30, 35, 39, 42, 53
Eigen, Manfred 82
Eildermann, Heinrich Arnulf 53
Einstein, Albert 82
Eisler, Hanns 51
Eist, Dietmar von 9
Engels, Friedrich 40, 41, 49, 83
Enzensberger, Hans Magnus 69, 98
Erasmus, Desiderius 6
Erdmann, Georg 51
Ernst, Karl 53
Eschenbach, Wolfram von 9
Euler, Leonhard 36

Falk, Johann Daniel 53
Fetscher, Iring 29
Feuerbach, Ludwig 40, 54
Fichte, Johann Gottlieb 23, 49
Fischer, A. 53
Fischer-Dieskau, Dietrich 44
Fleming, Paul 9
Fleißer, Marieluise 58
Fontane, Theodor 46, 47
Forkel, Johann Nikolaus 43
Forster, Georg 10

Fraunhofer, Joseph von 36
Freiligrath, Ferdinand 42, 53
Freud, Anna 62
Freud, Sigmund 54, 59
Freytag, Gustav 83
Fries, Fritz Rudolf 87
Frisch, Max 83, 90
Fröhlich, Hans J. 99
Fromm, Erich 62
Fühmann, Franz 87
Furtwängler, Wilhelm 43

Gandersheim, Hrotsvitha von 8
Gartenaere, Wernher der 4
Gaudenz, J. 53
Gauss, Karl Friedrich 36
Gebhardt, P. 53
Geibel, Emanuel 42, 53
Geiger, Theodor 61
Gellert, Christian Fürchtegott 42
Gerhardt, Paul 9, 53
Gerhardt, Uta 61
Gerth, Hans 61
Gervinus, Georg Gottfried 49
Gilm zu Rosenegg, Hermann von
    42
Glaßbrenner, Adolf 53
Gleim, Johann Wilhelm Ludwig 9
Glichezaere, Heinrich der 4
Gluck, Christoph Willibald 51
Gödel, Kurt 82
Görres, Joseph 21
Goethe, Johann Wolfgang von 11,
    18, 19, 20, 30, 39, 42, 53, 54,
    79, 83
Götz, Johann Nikolaus 9
Goldschmidt, A. 79
Gotthelf, Jeremias 37
Gottsched, Johann Christoph 11
Grass, Günter 93
Greiffenberg, Catharina Regina von
    7, 9

Grillparzer, Franz 31, 37, 83
Grimm, Jakob & Wilhelm 21, 29
Grimmelshausen, Hans Jakob C.
    von 7, 9
Groth, Klaus 42
Gruppe, Otto Friedrich 42
Gryphius, Andreas 8, 9
Grzimek, Martin 99
Günther, Johann Christian 9

Habermas, Jürgen 61
Hacks, Peter 83
Händel, Georg Friedrich 51
Hagedorn, Friedrich von 9
Hahn, Otto 82
Halm, August 43
Halm, Friedrich (Baron Elegius von
    Münch-Bellinghausen) 42
Hamann, Johann Georg 11
Handke, Peter 83, 86, 100
Hanslick, Eduard 43
Hartmann, Karl Amadeus 51
Hasenclever, Walter 66
Hasse, Johann Adolf 51
Hauff, Wilhelm 30
Hauptmann, Gerhart 38, 57, 83
Hausegger, Friedrich von 43
Hausen, Friedrich von 9
Hauser, Arnold 83
Haydn, Franz Joseph 51
Hebel, Johann Peter 35
Hebbel, Friedrich 31, 39, 83
Hegel, Georg Wilhelm Friedrich 24,
    43, 49, 54, 83
Hegel, Max 53
Hein, Christoph 87
Heine, Heinrich 32, 33, 39, 42, 53
Heinse, Wilhelm 10, 79
Heisenberg, Werner 82
Helmholtz, Hermann von 36
Henckell, Karl 42
Henze, Hans Werner 51

Herder, Johann Gottfried 11, 43, 49, 53
Hermand, Jost 43
Hermlin, Stephan 87
Herrosee, Carl Friedrich Wilhelm 42
Herwegh, Georg 53
Hesse, Hermann 42, 71
Hetzer, Theodor 79
Hey, Wilhelm 53
Heym, Stefan 87
Heyse, Paula Johann Ludwig 38, 42
Hilbig, Wolfgang 87
Hildescheimer, Wolfgang 83
Hindemith, Paul 51
Hochhuth, Rolf 83, 96
Hölderlin, Friedrich 21, 22, 39
Hölty, Ludwig Christoph Heinrich 39, 42, 53
Hoffmann, E. T. A. 26, 30, 43, 51
Hoffmann, Heinrich August: Hoffmann von Fallersleben 42, 53
Hofmannsthal, Hugo von 30, 83
Hofmannswaldau, Christian Hofmann von 9
Holz, Arno 69, 83
Horkheimer, Max 61
Horváth, Ödön von 58, 83
Hüsch, Hans Dieter 53
Hufeland, Christoph von 36
Humboldt, Alexander von 36
Humboldt, Wilhelm von 21, 86
Husserl, Edmund 62
Hutten, Ulrich von 6, 9

Ihering, Rudolf von 36

Jacobi, Friedrich Heinrich 23
Jahnke, Franz 53
Jaspers, Karl 49, 54, 62
Jean Paul 21, 34
Johannsdorf, Albrecht von 9

Johansen, Hannah 99
Johnson, Uwe 91
Jung, Carl Gustav 62

Kästner, Erich 50
Kafka, Franz 30
Kaiser, Georg 66, 83
Kant, Hermann 87
Kant, Immanuel 13, 43, 49, 54
Kaschnitz, Marie Luise 99
Kautsky, Karl 41
Keller, Gottfried 39, 42, 44
Kerner, Justinus 39, 42
Kipphardt, Heinar 83
Kirsch, Sarah 87
Klaj, Johann 9
Kleber, Leonhard 53
Kleist, Ewald Christian von 9
Kleist, Henrich von 21, 25, 34, 35
Klinger, Friedrich Maximilian 14
Klopstock, Friedrich Gottlob 9, 11, 42
Knepler, Georg 43
Knobloch, Heinz 87
Koch, Robert 82
König, Barbara 99
König, René 61
Königsdorf, Helga 87
Köpf, Gerhard 99
Kohlhaase, Wolfgang 87
Kokoschka, Oskar 66
Koloff, Eduard 79
Krenek, Ernst 51
Kroetz, Franz Xaver 83
Kürenberg, Der von 9
Kugler, Franz 42
Kuhlmann, Quirinus 9
Kuhnau, Johann 7
Kunze, Reiner 87
Kunert, Günter 87, 99

Laabs, Joochen 87
Langhoff, Wolfgang 53

Lappe, Karl 42
La Roche, Sophie von 10
Lassalle, Ferdinand 41
Leander, R. 42
Lederer, Emil 41
Lehne, Friedrich 53
Leibfried, Stephan 61
Leibniz, Gottfried Wilhelm 7
Lenau, Nikolaus 39, 42
Lenz, Jakob Michael Reinhold 11, 14, 83
Lenz, Siegfried 99
Lessing, Gotthold Ephraim 11, 12, 54, 83
Lettau, Reinhard 86, 99
Levy, Julius 53
Lichtenberg, Georg Christoph 36
Liebig, Justus von 36
Liebknecht, Wilhelm 41
Liebmann, Irina 87
Liliencron, Detlev von 42
Lingg, Hermann Ritter von 42
List, Friedrich 36
Liszt, Franz 51
Loest, Erich 87
Loewenstein, Rudolf 53
Logau, Friedrich von 9
Lohenstein, Daniel Casper von 7, 8, 9
Lorenz, Konrad 82
Lotzer, Sebastian 6
Ludwig, Christian Gottlieb 43
Lüchow, J. C. 53
Lukács, Georg 83
Luther, Martin 6, 9, 53
Luxemburg, Rosa 41

Mach, Ernst 82
Mackay, John Henry 42
Magdeburg, Mechthild von 5
Mahler, Gustav 51
Mann, Heinrich 64

Mann, Thomas 19, 43, 63
Mannheim, Karl 61
Marx, Karl 40, 41, 49, 54, 83
Matthison, Friedrich von 42
Mayer, Günter 43
Mayer, Karl Ulrich 61
Mayntz, Renate 61
Mayrhofer, Johann 42
Mechtel, Angelika 99
Meckel, Christoph 99
Mehring, Franz 41
Meinecke, Friedrich 49
Meitner, Lise 82
Melle, F. Hendrik 87
Mendelssohn, Moses 11
Mendelssohn-Bartholdy, Felix 51
Meyer, Conrad Ferdinand 38, 39
Michels, Robert 61
Moeller, Edith 53
Mörike, Eduard Friedrich 30, 37, 42
Mohr, Joseph 53
Mommsen, Theodor 49
Morgenstern, Beate 87
Morgenstern, Christian 50
Morgner, Irmtraud 87
Moritz, Karl Philipp 10, 11
Morungen, Heinrich von 9
Moscherosch, Johann Michael 7
Mosen, Julius 42
Mossmann, Walter 53
Most, Johannes 53
de la Motte-Fouqué, Friedrich 35
Mozart, Wolfgang Amadeus 51, 52
Mühsam, Erich 53
Müller, Adam 21, 36
Müller, Heiner 83, 87
Müller, Wilhelm 42, 53
Müntzer, Thomas 6
Musil, Robert 72

Nadolny, Sten 99
Neander, Joachim 53

Neefe, Christian Gottlob 51
Nestroy, Johann N. 31
Neutsch, Erik 87
Nicolai, Friedrich 11
Nicolai, Otto 51
Nietzsche, Friedrich 39, 43, 48, 49, 54, 83
Novalis (Friedrich von Hardenberg) 21, 30, 39, 42

Offe, Claus 61
Oken, Lorenz 36
Olearius, Adam 7
Opitz, Martin 7, 9
Overbeck, Christian Adolf 42, 53

Panofsky, Erwin 79
Pestalozzi, Johann Heinrich 36
von der Pfalz, Liselotte 7
Pfau, Ludwig 53
Pfitzner, Hans 51
Piscator, Erwin 83
Planck, Max 82
Platen, August Graf von 39, 42
Plenzdorf, Ulrich 87
Plessner, Hellmuth 82
Preradovic, Paula von 53
Pyrker, Johann L. von Felsö-Eör 42

Quantz, Johann Joachim 51

Raabe, Wilhelm 38, 45
Radbruch, Gustav 82
Radin, Leonid P. 53
Ramler, Karl Wilhelm 9, 43
Rahner, K. 54
Ranke, Heinrich 53
Ranke, Leopold von 36, 49
Rebhun, Paul 8
Redwitz, Oskar Freiherr von 42
Reinick, Robert 42
Reinig, Christa 99

Reinmar der Alte 9
Rellstab, Ludwig 42
Reuenthal, Neidhart von 9, 53
Reuter, Christian 7
Richter, Johann Paul Friedrich 21, 34
Riedel, Carl 53
Riegel, Alois 79
Rilke, Rainer Maria 70
Rinckart, Martin 9, 53
Rist, Johann 9
Ritter, Carl 36
Rosenzweig, F. 54
Rubianus, Crotus 6
Rückert, Friedrich 42
Rülicke, Käthe 87
Rumohr, Carl Friedrich von 79

Saar, Ferdinand von 39
Sachs, Hans 8, 9
Salis-Seewis, Johann Gaudenz von 39, 53
Santa Clara, Abraham a 7
Sauter, Samuel Friedrich 42
Savigny, Friedrich Carl von 36
Schack, Adolf Friedrich, Graf von 42
Schanz, Ludwig 53
Scheidt, Samuel 51
Scheler, M. 54
Schenkendorf, Max von 53
Schenker, Henrich 43
Scherer, Georg 42
Schering, Arnold 43
Schelling, Friedrich Wilhelm L. 23
Schiller, Friedrich 11, 14, 15, 16, 17, 39, 42, 49, 83
Schirmer, David 9
Schlegel, August Wilhelm 21, 82
Schlegel, Friedrich 21, 79
Schlegel, Johann Elias 8
Schleiermacher, Friedrich 21, 54

Schlippenbach, Albert 53
Schlosser, Julius 79
Schmid, Christoph von 53
Schmidt, Georg Philipp, a.k.a.
   Schmidt von Lübeck 42
Schmidt, Hans 42
Schnitzler, Arthur 38, 55
Schnurre, Wolfdietrich 99
Schober, Franz von 42
Schönberg, Arnold 51, 52
Schopenhauer, Arthur 27, 43, 54
Schrödinger, Erwin 82
Schubart, Christian Daniel 42, 43
Schubert, Franz 51
Schütz, Alfred 61
Schütz, Heinrich 51
Schütz, Helga 87
Schulze, Ernst Konrad Friedrich 42
Schumann, Felix 42
Schumann, Robert 51
Schwarz, Sibylla 9
Schweitzer, Albert 54
Seghers, Anna 87
Seidl, Johann Gabriel 42
Seuse, Heinrich 5
Sevelingen, Meinloh von 9
Siemens, Werner von 36
Silesius, Angelus (J. Scheffler) 5, 9
Simmel, Georg 61, 82
Spee von Langenfeld, Friedrich 9
Speier, Hans 61
Spener, Philipp Jacob 7
Spengler, Oswald 49
Spohr, Louis 51
Stachowa, Angela 87
Stamitz, Karl 51
Steinmar 9
Sternheim, Carl 66, 83
Stieler, Kaspar 7, 9
Stifter, Adalbert 37
Stolberg, Friedrich L., Graf zu 42
Storm, Theodor 30, 38, 39, 42

Stramm, August 66
Strassburg, Gottfried von 3
Strauss, Richard 51, 52
Strittmatter, Erwin 87
Stuckenschmidt, H. H. 43
Süverkrüp, Dieter 53
Suhrkamp, Peter 53
Sulzer, Johann Georg 43

Tauler, Johannes 5
Telemann, Georg Philipp 51
Tepl, Johann von 6
Tieck, Ludwig 30, 39, 42
Toller, Ernst 66, 83
Treitschke, Heinrich von 49
Troeltsch, E. 54
Tucholsky, Kurt 50

Uexküll, Jakob von 82
Uhland, Johann Ludwig 39, 42
Ulrich, Anton (Herzog
   Braunschweig-Wolfenbüttel) 9

Vallentin, Maxim 53
Veldeke, Heinrich von 9
Virchov, Rudolf 36
von der Vogelweide, Walther 9
Voßler, Karl 82

Wackenroder, Wilhelm Heinrich
   30, 43, 79
Wagner, Heinrich Leopold 14
Wagner, Richard 51, 52, 83
Walser, Martin 83
Walter, Bruno 43
Waltgher, Joachim 87
Walther, Johann 51
Wander, Maxie 87
Warbug, Aby 79
Weber, Alfred 61
Weber, Carl Maria von 51
Weber, Max 43, 60, 61, 82

Complete Author Listing in The German Library

Webern, Anton 51
Wecker, Konstantin 53
Weckherlin, Georg Rudolph 9
Wedekind, Frank 58
Wegener, Bettina 53
Weill, Kurt 51
Weinert, Erich 53
Weise, Christian 9, 7
Weiss, Peter 83, 92
Weizsäcker, Carl Friedrich von 82
Wesendonck, Mathilde 42
Weyl, Hermann 82
Wickhoff, Franz 79
Widmer, Leonard 53
Wieland, Christoph Martin 10, 11
Winckelmann, Johann Joachim 79

Winkler-Oswatisch, Ruthild 82
Wittgenstein, Ludwig 54
Wohmann, Gabriele 99
Wolf, Christa 94
Wolf, Friedrich 87
Wolf, Hugo 42, 51
Wolfram von Eschenbach 2
Wölfflin, Heinrich 79
Wolkenstein, Oswald von 9
Wolter, Christine 87
Würzburg, Konrad von 4

Zesen, Philipp von 7, 9
Zetkin, Clara 41
Zuccalmaglio, A. W. Florentin von
  42, 53